Build, Upgrade, and Repair Your Computer

To my son, Tony, who co-authored this manuscript,
To Linda Kay, who makes all things possible,
and
To Sedona, Arizona, the achievable goal.

Build, Upgrade, and Repair Your Computer

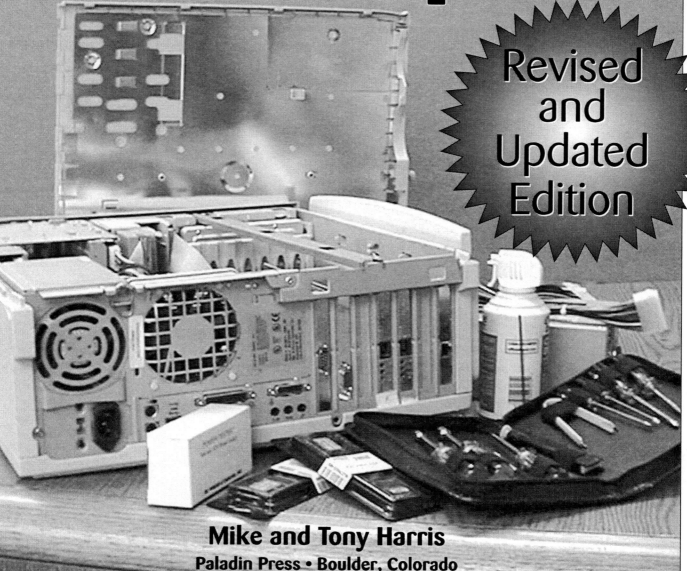

Revised and Updated Edition

Mike and Tony Harris
Paladin Press • Boulder, Colorado

Build, Upgrade, and Repair Your Computer: Revised and Updated Edition
by Mike and Tony Harris

Copyright © 2002 by Mike and Tony Harris

ISBN 1-58160-356-8
Printed in the United States of America

Published by Paladin Press, a division of
Paladin Enterprises, Inc.
Gunbarrel Tech Center
7077 Winchester Circle
Boulder, Colorado 80301 USA
+1.303.443.7250

Direct inquiries and/or orders to the above address.

Visit our Web site at www.paladin-press.com

Table of Contents

Warning

This book is intended to assist people who want to understand, build, repair or upgrade an IBM-compatible computer, but it is not intended as the sole source of information on this subject. This book supplements other available information, and you are urged to read all available material and tailor the information presented here to your unique needs. For more information, check your local library and the book section of your local computer retailer.

Every effort has been made to ensure the accuracy and completeness of the information presented. The author, publisher, and distributors have no liability or responsibilities to any person with respect to any loss or damage caused, directly or indirectly, by the projects described in this book.

Preface

This book has been enjoyable to put together and I hope you get satisfaction from reading it.

More importantly, I hope this book opens a door for you, as building my first computer did for me.

It always seemed to me that the price for a computer was about 30 percent out of my reach. One day, I found out I had the capability to build a computer, and suddenly I could afford one.

This book represents everything I have read on the subject; everyone I have talked to or learned from has contributed. It is only a small subset of the knowledge available on computers, but it is the most important information for the new computer builder to know.

There are few books that actually instruct you how to put together a computer, and none that walk you through the process with the depth this book presents.

I have listened to about 100 computer builders and people who upgrade their own systems, and they agree with me that the text and pictures in this book accurately convey the process.

The examples of systems I included are a great reference for anyone not sure of the exact configuration they desire.

—Mike Harris
Shadows-Lair@cox.net

Introduction

You purchased this book to learn how to evaluate your computer requirements and build, upgrade, or purchase a computer to meet your exact needs. Believe it or not, if you decide to go forward you have already performed the most difficult part of the task.

Most people have the misconception that a computer is internally similar to a television set and the mere mention of opening the cover conjures up visions of unspeakable horror. The greatest fear is wondering if the darn thing will ever work again when (if?) you ever get it back together. A look through this book will quickly put those myths to rest. If you can operate a Phillips-head screwdriver and follow instructions, you can build the most complicated PC.

This book profiles the IBM-compatible PC and covers the options and variations of the basic computer. It describes software, hardware, and interconnection possibilities as well. You will learn about the spectrum of add-on items that you can easily install to customize your computer to cover your special needs. Learning how to upgrade and customize gives you the power to keep your system current, so these two areas are covered extensively.

Many people have asked me if building a Pentium-platform computer is much harder than creating a simple (and obsolete) 486-based system. The truth is that a Pentium system, or any currently available processor platform, is considerably simpler to build than its ancient predecessors were. The plug and play features in the new motherboard BIOS make a blazing-fast system just as simple to build as the bare-bones systems of a few years ago. (BIOS is the instruction set built into the motherboard that allows the motherboard to recognize the add-on components you will install later.)

This is why this book was written—to demonstrate that regardless of which processor or system speed you choose, the actual assembly is exactly the same. The only variables are the number and configuration of optional add-on components.

Let's talk about complexity again. I built my first computer in 1986 with a number two Phillips screwdriver, a small slot screwdriver, a medium slot screwdriver, a small pair of standard pliers, and a small pair of tweezers. Last month I assembled a Pentium 4 1GHz computer in about 20 minutes with only these tools and saved about $1,000 or so compared to the best nationally advertised system with similar components.

Now seems a good time to mention a very important feature that makes building or upgrading the IBM-compatible computer significantly easier than in years past. Plug and Play (PnP) is the current standard built into hardware devices and add-on components and is the current standard in Windows. It is a set of hardware recognition instructions residing on the motherboard that allows the motherboard to set up the hardware, i.e., the modem or video card that you choose and install in your computer. This single standard revolutionized the computer industry by severely reducing the hardware and software conflicts that installing new hardware once caused.

When I built my first computer, I had to manually configure each item with a unique interrupt request address (IRQ). There are 16 different addresses available, but no two items can have the same IRQ. Many add-on components must also have a unique direct memory access (DMA) setting. (DMA is method of transferring data from main memory to a device without it passing through the CPU.) When I began building my first computer, I had to be certain that each item was unique in its IRQ and DMA settings. My

tweezers came in handy for setting the switches on the components before installation. Fortunately the newer components don't require this level of attention.

When I built my Pentium 4 all the items installed were PnP, so the first time I turned the computer on it automatically configured everything. The record of each DMA and IRQ setting configured by the PnP BIOS was saved, either on the motherboard or on each item installed. The beauty of this system is that, depending on the complexity of the computer, one may never have to worry about DMA or IRQ conflicts.

PnP in Windows goes one step further and configures —or specifies configurations for you to set—on items not PnP compatible. The first time Windows runs, it maps each installed item for conflicts and notifies you if there is a conflict that you must manually correct. The correction normally involves setting a component's jumper or switch to a different setting. PnP is a true blessing for the beginning computer builder or anyone interested in upgrading, and will eliminate hours of frustration.

Somewhere along the line you may ask yourself the big question, "What do I think I am doing?" followed immediately by the statement, "I can't possibly build a computer!" Ignore such concerns and let me show you how easy it can be.

Building instead of buying will save you a ton of money, and the experience will enable you to repair your PC and successfully upgrade to keep it current, if you wish. Many people I know are satisfied with their existing computer but would like a larger hard drive or more memory. The ability to perform upgrades yourself will save you even more money since some retailers would rather sell you a new computer than provide the information you need to perform a simple upgrade.

One of the objectives of this book is to help you understand exactly what you want in a computer before you spend a dime. Many people just need a basic system for word processing and running a few games, while those writing programs or performing operations with complex graphics, for instance, will require a more sophisticated and powerful system.

A couple of authors that I've read advise the buyer to purchase the most expensive computer that he or she can possibly afford. I have to disagree with that philosophy. I believe you should understand your computer needs right now and make an educated guess at your future needs; however, don't make any projections past three years, as technology advances can cloud up our crystal balls. Build the computer you want now and upgrade storage, memory, speed, and other functions as required to satisfy your advancing requirements. This realistic and cost-effective approach will not put you in the poorhouse.

With the help of this book you can determine what kind of computer you want, purchase and successfully assemble the hardware, and install the software. When you finish you will have the system you need and hundreds of extra dollars in your pocket.

This book also covers upgrades for improved performance on older machines in easy-to-read language and with sufficient detail to let you easily master the task. Included are tips and basic troubleshooting techniques used by experts to repair and tune up computers and peripherals.

ABOUT MIKE HARRIS

Who am I and why did I write this book? I am currently a business development director and engineer for a specialized engineering company, one of many involved in designing the next generation of digital communications equipment. We specialize in high-speed fiber optic communications links between computers.

You might have noticed that computers and related products are in a constant state of revision and improvement. The computer industry is always trying to convince the public that year-old products are obsolete!

My interest in computers and instrumentation control software presses me to constantly update my computer hardware and software knowledge. One of the required parts of my job is to be just ahead of technological advances in the computer field. This spills over into my personal life, and my primary hobby is designing and building computer systems. On this subject, I serve in an advisory or consulting capacity with several progressive firms specializing in IBM-compatible hardware and software. I have upgraded and repaired more than 1,000 computers at this writing.

I built my first IBM-compatible computer in the early 1980s to use as an engineering aid and typewriter. Saving money was high on my list of priorities, and by building my own computer I saved about $1,400. Recently, when I built my Pentium 4, I saved about the same percentage—around $2,000. Needless to say, I was quite astounded by the savings.

Today, due to the simplicity of design, a computer can be built by anyone with a modicum of dexterity and a bit of patience. Knowing this and realizing how much money you can save by building your own system, I made the decision to share my 25 years of computer and electronic experience with you.

To confirm that the information presented in this text could help nearly anyone build a computer, I ran tests. The details are in the text but to recap briefly, I took as subjects a lawyer, an assistant manager from a local convenience store, a young marine, and a computer-illiterate author. With this book, all were successful in building or upgrading their computers.

1

Computer
Talk

This chapter covers the computer dialect used in the industry today. The buzzwords can be the most confusing and intimidating aspect of computer shopping, primarily since the computer terms are the salesperson's best tool to gauge the customer's knowledge. This chapter gives the reader a compass to safely navigate the sales pitches and serves as a tool to determine exactly what your computer requirements are. Readers tell me that the single most intimidating part of a computer sales pitch is getting past the computer-related terminology.

The following tables display the measurement units commonly applied to the computer terms you will learn next.

COMMON MEASUREMENT TERMS

Kilobyte	KB	1,024 bytes
Megabyte	MB	1,024 kilobytes
Gigabyte	GB	1,024 megabytes
Terabyte	TB	1,024 gigabytes
Kilohertz	kHz	1,000 hertz, or cycles per second
Megahertz	MHz	1,000 kilohertz
Gigahertz	GHz	1,000 megahertz
Terahertz	THz	1,000 gigahertz

COMPUTER DATA BY PROCESSOR TYPE

CPU	SPEED	BUS BITS	MEMORY	CACHE int/ext
XT (8086)	4.7-10 MHz	8	640 KB	0/0
80286	6-25 MHz	16	16 MB	0/64 KB
80386	16-40 MHz	32	4 GB	0/128 KB
486/5X86	25-133 MHz	32	4 GB	8 KB/256 KB
6X86/PENT.	60-233+ MHz	64	4 GB	16 KB/512 KB
Pentium 4	**1-2 + GHz**	**64-100+**	**1 TB**	**32KB/512 KB**
Athalon	**1-1.4 + GHz**	**64-100+**	**1 TB**	**32KB/512 KB**

(Yes! The Pentium 4 and Athalon are in a class by themselves.)

BUZZWORDS AND THEIR MEANINGS

Electronic terminology in general and computer-related buzzwords in particular can be confusing, misleading, and even incomprehensible. This chapter exposes you to most of the commonly used terms and provides definitions. After you finish this chapter, you will be able to communicate with anyone regarding any computer topic.

These terms by no means represent the entire working glossary of the computer industry, but they are the common descriptions most users and sales personnel are familiar with. You will be more capable of describing your needs and determining whether or not the salesperson is competent enough to help with them after reading this chapter.

This glossary of terms and definitions is a good start on the road to computer literacy. It is placed in alphabetical, not historical, order. As you go through the chapters to follow, you will probably have to refer back to this section often.

286—This is the original AT (advanced technology) computer you hear so much about. It was a quantum leap from the 8-bit computers preceding it.

The original IBM 286 introduced in 1984 had an 80286 microprocessor and the capability of addressing 16 MB of RAM. The most common processor speed was 12 MHz. I built a non-IBM equivalent and was pleased to get an AMD 16 MHz clone processor.

The 16-bit internal and data bus made the XT machines slugs by comparison, and the 80287 math coprocessor made this the high-speed machine of its time.

386—The 386 was the first processor in home computers to break the 32-bit barrier. The 386SX had an 80386 processor with a 32-bit internal and 16-bit external bus. The 386DX increased the external data bus to 32 bits.

The SX processor ran at 25 MHz and the DX clocked in at 33 MHz for the Intel version, with the most common clones running at 40 MHz.

The addressable memory size expanded to 4 GB and a new 80387 math coprocessor was introduced. An SX version of the coprocessor also came out of the closet.

486—The 486 family of computers is still alive today due to outstanding performance. Since nobody builds the 80486 microprocessor anymore, 5x86, Pentium, and 6x86 computers are replacing the 486 as the supply dwindles.

The 486SX computers house the 80486SX microprocessor. It is a 32-bit internal and external bus microprocessor running 25 MHz.

A 486SX2 computer boasts the faster 80486SX2 microprocessor, which runs at twice the SX speed due to doubling the microprocessor clock. Computers with 50 MHz are not uncommon with this configuration.

The 486DX family added an 8 KB

internal cache to the SX processors. The math coprocessor was also included within the microprocessor.

A 486DX computer has an 80486 microprocessor, which can move out at 50 MHz. The 486DX2 computers upgrade the processor to a 80486DX2 microprocessor running up to 66 MHz. The clock doubling technique utilized for the SX2 processors was used to double a 33 MHz clock to give the DX2 the 66 MHz clock speed.

Someone found a way to quadruple clock speeds and build faster processors, so the 486DX4 computer became a reality. The most common processor speeds in this line are the 100 MHz and 120 MHz systems, and I have seen a 133 MHz processor.

8086—The IBM computer had to start somewhere. This was the processor of choice at the time. With an 8087 coprocessor, 640 KB of RAM and a 10-MB hard drive, this was the premier home computer for some time. If you opened an IBM PS/2 computer, this is what you would see. This processor supported 8 bits externally and 16 bits internally, and could address 1 MB of RAM. It ran at a smoking 10 MHz.

8088—This 8 bit internal and external version of the 8086 found its way into most of the IBM XT computers. With the capability to address 1 MB of RAM and operate up to 10 megahertz, this system was the computer most people bought for home use.

AGP—*Accelerated graphics port* video cards use a proprietary bus structure and provide significant improvements on 3-D video performance. They work in hand with the MMX instruction set to provide previously unheard of graphics speed.

Adapter—An *adapter* connects two pieces of hardware and translates one form of connection to the other. It can be an interface cable such as a DB25 to a parallel printer cable, a 9 to 25-pin adapter for use with a mouse, or an add-in card whose purpose is connecting the motherboard bus to another device, like a hard disk.

The SCSI and IDE hard-disk drive controllers are both adapters. So is a video add-in card.

Add-in card—*Add-in cards* connect the motherboard to the devices you wish to operate with your computer. The video card, for example, connects the video monitor to the CPU through the motherboard. The sound card is an adapter that takes digital signals from programs and connects them to your speakers after processing them.

Address—Everything connected to your computer via an add-in card has a unique *address* if it is an input or output device. This address is how your computer knows where to send data or where to receive information.

Memory locations are also addresses. Programs use memory addresses to find stored information to retrieve and process.

Addresses can be hardware addresses for a physical device or software data addresses in memory on a computer. The microprocessor treats them all the same.

ANSI—The *American National Standards Institute*. This group controls specifications for many industrial applications, including the computer industry. The standards for displaying information, screen color, and positioning are part of this discipline.

The ANSI.SYS driver is often loaded as a line in your CONFIG.SYS file. If it is loaded, your computer can respond correctly to ANSI commands in the programs you execute. This DOS command is seldom seen in the Windows 98 environment of today.

ASP—An agency that provides software rental is often called an *application service provider*. They provide subscription services for applications that they maintain and keep current, and access is generally over the Web. Primary users are the businesses that are here today and gone tomorrow and do not wish to purchase anything that must be liquidated later.

Actionable—Once only a legal term, it now means anything you can take action on. "Looking at your to-do list, these two items are *actionable*."

Amazon-ized—A Web-based retailer has just taken over your industrial niche. You have just been *Amazon-ized*.

Application—An *application* is a program or programs designed to execute a particular operation. For example, a word processor is an application designed to perform writing, editing, spell checking, and publishing functions.

Astroturf—Spam directed against politicians in order to change their opinions. Ineffective, since most politicians are unable to read or understand the English language.

AT-compatible—If a peripheral or computer provides the basic function as its counterpart in the original AT computer, it is *AT-compatible*. This is a must for buyers who need to know the cloned programs and accessories are compatible with their computer or add-on device. IBM compatible is another way of describing compatibility.

AUTOEXEX.BAT—This is one of the principal DOS configuration files. Programs that set up hardware or allocate memory blocks often utilize it. You can use an ASCII editor, such as the DOS edit command, to add lines of code or change parameters in this file.

The *AUTOEXEC.BAT* file and all lines of code within it are executed in order of appearance. Some applications may be sensitive to the order in which commands appear in this file.

The most important feature of this file is the ability to set the *path statement*. This is where paths are created to directories containing executable code. Commands can be executed anywhere in your computer if a path command to the executable code exists.

For example, you exit Windows. You are in the d:\windows directory on a two hard disk system. In your AUTOEXEC.BAT file, a path statement has the following line:

path = c:\norton

You type the command *sysinfo*, a Norton Utilities Version 8 DOS utility program.

Without a DOS path to the directory c:\norton, you would get a *bad command or file name* DOS error message and the screen would be laughing at you behind your back.

BAU—*Business as usual.* Very commonly used in e-mail correspondence. Unlikely to be found in any intelligent discourse otherwise.

Backbone provider—The larger companies that provide leased Internet access to Internet service providers.

Bandwidth—This common engineering term has been redefined as the speed at which data can be transferred electronically from the Internet-based application into our computer. This data rate is determined primarily by your method of connection, whether it is modem, cable, or DSL.

Barn raising—This is a type of problem resolution that is accomplished by dragging everyone not doing anything from all company functions.

Base address—Everything has a starting point. The first location in memory where a program resides is the *base address* of the program. Installed hardware devices also have a base address.

Batch files—Like the AUTOEXEC.BAT file mentioned above, DOS recognizes filenames ending in *.BAT* as *batch files.* These files are normally ASCII files written by the computer user to make life easier.

For example, if you have an antivirus program and wish to run it occasionally but do not want to waste a path statement to the directory *antivir* on a program operated only once or twice a month, you can enter the DOS editor by typing:

edit clean.bat

The file clean.bat will be created. Now start typing the commands.

cd c:\antivir

The first command changes your working directory to c:\antivir.

f-prot

This will execute an anti-virus program called f-prot.

Now follow the DOS edit screen commands to save the file and exit the editor.

This is a simple batch program, but it will execute automatically if you type the command *clean* followed by the *enter* key.

BBS—*Bulletin board services* exist worldwide for your enjoyment. Not to be confused with the Internet, a bulletin board is normally a single computer or system you can dial up and obtain shareware from or a place where you can engage in chat groups.

BBSes became popular long before the Internet as a way groups could share files and information. Many companies still keep an open BBS to allow you to get the latest software updates and information.

One magazine that lists national BBS numbers every other month is the Computer Shopper, P.O. Box 51020, Boulder, CO 80321-1020.

Below zeroes—This is the customer that costs you immeasurable resources while yielding nearly nothing in financial return for your company.

Bench—Biological assets. This has become a commonly used phrase in the communications and electronic industry. The office manager that needs additional resources to finish a task on time will say, often in vain, "We need *bench* to wrap up on time."

Betamaxed—When the best technology falls victim to second best, primarily due to better marketing of number two, product one has been *betamaxed*.

BIOS—You will see this term used repeatedly throughout this book. The *basic input/output system* is the ROM where your configuration platform resides and is the first code to run when you turn on a computer.

The BIOS (pronounced "buy-ose") sets up hardware and software addresses and is the software interface between different devices in your computer. BIOS exists on your motherboard (and occasionally video adapters and other add-in cards) and provides interface services to and from the motherboard and these peripherals.

Bit—The *bit*, or BInary digiT, is the building block for all information transmitted to or from any element in a computer. A bit can be a 0 or a 1, where 0 and 1 are opposite logic states. Computers communicate by building *bytes* consisting of 8 bits, and grouping the bytes in groups of two or more called *words*.

Bluetooth—Aimed at unifying computing and telecom industries, *Bluetooth* is a method of connection that uses wireless technology to eliminate cabling between hardware devices. The wireless connection is established through low-frequency radio signals. (Use of this technology is royalty-free, so count on it becoming increasingly popular.)

Boot—The act of initialization a computer undergoes when you first turn it on is called "*booting up.*" The BIOS starts the boot process and performs basic initialization.

The CMOS memory then executes configuration information to identify the hardware in your computer and perform basic tests on memory and other components as specified in CMOS setup.

Finally, the initialization files CONFIG.SYS, AUTOEXEC.BAT and any other configuration files are run to set up components not specified in BIOS or CMOS.

Normally, programs modify configuration files so the programs know what hardware exists and can use it. This process occurs as the programs are being installed for the first time. The computer is ready for use after this process is complete.

Broadband—This technology allows multiple channels of voice, data, and/or video to be simultaneously broadcast over the Internet.

BSOD—*Blue Screen of Death*, aka Nightmare 101. You have just done something Windows doesn't like, so the screen suddenly goes blue and you are left with a cryptic message outlining what to do next (and it *never* works).

Bus—This is the pathway used by signals and data to travel to and from the microprocessor and all add-in cards and accessories in your computer. The *bus* transmits signals to control the video, disk, and I/O operations, connects the memory and the processor, and is used by programs to control all the above hardware elements.

Bus type is a primary reason some computers are faster than others. An 8-bit bus handles 8 lines of data simultaneously, and a 64-bit bus can handle 8 groups of 8 lines in the same amount of time. Imagine a ribbon cable, like the hard drive interconnecting cable. The more wires in the cable, the more data can be processed simultaneously.

Byte—In computer lingo, a *byte* is a group of 8 bits of computer information. The byte is the most common method to express memory size, hard disk capacity, and file size.

A kilobyte is 1,024 bytes of information, often called a KB, or Kbyte. A megabyte is 1,024 million bytes of information, often referred to as MB or Mbyte, and the primary measurement unit of hard drive, floppy disk, and memory capacity.

A recent addition to the measurement scheme is the gigabyte, which is 1,000 MB of information or capacity. With 10-GB SCSI hard drives becoming obsolete, there will be another step in memory measurement coming soon: the terabyte. Hard disks of 100 MB have become the standard in many new systems, both purchased and custom-built.

Capsizing—This applies to the famous fiber-optic industry's process of constantly downsizing companies without reducing workload. Eventually the company dies a horrible painful death.

CGA—This was the *color graphics adapter* in the first IBM color systems. The monitor and adapter combination was capable of 320x320 resolution and 16 colors, along with rudimentary text support. If you have one of these around its best current use is target practice.

Chortal—A Chinese Web portal. To define portal, consider that many Web sites consider themselves to be portals into the Internet. They hope you will set them as your default method of Internet access.

You, being significantly smarter than they hope, will use your own start page for Internet access.

CISC—*Complex instruction set computer*. Most PCs fit into this category, in which the CPU can handle as many as 200 instructions. RISC (reduced instruction set computer) systems, used by workstations and some PCs, handle fewer instructions.

Cisco—Think outside the box (router) for a moment. Cisco has embedded themselves into every aspect of telecommunications, including wireless, fiber, and everything to do with the Internet. Bet you thought Microsoft was a monopoly...

CMOS—*Complimentary metal oxide semiconductor* is a process for integrated circuit manufacture. The devices are normally low power consumption, and ideal for battery operation. This makes them usable in portable computers or laptops.

Two devices in your computer continue operating even when the power is turned off and the plug is removed from the wall socket. When properly set, the CMOS clock runs off the small battery on the motherboard, keeping the correct date and time.

Speaking of CMOS setup, a programmable integrated circuit saves the information you enter into the CMOS setup program and reuses it each time you turn on your computer. This device also runs off the small battery. When you operate the computer, the battery is recharged.

Cockroach—This can be a little problem that, upon further research, is actually the tip of the iceberg. It is often a virus that was detected after doing significant damage to your system.

Command line and command prompt—When you turn on your computer your screen displays a *command prompt* (unless you enter a program automatically during the boot process). This is the first character string on the *command line*. When you type, the characters appear after the prompt. The command prompt can be configured. A line in your AUTOEXEC.BAT file could read:

prompt = PG

This would give you a prompt designating the drive letter followed by the current path. If you were in the DOS directory on the first hard drive in your system, the prompt would be:

C:\DOS>

Now for an enjoyable and easy to read screen in DOS, I have a prompt line in my AUTOEXEC.BAT file that looks like this:

prompt = $e[0;37;44m$P$G

This gives me a blue screen with white letters. A must for this option is a line in your CONFIG.SYS file reading:

device = ANSI.SYS

The special characters in this prompt command are available in the MS DOS version 6.0 or later manual.

The *command line* is where the commands you type are shown.

CONFIG.SYS—This is the configuration file, which is executed after the BIOS and CMOS setup routines are processed. It precedes the AUTOEXEC.BAT file in order of execution. The hardware and software device drivers for video, CD-ROM, and sound add-in cards normally reside here.

You will have several lines in this file starting with *device =*. These are device drivers. They control programs like ANSI.SYS, EMM386.EXE and several hardware drivers.

The DOS initialization programs are called out in the CONFIG.SYS file. In Windows, these files are embedded in WIN.INI, SYSTEM.INI, and CONTROL.INI files in the Windows directory.

Controller cards—Controller cards are synonymous with adapter cards. They process data to and from the CPU. See *adapter* and *add-in card*.

Conventional memory—Often called low memory, this is the first 640 KB of RAM installed in your computer. DOS programs run in this portion of memory. Unfortunately, this area in memory normally houses all of the device drivers and *TSR* programs running around in your computer. This reduces the maximum program size you can run under DOS.

Fortunately, Windows 95 and other programs break the 640 KB barrier. Programs such as MS-DOS memmaker also push some of the TSR programs and drivers into *upper memory* and get some of the 640 KB back.

CPU—The *central processing unit* is the main device on the motherboard. The CPU can be anything from an 8086 through a Pentium Pro and beyond. The CPU determines the bus architecture and system performance and speed. The computer's price is also determined by CPU type. (These processors are for IBM and compatible computers.)

Critical mass—In the computer industry, when a program becomes feature-laden to the point that it is useless for nearly every one of the embedded tasks, it has reached *critical mass*.

As programmers add features, they often lose sight of the original program's purpose and seem to forget that ease of use is one of the reasons we buy software.

Cube farm—A *cube farm* is one of many features in the new business scene. Offices have been replaced by look-alike cubicles, which allows the company to maximize space utilization and headcount in space-restricted areas.

Current directory—Your *current directory* is the spot in your system path you are indexed to. Every operation you perform runs on files and programs in the current directory. The current directory is searched first for commands you execute, then the path statement is searched until the program you executed is found.

Current disk drive—If you have a prompt that displays your current directory, it probably also displays your *current disk drive*. If you are in the root directory of the hard disk you normally boot from, your prompt may look like this:

C:\>

You can change your current disk drive by typing the drive letter, followed by a colon, then pressing the *return* key. Example: To change to the A drive, type *A:*

Your current disk drive will be the *A* floppy disk. The prompt will change to:

A:\>

Your current disk drive is the one first searched by any commands you execute. The *path* statement takes over afterward. Note that your computer BIOS may set different resources in your computer to be your default current drive.

Cyberslacker—An employee that utilizes significant amounts of time and computer resources in the workplace is defined as a *cyberslacker*. It has been determined that approximately 15 percent of all workers involved in the computer industry spend a minimum of 10 percent of their workday cyberslacking.

Data dump—"In the unlikely event of a water landing..." Sound familiar? When your computer crashes, it is unlikely that you will have a chance to save any files that were open at the time, so the data is "dumped" onto the hard disk with no file association. Some programs automatically backup work as you process data but you should periodically save your work as you progress.

Defrag—This term refers to the act of *defragmenting* files and directories on your hard disk. When files are defragmented, they are quickly accessed. Fragmented files (meaning files scattered throughout the hard disk surface) require multiple read and access cycles from the hard disk heads to capture the file for use. This makes for a slow system, which will get slower over time. It is suggested that you run a good disk defragmentation program periodically to eliminate this problem.

Device—Hardware connected to or inside your computer is considered a *device*. Most devices are hardware and either accept or transmit data. A video monitor accepts data and a keyboard transmits it. Both are devices.

Some software programs set drivers for *virtual devices*. The virtual device accepts input or gives output, but is merely a subprogram and not hardware. This is common in sophisticated graphics programs, which swap output and input with other resident programs.

Device driver—*Device drivers* are pieces of software designed to configure hardware in your computer to perform certain tasks. You will find device drivers in your CONFIG.SYS file. *See CONFIG.SYS.* Some device drivers DOS uses are HIMEM.SYS AND ANSI.SYS.

Diagnostic programs—These programs, discussed in Chapter 8, are tools to identify and correct problems. Diagnostic routines range from full-blown burn-in programs that test all operational parameters of your computer, to simple memory test routines.

Directory—When you first install DOS on a virgin hard disk, your first *directory* is created. The root directory is the first place on the hard disk programs and data are stored. The second directory is normally the DOS directory, created by your DOS installation disk to store the DOS program files. As you install other programs they often create their own directories, or folders, to store the files required to run.

A DOS file system is like an upside down tree, with each branch representing a different directory and the root directory at the top. As you add programs, branches grow on the tree.

Why have directories? First, there is a limit on how many files can exist in the root directory. If you have 512 or fewer files, you may never need any sub-directories. If you have 513 files, forget it. Many programs have more than 512 files.

Second, for organization of files within programs, directories and subdirectories are necessary. If each program has its own area to store information, identical filenames will not be overwritten.

Disk—A magnetic medium that rotates on a spindle with read and write heads hovering over it. Refer to the next two entries for information on the two primary types: hard disks and floppy disks.

Disk, hard—Hard disks are multiple magnetic platters with a handful of read and write heads added, all sealed up in an enclosure with a circuit board for cache and sector translation attached.

This is an oversimplification, but a good analogy. The reason hard disks are sealed in a very clean medium is the small amount of area between the heads and platters. The smallest dust particle would jam between a head and one disk platter surface, destroying your recently installed DOOM 2 program. (Hard disks are discussed in detail in Chapter 1.)

Diskette—Floppy diskettes are removable storage media that consist of a single magnetically coated vinyl platter installed in a jacket. The drive for a floppy disk has a spindle that spins the floppy disk and read/write heads to transfer data to and from the floppy diskette.

Floppy diskettes are the most common way to transfer data to other computers.

Disk controller—A *disk controller* is the IDE or SCSI interface between the hard disk and floppy disk drives and the CPU. It can be an add-in card or built-in circuitry on the motherboard.

DMA—*Direct memory access* is one way to transfer data between computer memory and a hardware device installed in the computer. DMA does not require CPU involvement, making the process extremely fast.

DOS disk—A *DOS disk* is one that has been DOS formatted and one that can be utilized for data storage and retrieval on a DOS-based system.

DOS memory—*DOS memory* is considered the first 640 KB of addressable memory in your computer. See *conventional memory*. It holds boot data, programs, and system information.

DOS—The *disk operating system* is software written to perform on a specific type of computer. In the case of MS-DOS, the program was written to operate on IBM and compatible PC systems.

Applications unique to the type of hard disk, monitor and adapter, file system, and input/output devices are written and developed into a complete operating system package. (DOS recognizes commands typed in both upper and lower case. I mix upper and lower case in commands all the time, but many programming tools do not. Be careful.)

DOS boot diskette—A floppy diskette with the necessary DOS system files required to launch DOS is called a boot diskette. It may be necessary to have one if something happens to the boot block on your hard drive.

A *boot disk* is an invaluable tool. The DOS manual describes how to make one for yourself.

Dot-com—This is a virtual company with no doors, windows, furniture, etc. It lives in the domain of the Internet and consumes VC (venture capitalist) money. After it eats up the money, it dies and leaves the once-millionaires that invested in it without a penny to their name.

Drip irrigation—When you visit the computer store for the first time you will be exposed to this method of salesmanship, in which the salesman gives a customer just enough information to lead him to buy the most expensive thing the store has to sell. Hopefully with the aid of this book you will be able to set the sales personnel aside and shop for what you want, not what they want you to buy.

Drive—The assembly that transports a floppy diskette, or the entire hard disk *drive* assembly is often referred to as a drive. A CD-ROM transport system or tape transport system shares the same designation.

Dual Data Rate RAM—The fastest computers use *dual data rate RAM* or *Rambus-manufactured DRAM*. DDR RAM utilizes a "dual pumped" technique for increased performance. It allows data to be clocked both on the rising and falling edge of a clock pulse.

Dual in-line memory module—The DIMM is a circuit board that holds memory chips and has a 64-bit path. See SIMM.

Dub-dub-dub—Short for WWW. When technophiles pass on URLs, they precede with this nonsense. Obviously this is one of our many communications shortcomings.

E-business—Business is now conducted over the Internet in staggering amounts. More than 40 percent of my business is handled over the Internet through e-mail.

E-mail—Electronically transmitted mail (other than FAX transmissions) is commonly referred to as *e-mail*. It has far surpassed snail mail as a preferable method of intelligent communication between mammals.

EGA—IBM introduced the *enhanced graphics adapter* to improve graphics display quality in their computers. EGA offered a medium resolution alternative to the existing CGA system. EGA was compatible with both CGA and monochrome display units.

EIDE—Enhanced integrated disk electronics. A newer version of IDE that is three or four times faster than the old IDE standard.

EISA—The *extended industry standard architecture* definition of the internal bus structure on an IBM or compatible PC redefined the existing standard. It offered higher speed and more features than the *ISA* bus.

The real improvement was definition of a 32-bit architecture completely different from the existing and proprietary IBM MicroChannel system; one the clone industry quickly adopted as the 32-bit standard.

EMM—The software that controls use and allocation of high memory in a PC is referred to as an *expanded memory manager*. The specification is sometimes called *LIM*, for its developers, Lotus, Intel, and Microsoft.

The upper memory between the DOS memory (the first 640 KB) and 1 MB can be included in the expanded memory. The EMM sets aside 64 KB of upper memory as a map to the extended memory for certain programs to use. Extended memory usually starts at 1 MB and runs up to the amount of RAM installed on the motherboard.

EMS—The *expanded memory specification* is a standard that governs the hardware and software that comprises expanded memory.

ENTER—The *ENTER*, or carriage return key signifies termination of a command line. It is often called the *RETURN* key. Do not confuse the alphanumeric ENTER key with the numeric keypad ENTER key. In some programs they will have different functions. Normally, however, they are identical in function.

Environment—DOS sets aside a small amount of memory to store information. This information is available for use by other programs. Among the things in the DOS environment are the *path* information, *prompt,* and *set* information for variable definition.

ESDI—The *enhanced small devices interface* is a definition of the standards applying to the interconnection of a type of high-speed hard disk drive. It joins the currently utilized SCSI and IDE interface specifications.

Execute—When a program is running, it is being executed. A computer executes instruction sets when it runs software programs.

An *executable file* is a file normally having a .BAT, .EXE, or .COM filename extension. Files like this can be executed by typing the filename without the extension, then pressing the *ENTER* key.

Expanded memory—*Expanded memory* is the portion of RAM set aside and managed by the EMM. This memory is normally used as a scratch pad for database and spreadsheet programs.

The EMM sets aside a 64 KB portion of upper memory between the DOS memory and 1MB. This 64 KB of memory serves as an index to the larger portion of expanded memory above 1 MB. The expanded memory size is limited only by the motherboard capacity and the amount of RAM you have installed on the system. It can be up to 1 TB in current Pentium 4 systems.

Extended memory—In a 286 or higher computer, memory above 1 MB is referred to as *extended memory*. Disk caching is a principal use for this memory.

If you install HIMEM.SYS in your CONFIG.SYS file, you can set aside a 64 KB portion of extended memory for DOS and other TSR programs.

Face time—This is very rare in the telecommunications industry. It is time in front of a salesperson, serviceman, or other computer icon whose time is so valuable that you have to weed through a myriad of message buttons on your phone just to hear a real voice. In the unlikely event you actual get some *face time* with a sales or service person, bleed him dry.

Fast-food system—A computer system that's been preassembled by a computer manufacturer. These computers are far less effective and far more expensive than the one you'll be able to build after reading this book!

FAT—The file allocation table stores the location of each part of each file. It's how the computer finds files on the hard disk.

File—A *file* is a portion of a program or data occupying space in memory or on a disk. Some files are complete programs, but most files are data resulting from program execution.

A file stored on a disk is identified in the file allocation table, or FAT, by its starting location and size. This way the file can be accessed, modified, or deleted as required by you or program execution.

Filename—The *filename* is a group of ASCII characters you assign to a file to identify it. In a DOS system, a filename can be up to eight characters with a three-character extension identifying the type of file.

In Windows 95, the eight-character limit is gone and you have infinitely more flexibility naming files.

Filenames must be unique in the same directory, lest they be overwritten by another application.

First eyes—On the Internet, it is critical to be the first Web site or portal to capture users' attention (and money). ISPs pay a lot of money to be the first thing people see when they log onto the Internet.

Filename extension—A string of one to three characters following the period in a filename is the *filename extension*. The extension normally describes the type of file, so applications can use it.

If you look in your CONFIG.SYS file, you will see several types of DOS filename extensions. Those ending in .EXE and .COM files are ones DOS can load and execute. Filenames ending in .SYS are DOS system files and .DRV files are device driver filenames.

Fixed disk—This doesn't mean a repaired disk. Refer to disk, hard.

404—This is the error message you receive when searching for a Web page, only to find it has disappeared for some reason. It also is used to describe someone who is clueless about the subject at hand.

FUD factor—*Fear, uncertainty, and doubt.* This is the best tactic the second-to-market has at its disposal. Intel, when besieged by benchmarks of the Athalon processor showing clear superiority in performance per gigahertz, quickly inquired of the buying public: "Does it work well under load? Is it *robust*? Does it fit the current industry standard models?" Then they released the 2 GHz version of the Pentium 4, which finally outperformed the mere 1.4 GHz Athalon, but barely.

Geek—Once measured by the quantity of pencils in their pocket, *geeks* are now determined by the quantity of pocket computer interfacing gadgets they employ.

Gigabyte—A *gigabyte* is 1,024 MB of memory, storage, or information. Hard disk drives and tape backup systems have capacities in this range.

GUI—*Graphical user interfaces* (pronounced "gooey") are not messy, as the buzzword might indicate. The icons and display of your computer are your GUI.

Hacker—Someone that has refined the capabilities in the computer industry of manipulating a computer to do anything they wish, through either software or hardware, is a *hacker*. This is not always bad. Most hackers never create viruses or secretly enter forbidden computer space, at least so we say...

Hang time—Occasionally you will be typing away and for some reason your computer goes to sleep. You patiently wait, time goes by, and you try everything imaginable to get things going again. Finally, you give the three-finger salute (ctrl + alt + del) and you meet the BSOD (Blue Screen of Death).

Hardware interrupt—Interrupts alert the CPU of events requiring action. *Hardware interrupts* are asserted by a keyboard, mouse, hard disk, etc., to inform the microprocessor that software interaction is requested. The action may be to open or close a file on the hard disk, accept movement information from a mouse or input from the keyboard.

Hercules—Before IBM released the medium-resolution EGA system for PC color displays, Hercules Technology came out with one. To this day, most video adapters are downward compatible to the *Hercules* format.

Hexadecimal—Unlike the standard base-10 counting system most humans use, computers often use a base-16 system called *hexadecimal notation*. Four bits of information, represented by 1, 2, 4, and 8, make up the base-16 number system. The 15 "numbers" that comprise the system are 0 through 9 and A through F. An 8-bit byte, represented by (8 4 2 1) (8 4 2 1) represents 255 different items, 00 through FF.

High memory—*HMA*, or the *high memory area*, is the 64 KB area above the 1 MB address range that HIMEM.SYS creates. This area can be used by a program for storage of intermediate results during program execution. When this process occurs, you have more free *DOS* memory available for other applications.

Host adapter—Add-in cards that interface between hardware devices, such as hard disks or video monitors, are referred to as *host adapters*. They process data to and from these devices and the memory, allowing the CPU to expend effort elsewhere. This speeds up execution of programs.

IBM-compatible—If a computer or component provides the same function as the original component in an IBM computer, the device or computer is *IBM-compatible*. This means the software and hardware devices will behave the same in the clone and the original IBM machine.

IDE—The *integrated drive electronics* standard for hard-disk control is the most popular today. It regulates the definition of a high-speed integrated drive and controller assembly, hence the name. An adapter to transfer data to and from the hard disk is normally integrated into the motherboard, but is also available as an add-on card.

The IDE specification is part of the ATA standard. AT-Attachments is the specification used in the interface for hard disk drives to the IBM PC/AT bus.

I/O—*Input/output* is the ability of a computer to transfer data to and from internal and external devices. This capability can be inherent in both hardware and software. Video cards and USB adapters are I/O devices.

I/O often refers to a special add-in card or function embedded in the motherboard. This function controls data transfer between devices inside the computer and outside, and includes interaction with other computers through a modem or external port.

IRQ—*Interrupt requests* (IRQs) are signals transferred over the bus between add-in cards and the CPU. They instruct the CPU to perform immediate action.

Normally IRQ lines are asserted to request the CPU coordinate transfer of data between add in devices and memory.

ISA—The 8- and 16-bit bus utilized by IBM and compatible computers is the *industry standard architecture* bus. It can accompany a VESA or PCI system. Most computers have up to three ISA connectors to ensure compatibility with older add-in cards.

Java—*Java* is the one programming language that migrates across computer systems. There was a time everyone thought it would give Microsoft a run for the money...

Killer apps—Applications that excel in one manner or another are called *killer apps*.

Legacy system—This term applies to older

computer systems, such as the 486, Pentium, 386, and AT.

LoadHigh—This statement describes the action of setting an executable file or device driver in the upper memory area or in high memory. With this command in your CONFIG.SYS or AUTOEXEC.BAT file, you can specify the start memory address the command must use.

Before you use this command, you must initialize a memory manager such as EMM386 or QEMM. The line to start the memory manager must precede this line in the batch file.

Local bus—The VESA standard (set down by the Video Electronics Standard Association) is a high-speed I/O to CPU interface that maintains compatibility with the ISA standard interface.

Logical devices—Partitioning a large hard drive into smaller ones creates a *logical device* for each partition. DOS treats each partition as a physical device, not as a portion of one drive.

A logical drive is a partition, as mentioned above. Other logical devices are RAM drives created in RAM and maintained by software control. Network drives are considered to be logical devices by your computer.

Loopback adapter—This is a special connector wired to allow you to test communications ports without actually going online.

Lower memory—See DOS memory.

M-commerce—Now that cell phones are part of the Internet, you can change your dental appointment and reorient your stock portfolio just before rear-ending the car in front of you. Not for me!

Math coprocessor—The *math coprocessor* is integrated into 486DX and all faster microprocessors for IBM and compatible computers. The 486SX, 386 and earlier computers had an expansion slot to accommodate one if required.

The math coprocessor performs all the complex math operations, allowing the CPU to perform other tasks.

MCA—*Micro channel architecture* is the standard utilized in the IBM PS/2 computer line. It is an IBM trademark and is incompatible with all other architectures past and present in any other system.

MCA systems use different adapters and add-in cards, none of which will work in anything else.

MCGA—Put simply, this refers to the *multicolor graphics array* system that was used in IBM PS/2 computers. It was noted for great gray-scale and improved resolution over CGA.

Meatloaf—Homemade spam consisting typically of jokes and/or obscene pictures, normally sent during work hours to your unwitting coworkers.

MDA—The first IBM computers had the *monochrome display adapter*. The display was either green or amber. See *target practice*.

Megabyte—A *megabyte* (MB) is 1,024 KB of information, storage, or memory.

Megahertz—This measure of frequency is in millions of cycles per second. It is abbreviated as MHz. Clock speeds are measured in *megahertz*.

Memory—*Memory* is any form of storage area for program use that resides in your computer. RAM, hard disks, floppies, and CMOS are types of memory. So are tape cartridges or CD-ROMs. Cache is the fastest memory in your system, and the floppy disk is the slowest.

Microprocessor—See *CPU*.

MIDI—The *musical instrument device interface* is the industry standard driving the computer interface for musical devices. It specifies connections, hardware, and software protocol.

Mips—Stands for million instructions per second.

MMX—This term refers to the first significant extension to the 1985-era instruction set inside the CISC processor family. The additional 57 new instructions are used to accelerate calculations in graphics and audio applications, including 2-D and 3-D graphics, speech recognition and synthesis, and video processing and types of compression. The performance expectations are an increase of 50 to 100 percent in speed while using multimedia programs and equipment.

Intel upgraded its product line to *MMX* in 1997 and released a Pentium Pro in RISC format with embedded MMX.

Modem—This name is an abbreviation for the actual function of the device. The *modulator demodulator* is an analog to digital and digital to analog converter. The modem converts digital information from a computer to analog signals that can travel through the phone lines. It accomplishes the reverse upon receiving signals from another computer.

Motherboard—The heart and soul of a computer is the *motherboard*. Everything plugs into it and it serves as the information pathway to and from the CPU and each device connected to it.

A motherboard typically has the CPU, RAM, cache, and IDE I/O function installed. Add-on functionality in the form of video support, hard and floppy disks, keyboards, and mice complete the computer.

MS-DOS—Bill Gates before he became a millionaire. MS-DOS was the de facto standard in the 1980s for computer software.

Multitasking—Performing more than one operation at once is *multitasking*. This is normally a software process in which programs and data are quickly swapped between a reserved portion of memory and the active memory a microprocessor is using.

In a process like this, the software determines how long each operation remains on hold in reserved memory and how long the operation gets CPU attention. If you have a faster computer, you may never notice any slowdown in operation while your computer is performing multitasking operations.

The *foreground* process, the one you can see on the screen, is typically the one getting most of the CPU's attention. Examples of programs that use

multitasking are Windows, Windows 9X and DESQview.

Network—When you connect two or more computers, you are establishing a *network*. Networking computers is essential when multiple users must access common data and programs. The workplace is your most likely place to encounter a network.

Network interface—An add-in card to interface between your computer and a network communications hub is called a *network interface* card. This add-in card processes digital signals from your computer and sends them to a common node all other users share with you.

Offline—A computer not connected to another computer, network, or the Internet.

Online services—*Online services* are pay-for-use BBSs with advertisements. They do, however, offer connectivity to a large number of useful and enjoyable sites. Access to shareware, electronic mail, software support, and online games and chat groups are included. America Online, CompuServe, Prodigy, and the Microsoft Network are examples of online services.

Page frame—On a DOS machine, the location in memory between DOS memory and 1 MB where expanded memory is indexed is called *page frame* memory.

Parallel I/O—Transferring data using the parallel port is extremely fast. Eight or more bits of information can be sent simultaneously using the *parallel I/O* port on your computer. Data transfer rates of 100 KB are not unusual using this technique. The computer's parallel or printer port is the vehicle of transportation.

Parameter—Some commands allow you to specify how the program executes. Setting different *parameters* in the command line does this.

Example:
pkzip -ex -rp aargh.zip b:*.*

The PKWARE program pkzip has been executed. The parameters -ex and -rp specify how the program will be executed.

PC—The first model designation IBM gave to its personal computer family was *PC*. All personal computer manufacturers that made IBM compatible computers and accessories adopted this term.

The base IBM machine had 64 KB of memory, an optional tape drive instead of hard drives, and a monochrome display. Data was transferred between computers using a floppy disk storage device.

PC-compatible—See *IBM-compatible* and *AT-compatible*.

PCI—The *peripheral component interconnect* standard developed by Intel specifies a very fast interface between I/O devices and the CPU. The primary add-in cards using this interface are the video adapter and the IDE I/O cards.

PCMCIA—Portable computers brought with them a new specification. The *Personal Computer Memory Card Industry Association* I/O interconnect specification is the standard for interfacing memory, disk drives, modems, and network cards to portable computers.

Pentium—This 64-bit microprocessor is capable of operating beyond 233 MHz, and contains 16 KB of instruction cache and an internal floating-point processor. It is the current mid-range processor, replacing the 486 of yesteryear.

Pentium II—The replacement for the Pentium Pro, this CPU has MMX instruction sets included and has the capabilities of the Pentium and Pentium Pro. It is packaged more like an add-in card than a processor. Current versions run at speeds beyond 400 MHz and have L2 caches of 512 KB. Offshoots of this design included the Pentium 3 and the Pentium 4.

Peripheral—A device (e.g., a scanner or printer) that is not necessary for the computer to operate is a *peripheral* device. Internal tape drives and CD-ROMs are peripheral devices, as are the external versions.

Physical drive—The hard disk drive containing your partitions is a *physical drive*. Your floppy drives, tape drive, and CD-ROM drive are physical drives. A physical drive is hardware, not a software managed partition on your (hardware) disk drive. The partitions on your hard drive, if any, are not physical drives.

Ping—Swiped from sonar technology, to *ping* an Internet address is to determine if it exists and is accepting requests.

Port address—The address in memory through which any hardware device allows access is its *port address*.

POST—When you turn on a computer, the first thing it does is a *power on self test*, or POST. It runs diagnostic routines on various hardware components as specified in BIOS or CMOS setup. If errors are encountered, the test provides error messages or beep codes, or both.

Prompt—Your computer indicates when it is ready for commands by displaying a command *prompt*. The prompt visual indicator can be changed using the DOS prompt command as specified in your DOS manual.

PS/2—IBM recently released a new version of their *Personal System/2* computer. These systems had new bus and adapter designs and were the current state of the art when introduced.

RAM—*Random access memory* is the primary storage computers use to store intermediate results. When a program is executed, data flows into and out of RAM during the processing portion of the program. Only after all operations are performed is the data stored on a hard disk or floppy drive.

RAM is identified by its storage capacity and speed. (I have 16 MB of EDO 60 nanosecond DRAM in my computer.) DRAM must be *refreshed*, or repeatedly written to with the same data, in order to retain information.

Cache memory is also RAM. Cache is extremely fast SRAM, which requires no refreshing, hence the speed. Eight nanoseconds is the average pipeline cache RAM's speed.

RISC—See CISC.

ROM—The ROM (*read-only memory*) in your computer consists of one or more programmed EPROMS with setup information specific to your computer. The programs in ROM execute when you boot the computer. ROM cannot easily be altered or erased.

ROM BIOS is the set of programs loaded in the ROM. Often, certain video adapters and add-in cards may have their own ROM BIOS.

Some computers today come with *FLASH BIOS*. Running a software program can change EPROM memory. This is ideal as the new BIOS is released to support more hardware devices and faster CPUs.

Root directory—The first directory on a hard disk or floppy diskette is the *root directory*. See *directory*.

Scalable—Expandable to meet future needs.

SCSI—The *small computer system interface* (pronounced "scuzzy") was the fastest thing around until the high speed IDE drives became a reality. SCSI drives still hold the size record with drives in the 10 GB range commonplace.

SCSI hard drives require a special interface to run in a PC. The interface supports many more drives than are possible with any other drive architecture.

SDRAM—*Synchronous dynamic read-only memory* is the current standard for fast computer memory. It is nearly as fast as pipeline burst cache, at 10Ns access speed. Significant improvements in application speed can be achieved with SDRAM installed in a Pentium 200, 200 MMX or Pentium Pro system.

Serial I/O—Serial data transfer occurs one *bit* at a time, unlike parallel I/O, which transfers one *byte* (8 bits) at a time. The good side of serial transfer is compatibility with modems and existing data-transfer protocol.

Though it is fairly slow at 115 KB per second, it is the most common method of interconnection between computers for data transfer.

Communication occurs through one of the *serial ports* in your computer. A mouse or other serial device can use the other ports.

Shadow RAM—Many computers map BIOS information into faster RAM devices to speed up various operations. The RAM locations specified in CMOS setup as *shadow RAM* are where this information is stored and executed.

Single in-line memory module—A SIMM is a 32-bit path circuit board that holds memory chips. See DIMM.

Software interrupt—An interrupt command from a program that requires CPU attention is a *software interrupt*. These can occur upon completion of part of a program or when device drivers are invoked. Keyboard operations, drive access and certain timing services are available to programs as software interrupts.

SRAM—*Static RAM* holds data until it is changed, eliminating refresh cycles.

Subdirectory—Any directory within another directory is a *subdirectory*. Therefore, all directories other than the root directory are subdirectories. Subdirectories allow programs to organize data and files by the application they are associated with.

Target practice—See *EGA* and older monitors. Take 30 paces, turn, and shoot!

TSR—*Terminate and stay resident* programs are programs that remain in memory so that you can easily call up applications within them with a hot key or other command. Some device drivers, for example mouse drivers and the DOS *setver* command, fall into this category.

Turnkey—"Just turn it on and it works." This is the primary method utilized by computer system manufacturers to sell you a complete system. Since everything usually works anyway, this should not be a unique selling point for purchased systems, but it is perceived to be so.

UAR/T—The *universal asynchronous receiver/transmitter* converts parallel bus information into serial data for transfer using a modem. The device reverses the process upon receipt of serial data from a modem.

UMB—*Upper memory blocks* are made available by memory manager programs. They reside in the addressable memory area between DOS memory and 1 Mb. TSR programs and part of DOS can be placed in upper memory to free up conventional memory for applications.

uP—See *CPU*.

USB—The *universal serial bus* has become the standard for peripheral interconnect. (Mine has four in front and two in back. All but two have stuff hooked up.) USB replaces standard scanner, printer, tape backup system, keyboard, and mouse connectors.

Utilities—Programs that help with routine operations like backups, virus testing, and file and hard disk testing are normally either *utilities* or diagnostic programs. See Chapter 8 for diagnostic programs and utilities.

Vaporware—Watch out for this stuff. It is advertised before it's available, normally doesn't work when finally released, and always falls short of expectations. Example: the first release of Windows 95.

VGA—*Video graphics array* is a high-resolution graphics and text system that supports the previous IBM standards. It uses an analog video monitor as a display unit.

Video adapter card—This add-in card connects the video monitor with the CPU. *Video adapters* come in a wide range of performance and price ranges and support all bus types.

Video memory—This is a great hiding place for polymorphic viruses. It is often fast memory and speeds up graphics applications by taking the CPU out of the loop when processing video information. *Video memory* can be DRAM, or the faster VRAM.

WASP—*Wireless application service providers* are the service providers for the well-endowed cellular phone/Internet calling card market. This industry has come to fruition with the advent of cellular phones that double as information storage and retrieval units.

Windows—The first GUI program I used was *Windows*. It opened up the multitasking world to me. Windows supports multiple programs sharing the same resources.

Windows 9x—The latest release of Windows is *Windows 9x*. It has more resources available and 32-bit performance. Multitasking programs run smoothly under Windows 9x. Of course, it has been replaced by Windows 2K. (In the text of this book, when I refer to Windows 9X or Windows 2K, I mean Windows 95 or 98 and Windows 2000.)

Windows NT—*Windows NT* is the true 32-bit engine from Microsoft. It has become commonplace in power systems. Windows 2K is an offshoot.

XMS—The *extended memory specification* is the standard that defines control of any memory above DOS memory. When you load the HIMEM.SYS driver in the CONFIG.SYS file, XMS is set up. Other memory management programs and utilities can also set up XMS.

XT—This version of the IBM PC provided *extended technology*, enabling the user to add a hard drive to the machine. Up to 256 KB of memory could be installed.

2

Computer Cost and Performance

HOW MUCH CAN YOU SAVE?

This is the real question, and the reason for writing this book. Let's look at some sales literature...

Another big sale weekend and I have the advertisements in front of me. Disregarding the department store advertisements because the prices I see are too high, I peruse the electronic specialty stores and computer outlets for the best current prices on several systems.

Electronics Superstore No. 1

Prepackaged complete home office system:
Pentium 4, 1.7 system with 40-GB hard drive
17-inch .28 dot pitch monitor
Mini-tower case
32-MB NVIDIA GeForce 2 video card
56K fax/modem
256 MB of RAM
48-speed CD-ROM and SB Live! sound card
Satellite speakers
3.5-inch 1.4-MB floppy drive
Mouse and keyboard
Software: Windows ME (with manuals), Microsoft Money, and several generic shareware programs worth $20

Total: **$1,359.99**

Do It Yourself

Motherboard with **Pentium 4, 1.8 :**	$319
Mid-tower case:	$29
256 MB of PC-133 RAM:	$22
3.5-inch 1.44-MB floppy drive:	$10
Internal 56K fax/modem:	$12
104-style keyboard and three-button mouse:	$15
NVIDIA GeForce 2, 32-MB video card:	$69
60-GB hard drive:	$149
17-inch digital super VGA monitor .27 dot pitch:	$124
52X multimedia CD-ROM package with Sound Blaster Live! sound card, speakers, and 10 CD-ROM titles:	$79
Software: Windows, Millenium Edition:	$89
Microsoft Encarta and 10 titles:	$39

Total:	**$956**
Your savings:	**$403.99**

Bold type in the Do-It-Yourself sections indicates components that are of higher quality than the ones available in the preassembled computers.

You also get much more software—10 titles with the Encarta bundle and 10 titles with the CD-ROM bundle. The important hardware improvements in your package are a better motherboard, a faster processor, a larger hard drive, and a faster CD-ROM drive. Remember that most systems from an electronics store will not come with the best components because it is difficult for these outlets to get good prices on high-performance components. Building your own system allows you to avoid the nightmare of chasing down a hardware interrupt or DMA conflict because of these components. You also get a 52X CD-ROM!

The superstore's offering is a fairly good price on a system, but can be beaten, and without doing a lot of running around. Now, let's look at some more locally advertised bargain-priced systems and see if they can be beaten, too.

THE HOT-ROD SYSTEM

John Q. Public just won the lottery—not enough to quit his job or buy that new Rolls, but he must reward himself somehow…

The computer catalog shows a full-blown Pentium 4, 1.8 GHz computer. He knows Pentium 4 chips are coming out that clock at 2 GHz and faster but realizes they are not cost-effective; they should benchmark about the same as the 1.8-GHz chip when installed in a system. He goes the safe route and decides to get a faster chip when prices fall.

Computer Catalog Price

Complete audio/video/office desktop system:
Pentium 4, 1.8-GHz system with 512 MB of RDRAM
Mid-tower case   60-GB hard drive
17-inch SVGA monitor with .28 dot pitch
32-MB ASUS V7100 GeForce 2 video card
52X speed CD-ROM multimedia system with speakers
56K fax/modem with voice capability
Mouse and keyboard   Bookshelf
Software: Microsoft Windows ME, Office 2000,

Total:	**$2,579.99**

He comes to you gloating, informing you this is a one-of-a-kind super sale, and you will never find a system this good for the price. It is a good price indeed, but let's just see.

Do It Yourself

Motherboard with **Pentium 4, 2 GHz CPU:**	$519
Full-tower case (300W power supply):	$45
512 GB of 800 MHz RDRAM:	$178
Two each, 3.5-inch 1.44-MB floppy drive:	$20
Internal 56K fax/modem:	$12
104-style keyboard and three-button mouse:	$15
ASUS V8200 GeForce 3, 64-MB video card:	$175
Western Digital 100-GB IDE hard drive:	$249
19-inch KDS digital video monitor, .22 dot pitch:	$193
52X multimedia package with Sound Blaster Live! sound card, 52X CDROM, 16X DVDROM (2 drives):	$115

And, optionally, add these: Altec Lansing sub-woofer and surround sound system with five speakers: (price shown below)

Software: Windows 2000 Professional:	$89
Microsoft Office 2000 Pro with Bookshelf:	$189
Total to match John's system:	**$1,799**
Your savings:	**$780.99**

Now, add the optional explosive speakers mentioned above:	$55

Total to blow away John's system:	**$1,854**

And so once again, we beat the unbeatable price with quite a bit of margin.

BEATING A BARGAIN-PRICED PENTIUM SYSTEM

Why would anyone want a bare-bones Pentium computer today? Ask any student who needs a computer but doesn't have $1,000 to spend.

Most stores have the come-in computer priced extremely attractively. It usually does not have an upgradable processor and comes with a minimum of bells and whistles. Here's a sample.

Local Computer Outlet

Mini-tower or desktop Intel Celeron 900 MHz computer with 64 MB of RAM
15-inch .28 dot pitch monitor
20-GB hard drive
3.5-inch 1.44-MB floppy drive
48X CD-ROM
Windows 98 pre-installed
16-MB RAM video card
Mouse and keyboard

Total: **$699.99**

I wouldn't even think of buying a new system with these parameters. There are too many places that sell used systems like this for $200 to $400 as excellent starter systems. You can even find good Pentium 3 systems for around $550 if your needs are simple. Our objective now is to beat the price, with margin, while maintaining the option to easily upgrade to a faster computer later. The add-on components will also be Pentium-compatible. We will also include a much better video card and larger hard drive as well as more RAM.

Do It Yourself

Intel Pentium 4, 1.5 GHz and motherboard:	$199
Mini-tower case:	$19
128 MB of SDRAM:	$13
3.5-inch 1.44-MB floppy drive:	$10
104-style keyboard and three-button mouse:	$15
nVidia 32-MB AGP video card:	$35
52X CDROM:	$29
40-GB hard drive:	$91
15-inch SVGA monitor **.28** dot pitch:	$102
Software: **Windows ME:**	$89

Total: **$602**
Your savings: **$97.99**

The real importance isn't savings but the ability to upgrade this system later. Everything is upgradable, which means all components will work with the faster Pentium 4 processors. For example, the 2-GHz Pentium 4 is a drop-in upgrade and will hop up this system beyond current speed. If you would rather upgrade to an Athalon instead, the motherboard and processor are all you need to change since the video card and all other components are compatible.

The three systems whose cost I beat are priced about 10 to 30 percent below similar systems at most retail outlets. I selected these systems for comparison pricing because nobody looks for the most expensive system when selecting a computer. By building it yourself, you will save 10 to 30 percent more than this on typical computer prices.

By now you're probably convinced it is possible to build a computer and save money. I have looked at this reality several times through the years and come to the same conclusion each time. Whenever I see an advertised deal on a super system, I find it easy to beat the price by building it myself. Hence, this book.

But the most important fact remains undisclosed. I have been pricing complete systems that have generic components from inexpensive parts wholesalers. The components in most of these preassembled systems are not what you would pick if you had the choice. In fact, when I price components for a system to build, *I use prices of components I want in my system*. I purchase high-quality components that can be upgraded if possible. PnP components and current model items are the standard.

My systems normally are three to six

months more current than the computers sold in the stores. Why? I buy the newest components available at reasonable prices. Systems in most stores have been assembled and put in storage somewhere, then are purchased by the retailers in bulk. I buy components a matter of hours before I build the computer. Innovations are slow to filter into the retail computer marketplace; recent examples are DDR RAM for the Athalon processor and RDRAM for the Pentium 4.

The article that I wrote to local retailers and a local news group several years ago follows and explains my frustration with some computer retail outlets. It is an old example, but representative of current issues involving processor speed versus complete system speed. Since most currently purchasable systems do not have either RDRAM or DDR RAM installed, the article is again coming of age. Nothing foretells the future like the past.

THE CASE OF THE SLOW PENTIUM

Nowadays, the hot thing is to buy the fastest machine on the market when you upgrade to keep it from being obsolete before you reach the parking lot.

There are, however, some other serious considerations often ignored by the need-for-speed crowd currently purchasing the "fast" systems.

When purchasing a packaged system designated as "upgradable," assume your purchase is set up with some of the slowest components available and consider the cost of faster RAM, faster cache, and a faster video card in the projected upgrade cost. Why? Because it is not cost-effective for computer retailers to put the fastest and most expensive add-in components in their systems.

Never purchase a system based on processor speed alone. The benchmark data provided with this document shows why.

Note the top benchmark. This is a purchased Pentium 133 MHz system compared to a Pentium 90. The difference is insignificant—certainly not worth the significant difference in price.

The bottom benchmark compares a Pentium 120 against the same Pentium 90 tested above. This is the expected increase in performance one would like to see from a faster processor. The primary system difference is that I have set up my system BIOS parameters for faster performance and purchased the faster pipeline burst cache memory. The 7 Ns cache memory is a necessary addition to any processor faster than 90 MHz, and is seldom provided on the cookie cutter 100 MHz and faster systems. The cost of upgrading cache memory runs about $85.

The moral: Don't buy until you have a clear idea of the actual performance improvement you can expect, and never buy a system based on processor speed alone.

The Pentium 133 shown in Figure 2-1 is not really optimized, as you can see. Tested while running 32-bit applications, the primary code it was designed to run, it performs barely better than a one year old Pentium 90.

Now look at Benchmark 2 in Figure 2-2. This is more like it. The computer benchmarked here is a Pentium 120. I wonder why the store-bought Pentium 133 benchmarked so poorly in the test above?

We learn why upon opening the case. The Pentium 133 does not have pipeline burst cache! It still has the obsolete dip cache, but the Pentium 133 is six months *newer* than the Pentium 120 used here.

This is exactly why I build my own systems. Don't get the idea I am a supreme expert whose intuitive senses ferret out the best deals; rather, I am a horribly impatient shopper and will spend $5 more if I can avoid going to the store next door. The deals out there scream from every component distributor's handout and every computer magazine. (There is an extensive list of computer and trade magazines listed at the back of this book.)

BUILDING THE COMPUTER YOU WANT

We have examined how much can be saved by building our computer and found out that some packaged systems are not what they

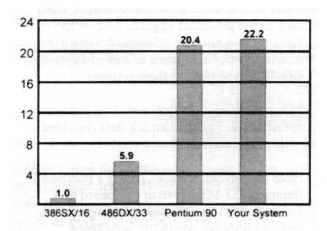

Figure 2-1. Benchmark 1.

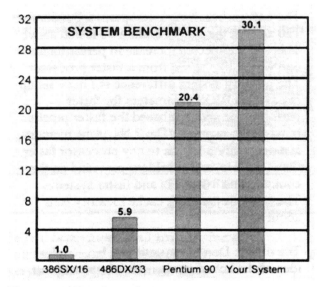

Figure 2-2. Benchmark 2.

seem to be. We have taken a good look at hard performance data from a recognized software company proving a take-out computer does indeed have that fast-food quality. Now let's take a good look at what is out there in the component categories and then buy the components we want for our custom system.

John, an attorney, came to me last year wanting a good, fast computer. He was primarily interested in a Pentium system but thought a fast Pentium system was too expensive. I had been interested in several clone systems, strictly from a performance standpoint, and suggested he build one.

**The Computer He Wanted
at the Best Price He Could Find on Sale**

Pentium 4, 1.8 GHz mini-tower multimedia system
128-MB RAM, 40-GB hard drive, 3.5-inch 1.44-MB
floppy
48X CD-ROM drive
16-bit sound card
AGP 32-MB video card
Speakers
Keyboard and mouse
Win ME and MS Works
17-inch .28 dot pitch monitor
56K fax modem.

Total: $2,199

A couple of quick moves with a screwdriver opened the case to reveal the inner workings. We found a generic 32-MB video card, which is an inexpensive moderate-speed video adapter. Two other cards were installed—a generic modem and a generic Sound-Blaster-compatible 16-bit sound card. The motherboard was a good one, with enhanced memory support onboard. It had 128 MB of RDRAM—the fast stuff. Nothing else of significance was revealed.

After having a peek at the innards, I concluded it would be cost effective to look into building an Athalon-based system as an alternative. John just sat there with a puzzled look on his face, as he was unaware that there was life beyond Intel parts and accessories. He was about to get quite an awakening...

I suggested an Athalon XP 1800+ system with a 100-GB hard drive, a DVD-ROM, a CD-RW, and a network card so he could connect to the Internet via cable. I knew this was a good system, having recently made one about a week before the lawyer's urgent request. If you look closely, you can determine that the computer in question is the star attraction of this book.

I outlined the minimum requirements for an Athalon-type system. A case, mouse, keyboard, motherboard, RAM, a floppy drive or two, modem, video card, hard drive, monitor, and CD-ROM. Speakers and a sound card wrapped up the package. Figure 2-3 is the benchmark for the "Pentium Killer" processors commonly available. I decided to let John go it alone this time.

Needless to say, this system is extremely fast. Even the slower Athalon chips are very fast.

John was beside himself. He was torn between buying the much slower system (out of fear) or jumping into the exciting world of building his own system. Deep inside, I knew his killer instincts would kick in, especially where money was concerned. He knew he could save money and get a better system, too.

I helped him with the shopping—my least favorite part. He taught me some patience in this department, so I learned something, too. I would prefer to go one place and get all the components, but John is a miser and got some really great deals. (Notice that *everything* on this list is boldface, indicating that all the components are of better quality than he would have gotten with the preassembled computer.)

Motherboard with Athalon XP 1800+	
processor and fan:	**$319**
512 MB of DDR RAM:	**$68**
High-end case:	**$49**
Floppy times two (both 3.5-inch drives for	
copying office records):	**$20**
56K fax modem:	**$12**
Keyboard and mouse bundle:	**$15**
ASUS V8200 GeForce3 video card:	**$259**
15-inch LCD monitor (3 inches thick!)	**$299**
Ethernet card:	**$7**
Toshiba 16X DVD-ROM, IDE:	**$55**
Sony 32X CD-RW:	**$59**
Windows 2K (free with stuff):	**$0**
Western Digital 100-GB hard drive:	**$249**
Sound-Blaster Live! sound card:	**$29**
Altec Lansing surround sound system:	**$55**

Total: $1,495

John just saved nearly $1,000 and got a superior system he designed himself.

Now comes the easy part. To give John an idea of what he was undertaking, I showed him the huge stack of boxes containing the parts for the project—the tower, the monitor, the accessories, the whole shebang. If that didn't terrify him, nothing would.

WHICH COMPUTER IS FASTEST?

That question is best evaluated by looking at some benchmarks of manufactured systems. Fast-food systems will not reach these benchmarks, but they can be achieved by making your own computer. (It *is* possible to achieve these benchmarks with a name-brand computer. High-end Dell, Hewlett-Packard, Sony, and Gateway computers reach similar levels, but count on spending lots of money for this performance.)

The benchmarks in Figures 2-4 and 2-5 outline processor speed in both office and games applications. Select the computer processor to fit your needs with this information and you will be more satisfied with your choices.

These two benchmarks depict clearly how your specific applications might determine your choice of processor. The youngster that lives in the 3-D world of game animation will opt for the Pentium 4, whereas an individual more interested in a stable environment for writing or performing business-related tasks might prefer the Athalon selections.

Note that the newest Athalon processor, shown in a benchmark on Figure 2-3, outperforms even the Pentium 4 2-GHz processor, but the jury is still out on which processor performs best in gaming applications with extensive 3-D rendering. I ran some tests of my own that showed that the Pentium 4 platform is still slightly better overall in gaming applications and 3-D modeling involving motion and repetitive iterations of movement and redraw.

As for any other architecture differences between a Pentium-based and an Athalon-based system, I have found none. The motherboards are different, as are the support chipsets and RAM types but beyond differences that live on the motherboard, I find no unusual quirks from either architecture. All of the peripheral devices I have purchased will work with either motherboard, including the case, all plug-in modules, and all peripheral devices that are installed in the case. From a cost standpoint,

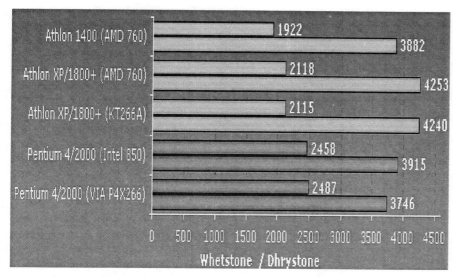

Figure 2-3. Benchmark for Athalon-based computers.

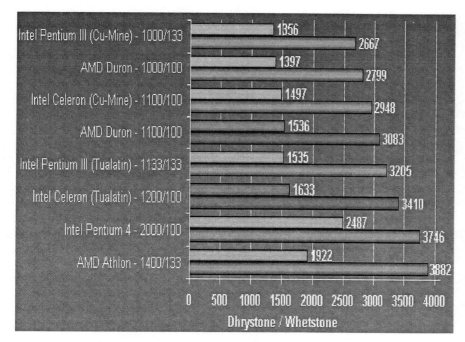

Figure 2-4. System benchmarks running office-related applications

find parts. Many vendors increase their public exposure by renting booths at local swap meets and user-group gatherings. Many computer shows also have a vendor section where the latest available components are shown. Watch the local newspapers to find out when these shows pass through your area.

Back to John.

Like Lisa two weeks before, John had a pile of unfamiliar parts in front of him and no idea of what to do with them. That is where this book came into play. John read Chapter 3 to review what he bought and why. (He already had read Chapters 4 and 2. That's why he knew to pick up a good video adapter and sound card.)

He followed the instructions in Chapter 4 to procure the components, then read Chapter 6 on Lisa's exploits in building her computer.

Then he was ready. He installed the Athalon motherboard per the directions in the included manual, added the RAM, double-checked the jumper settings and then installed the video card, modem, and sound card.

He installed both of the 3.5-inch floppy drives, the hard drive, CD-ROM, and DVD-ROM. When he finished this portion, I took a look at his progress and found every jumper and cable properly placed.

He finished connecting up the IDE hard drive cable and IDE CD-ROM cables, then wrapped up internal installation by connecting the I/O cables to the rear panel of the case. I suggested he leave the cover off.

the Athalon-based computer will cost you hundreds of dollars less.

Before I go any further I want to discuss where you can find components. Most vendors like to advertise in those magazines that are distributed at no cost at electronics stores; they are prime sources for finding components.

Local swap meets are also good places to

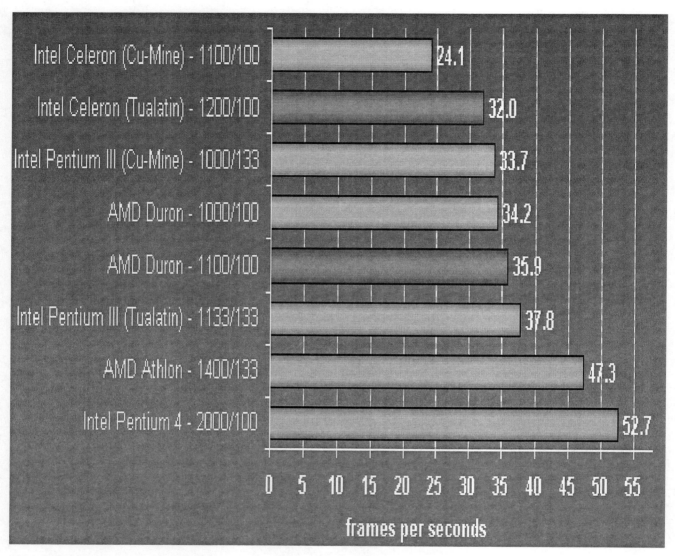

Figure 2-5. System benchmarks running games-related applications

He was one hour into the project when he finished connecting up the mouse, keyboard, and monitor. That's how long I take to build one, I thought to myself. I noted that Lisa took 45 minutes to get to this point and wondered if it would be this easy for anyone.

He turned the computer on and went into the setup routine. (He had done this before when he installed a new hard disk in his old Pentium.) He set up the hard drive, floppy-drive parameters, date, and time. (All initializations and setup procedures are discussed in Chapter 6.)

He booted up on his Windows 2K disk, ran fdisk, then formatted his hard drive. He installed Windows 2K and had a perfectly operational computer within two hours. Everything worked the first time.

I have built many computers and have only had to return two defective items, so I was not surprised. One was a hard drive that died after 24 hours, and the other was a motherboard with a bad CMOS battery. With today's quality control, you can be reasonably certain your components will work properly if you follow basic handling precautions.

3

Shopping for a Computer

The first order of business in building your computer is figuring out what you want. The easiest way to understand your computer needs is to go out and try someone else's system, and the easiest way to try lots of systems is a trip to the computer store. This computer store may be a specialized computer and electronics outlet, a chain department store with a computer electronics section, or any other store with a moderate supply of varied computer systems.

Before you go shopping, review this chapter for information on options and accessories, Chapter 5 for software, and Chapter 1 for terminology.

At the store, you can get lots of mileage from sales personnel, whose objective is to keep your interest. They will, however, attempt to get you to purchase an expensive system you may not need. This is their sole purpose in life and the reason so many people return their first computer purchase. Their intent is seldom to provide you the computer you need; rather, it is to offer you the computer they want to sell.

Try many computers of varying processor types, speeds, and with as many different accessories as possible. Get a feel for the IBM-compatible computer, the wide variety of configurations and options, and the tremendous number of software products available. Do not be afraid to ask questions and get second opinions on everything any salesperson tells you.

After you cut through the sales hype, categorize the systems you have looked at into groups you can evaluate.

WHAT IS A COMPUTER?

THIS BLOCK DIAGRAM WILL GIVE YOU SOME IDEA

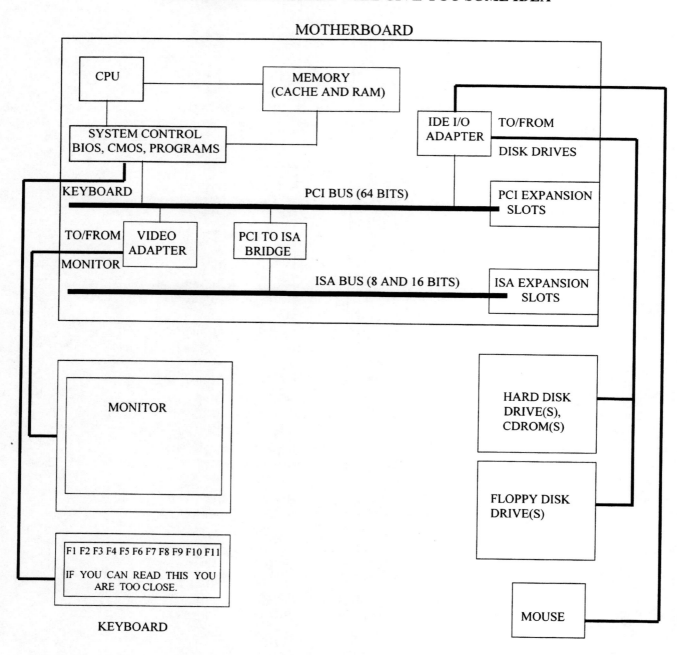

I'll discuss my categories and the reason for the groupings. Your individual requirements may necessitate making categories different than mine. The objective of this exercise is to determine which computer is right for you.

BARE-BONES SYSTEM

Beginning computer owners may wish to build a "basic system" to minimize expenditures as they develop an understanding of their total computer requirements. They can add hardware or software options later as they begin to use the system and define their long-term needs. A bare-bones system will have a minimum of RAM, a small hard drive, a basic video card, basic I/O capability, a small monitor, a keyboard, and a basic mouse. Software operating systems may or may not be included. Bare-bones systems are available in Intel Celeron, Pentium 3, and Pentium 4, as well as AMD Duron and Athalon versions.

DESKTOP PUBLISHING SYSTEM

Compared to the basic system, the components that create a desktop publishing system include more RAM (at least 256 MB), a larger hard drive (60 GB), a good video card, a larger monitor, (17-inch digital), and a modem (56K fax/modem). The desktop publishing system typically has Windows 2000 and one or more publishing or office suite programs included. A good quality laser or color ink jet printer is normally added to such a package.

PUBLISHING AND MULTIMEDIA SYSTEM

In addition to the improvements listed above, the multimedia system adds a CD-ROM, a sound card, 246 MB more RAM, an even larger hard drive (100 GB), and often a 19-inch or larger digital monitor. Speakers to reproduce the stereo multimedia effects are added, and a joystick or flight controller or both are included. Few people need all this in a system but many purchase it, only to realize later they have made a mistake.

Each one of these groups can have a Pentium 4 or Athalon microprocessor-based computer as the core system, and basically the only difference in performance will be the speed at which each system is capable of operating. Most of the software out there runs well on a Celeron or Duron and great on a Pentium 4 or Athalon-based system. When deciding which speed is right for you take everything into consideration, including the software you intend to run.

Processing speed is the biggest selling point of most systems. The data throughput, or actual processing speed, is measured in millions of instructions per second (mips). It is useful to compare the speed of an old XT computer with today's Pentium 4. The XT processes data at 0.75 mips, while the slower Pentium 4 processors run about 10,000 mips. A Pentium 4 2-GHz microprocessor-based system is approximately 15,000 times faster than my first PC and infinitely easier to build.

By this point in your exploration you have

CPU DATA

IBM XT 8086	IBM AT 286-16	AMD 386-40	AMD 486-100	INTEL Pentium P4, 2 GHz	
30,000	135,000	275,000	1.2 million	42 million +	# GATES (approx)
0.75	2.7	11.5	54	12,000 +	MIPS
8	16	32	32	64	# BITS

hopefully tried out several computers and know which processor best fits your needs and budget. Remember, Celeron-based systems can generally be upgraded to Pentium 4 speed with the simple installation of an Athalon processor and motherboard, and that makes the Celeron system a good place for the budget-minded person to start.

The Pentium 4 system, though more expensive, is still open-ended and has no speed limitation. Faster Pentium chips are constantly being offered. The Pentium 4 2-GHz system is running about 420 times faster than my XT, and 2 GHz (and faster) chips are available as a drop-in upgrade for most motherboards. One final look at processor speed is available with the CPU Data Chart on the previous page.

THE CLONES OF NOTE

AMD offers microprocessors that are compatible or better in performance than motherboards that support Intel's Pentium 4 line. The chips are both cheaper and faster than their Pentium counterparts according to certain brands of benchmarking software. Across the entire domain of processor platforms, the AMD product line is dominant in performance.

In 1987, a 133 MHz system with 8 MB of RAM, a 1-GB hard drive, and no monitor was about $300 less than a comparable Pentium 75 system, and it was faster. This fact still holds true today; the Athalon 1.4-GHz processor and motherboard is faster than a Pentium 4, 2 GHz processor and motherboard and costs $375 less.

How much CPU do you need? Weigh the options available to you against your budget. If a CPU selection drives you to the poorhouse, that's not the processor for you.

Build or buy the most open-ended (upgradable) system you can afford. If you upgrade a Celeron or Duron-based system, insist on a motherboard with onboard sound card support and USB or Firewire. Onboard USB support enables you to configure your PnP I/O components more easily. USB is becoming the standard input/output controller

for printers, modems, and game adapters. The built-in interface is faster than an add-on card and frees up a slot for more options.

If you build a Pentium 4-based system, buy the fastest motherboard you can *but don't buy one with an integrated sound card*. You may not be satisfied with its level of sound card performance for the life of the motherboard. In general, do not lock yourself into a level of performance you may later regret. I mention this now because the price of a motherboard with an integrated sound card may influence you to purchase one, particularly if you associate a high price with a better motherboard.

Now is a good time to talk about hardware and options. I separate hardware into two groups: internal options and external add-ons. Obviously, internal options require more work on your part, so we will look at them first.

INTERNAL OPTIONS

Here is a list of the hardware required to build a basic computer, starting with the motherboard, case, and everything that goes inside. This is just a list; detailed descriptions of the components, as well as pictures, can be found later in this chapter. These are the standard required components, to which you may add options—such as a memory stick reader for your digital camera or a DVD-ROM drive—as your needs grow.

Motherboard
The CPU is the main component of the motherboard. The microprocessor, RAM, BIOS, cache, and all add-on cards plug into the motherboard. It is the heart of any computer and determines the speed and flexibility of your system. The microprocessor can be anything from a Celeron to a Pentium 4 and beyond.

Case
All components except the monitor and external items fit inside the case and operate from a power supply inside the case. A fan integrated into the power supply cools the power supply and all internally installed

components. An additional fan is often mounted on the microprocessor for additional cooling.

Memory

The memory is installed on the motherboard and consists of *single in-line memory modules*. SIMM modules are discussed in detail later in this chapter. Included on the motherboard is cache memory, the fast RAM that stores information passing to and from the microprocessor.

IDE I/O

This function is normally integrated into the motherboard, and all disk operations and all external input/output functions are controlled by it. The integrated disk electronics and input/output functions are available as a separate add-on card for motherboards without a built-in IDE I/O or for those people that like multiple hard disks and multiple CD-ROM or DVD-ROM drives.

Video Card

This add-on card allows the computer to display text and graphics on your monitor. The range of performance in video cards is remarkable and will be discussed later in this chapter.

Hard Disk Drive

Most of the primary information, including the operating system, is stored on your hard disk drive. The basic exception to this is the setup information, which is stored in the BIOS ROM discussed later in this chapter. Most new motherboards and cases support multiple hard disk drives. All installed programs and data you create are stored and run from the hard disk drive.

Floppy Disk Drive

When installed, a hard disk drive has no information on it. You will install programs and operating systems on your hard disk using either a floppy disk drive or a CD-ROM. All programs you acquire will be installable using a floppy disk drive or CD-ROM.

Sound Card

Sound cards were invented to expand the computing experience by processing sound from digital information. Certain programs and games provide sound and music during execution. The sound plays from either headphones or external speakers. A sound card is one of the most important pieces of a multimedia system and most new games would be useless without one.

Modem

The primary way your computer talks to other computers is through the telephone lines using a modem. (The modem gets its name from the operations it performs on communications signals passing through it to and from your computer. *Modulator* and *demodulator* operations are discussed later in this chapter.) The modem takes information from your communication program and converts it to analog signals for transmission over telephone cables. The signals are sent through the phone line to a destination you select. Most modems have FAX and voice capability as well.

CD-ROM drive

Large amounts of data and visual information can be stored on a compact disk and later accessed using a CD-ROM (*compact disk read only memory*) drive. This read-only type of media is the heart of the multimedia experience because programs up to 650 MB in size can be stored on a single density CD-ROM. This opens up avenues for extensive graphics, including moving pictures and sound. The medium is similar to the compact disks you enjoy in your home stereo system.

Tape Drive System

The tape drive backup systems currently available are the most important protection available for today's computer systems. For under $100 you can protect the contents of your hard drive from data loss. A tape drive and the tapes are cost-effective, easy to use, and reliable.

EXTERNAL OPTIONS

Monitor

The display monitor is one of the most important parts of the computer, and one of the most expensive. You will see and use the monitor more than any other part of the computer, so it had better suit your needs. You will upgrade the motherboard, keyboard, mouse, and most of the internally installed components long before you upgrade or replace the monitor. The sizes and options will be discussed later in this chapter.

Mouse

Most programs today make use of the mouse, a pointing device. It is primarily used to select options in programs and to start programs. Several options and configurations are available and are discussed later in this chapter.

Keyboard

The keyboard is the primary device you use to input data and control programs into a computer. It is set up similar to a standard typewriter keypad, but has several other options and keys to expand its capabilities for use on the PC.

Modem, CD-ROM, Tape Drive

These three devices, discussed above as internal parts, are common items you can also purchase as externally mounted accessories. They interface through cables attached to I/O ports on the back of the computer.

Now let's take a more detailed look at the options within each component category. This is where you make an informed decision on exactly how much computer you will build. Remember, maximum performance usually means more cost, but weigh your requirements against the future and your pocketbook when deciding. Remember, you normally do not have the option to select any of the components if you purchase a packaged system from a retail outlet.

IN DETAIL

Case

The cabinet and integrated power supply constitute the case. There are several different case styles available, such as mini-, medium-, and full-tower cases. Flat desktop styles commonly used in older systems are still available. Choose the case type only after you have selected everything else, since the case size can limit your options. A mini-tower case, for example, will not house two floppy drives, a CD-ROM drive, and a tape backup system, and neither will most basic desktop cases.

Power consumption is also a factor, but case designers typically take this into consideration when they make the cases. A mini-tower case should be rated at 200 watts minimum. A medium-tower case should be rated at 250 watts, and a full-tower case should support at least 300 watts of accessories. The larger cases have more drive and accessory bays, so the power supply must provide more power.

The power supply inside the case takes the 117 VAC from your wall socket and converts it to the +5, +12, -5, and -12 volts the computer requires.

The power supply fan must be kept free of dust and obstructions, so don't let anything block the part of the case where the fan is mounted. Blocking the airflow through your computer will result in heat damage to one or more of the internal components. This fan is the only source for cooling in most computers.

As is true with all computer components, prices for cases cannot be depended upon to

IMPORTANT NOTE: Some tower system cases, when packaged, do not have the power switch installed. It typically interferes with the packaging. To install the switch, follow the wiring information carefully. *This is the only part of the installation that can cause you harm.* If you have any doubt whether the switch is wired properly, consult the sales personnel where you purchased the case.

remain constant. Advances in technology and market forces drive costs down steadily. Use the following prices for reference only.

Desktop cases run about $22 with a 150-watt power supply. You can get a 200-watt version for about $37. Mini-tower cases start at around $30 with a 230-watt power supply. Both mid-tower and full-tower cases with 230-watt power supply go for about $45. The same case with a 300-watt power supply is $55.

You can spend more for cases with special colors, styles, or other gimmicks, but I don't recommend it generally. If you spend a few dollars more for a case with an extra fan, however, it is money well spent, since two fans are safer than one. *Nothing kills a great computer faster than an uncorrected fan failure.*

Motherboard

The biggest difference between PC models is the motherboard and central processing unit, or microprocessor. The CPU type commonly gives its name to the system. A *Pentium 4* system has a Pentium 4 CPU loaded on a Pentium-style motherboard. Athalon-style CPU bundles have Athalon microprocessors and motherboards installed.

Motherboard/Processor Compatibility

A motherboard capable of accepting each grouping of processors within a family will accept higher or lower speed processors in the same family. Example: a motherboard capable of handling a Pentium 4, 2 GHz processor will accept a slower processor in the Pentium 4 family. For cost reasons, this is good information. The same goes for the Athalon family of AMD processors. The basic groupings currently available are Athalon and Duron, from AMD, and Pentium 4, Pentium 3, and Celeron, from Intel. For the time being, this is what is available. Benchmarks for each type of processor can be found in Chapter 2.

The BIOS is information stored in a programmable memory device on the motherboard. This information allows you to initially set up your motherboard's configuration for various options. CPU speed, RAM type and quantity, and other information

necessary for proper computer operation is configurable in BIOS. More information on BIOS setup parameters is available in Chapter 8.

The manual included with the motherboard will tell you if your BIOS will support a specific microprocessor. Certain processors, like the AMD Duron and Athalon, are as fast as a comparable Pentium-type. Try to get this type of upgrade information in a computer store!

The Athalon motherboard will support both the standard Athalon up to 1.4 GHz, and the XP version, which operates at 1.8 GHz. Figure 3-1 shows a standard Athalon motherboard. This motherboard has onboard sound and modem capabilities. It includes a slot for the AMR (audio modem riser).

This is a motherboard with jumperless configuration capability, meaning that the BIOS can auto-detect and set up your processor and RAM. Ideally, this is the best option you can have at your table when building for the first time. It is an extension of the PnP technology.

Fast Processor, Slow Computer

Why does a fast processor like the 2 GHz Pentium 4 run slowly on the average home user's system?

Most of us are currently using programs written with 16-bit code embedded in the operating system and programs we use or plan to use. Even Windows 98 has both 16-bit and 32-bit code. Windows NT, however, is a true 32-bit operating system. How many of you are using or planning to use Windows NT? Not many, I'll bet. Windows 2000 Professional or XP are better 32-bit choices. The speed of the 2 GHz Pentium 4 processor will be more evident with updated software.

It used to be that the bulk of PC software available was 16-bit software, written in 16-bit code, with 16-bit compilers, using 16-bit drivers. Many hardware devices did not have 32-bit drivers or software available. If you are hanging on to old components, don't expend the money for a Pentium 4 or Athalon-based system for this reason.

The average home system must be capable

of efficiently processing both 16- and 32-bit code. The Pentium 4 can do this, but since it is optimized for 32-bit code, it slows down considerably running 16-bit code. It normally runs *slower* than an Athalon-based system running the same 16-bit program.

Most motherboards have a feature for energy savings called "the green feature." It enables you to set the shutdown time in BIOS. This can save quite a bit of energy on a system left unattended.

The green feature can be found in many peripherals for today's computers, including monitors, printers, scanners, and some high-end cases.

Figure 3-1 has both AGP and PCI bus slots. The next few paragraphs describe the bus types. These slots are for the various add-on cards. Add-on cards provide video display capability, sound support, hard-disk control, and many other functions. These cards and others are discussed in detail later in this chapter.

Most of the add-on cards used in different system types are similar. The primary difference between cards is the bus type. This is why it is just as easy—or easier—to build a Pentium 4 screamer as an ancient 386 system. The primary reason is that current motherboards for all processor types are more flexible in ease of configuration, and support an increasingly large number of add-on cards. The only real differences in computer architecture are determined by the motherboard. The architecture mentioned above refers to the parallel data bus to and from the components on the motherboard. Data in an XT computer traveled on an 8-bit parallel bus. Envision eight lanes of traffic. To increase data throughput, a 286 system doubled the bus to 16 bits of parallel data transfer.

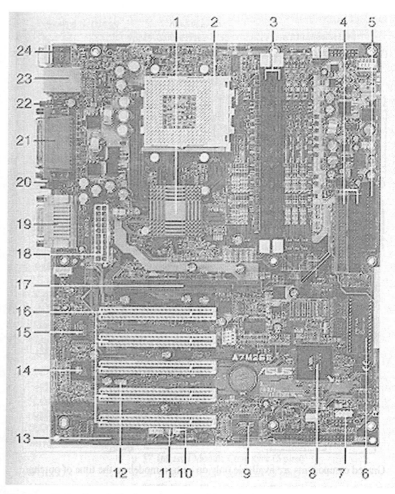

Figure 3-1. An Athalon motherboard for AMD Athalon 1400 + CPU.

The 386 and 486 had a 32-bit bus, and the Pentium 4 has a 64-bit bus. Even if there were no other advantages, the 64-bit bus (64 lanes of traffic) moves data eight times faster.

The ISA (Industry Standard Architecture) bus was introduced in the first PCs and remains one of the standards. This standard, however, limits the I/O bus size to 16 bits and the I/O speed to 8 – 10 MHz. Currently available motherboards no longer have slots other than PCI (peripheral component interconnect) and AGP for add-in cards, with few exceptions. The AMR slot (13) on Figure 3-1 is an exception to this rule.

All Athalon and Pentium motherboards incorporate a PCI bus that is 64-bits wide. This bus is stand-alone and is not downward

Motherboard Components

		LOCATION
Processor support:	Socket 462 for AMD Athalon/Duron Processors	2
Chipsets:	AMD 761 System Controller	1
	VIA VT82C686B PCIset	8
	2 Mbit Programmable FLASH EEPROM	6
Main Memory:	Maximum of 2 Gigabytes	
	2 DIMM Sockets	3
	PC2100/PC1600 DDR memory support	
Expansion Slots:	5 PCI slots	16
	1 *Accelerated Graphics Port* (AGP) Pro slot	17
	1 *Audio Modem Riser* (AMR) shared slot	13
System I/O:	1 Floppy Disk Controller Driver Connector	5
	2 IDE Connectors (UDMA/100 Support)	4
	1 Parallel Port Connector (top)	21
	1 Serial Port connector (com1, bottom)	22
	1 Serial Port connector (com2, bottom)	20
	USB Connectors (Port 0, 1)	23
	USB header (Port 2,3)	7
	1 PS/2 Mouse Connector (top)	24
	1 PS/2 Keyboard Connector (bottom)	24
Audio:	PCI Audio Chipset	15
	1 Game/MIDI Connector (top)	19
	1 Line Out Connector, 1 Line in Connector (bottom)	19
	1 Microphone Connector (bottom)	19
Network Support:	3Com Fast Ethernet Controller	14
	1 LAN (RJ45 Connector (top)	23
	Wake-On-LAN connector	12
	Wake-On-Ring connector	10
Other:	ASUS ASIC	9
	ATX Power Supply Connector	18
	Onboard LED	11

Table 3-1. Motherboard components for Figure 3-1.

compatible to the ancient VLB 16- or 8-bit buses. It has one great feature: it supports PnP compatible add-on cards. As previously mentioned, PnP means you install the card and the computer interface sets the DMA and IRQ settings for you. Unfortunately, all PCI motherboards also exclude the 8- and 16-bit bus slots for your 8- and 16-bit add-on cards. Looks like time to clean house...

Speed is the most significant difference among CPUs, and the reason faster processors are more expensive. One factor in CPU speed is how the CPU handles instructions. Of the CISC processors, the Athalon and Pentium are kings. CISC, or complex instruction set processors, have a large instruction set built into the chip. When the CPU is asked to perform a task, it must sift through a built-in list of instructions to find the ones necessary to perform the task. RISC (reduced instruction set) processors, like the DEC Alpha AXP and Apple's PowerPC, have a much smaller instruction set. They can process data at speeds of 1,500 mips. These RISC processors are faster than the Pentium, but...

There are more than 75,000 programs that run on a Pentium. Nearly all of these programs must be translated if they are to run on a RISC machine, because the RISC processor only understands instructions written in its unique language. The chore of translation slows the program to a crawl, so the RISC processor running a Pentium-based program is up to 50 percent slower. In other words, an Indy race car runs great on a closed racetrack, but will never survive New York's pothole-laden city streets. For the time being, if you want speed and compatibility, select a fast Athalon or Pentium-style motherboard.

Intel, in its infinite wisdom, decided to utilize its 0.18-micron technology, MMX and X86 instructions, and the finest aspects of both the Pentium and the Pentium Pro, and go back to the drawing board. What evolved from these efforts is the currently unsurpassed CPU called the Pentium 4. With speeds exceeding 2 GHz, the Pentium 4 is the current state of the art for the high-end computer owner, sharing that distinction with the slower clocked, but

faster operating, Athalon XP 1800+ processor from AMD.

Built-in functions available on the newer motherboards include the EIDE interface for IDE hard drives. A floppy disk controller and support for four IDE devices, including IDE CD-ROM drives, is part of this package.

Support for two serial ports, a 16550 UAR/T, one parallel port, and one game port complete the IDE I/O functions built into this group. This group of built-in connectors eliminates the need for an I/O add-on card and an IDE add-on card, freeing up one or two PCI slots in your computer for other options. Add firewire and USB ports, and you finish the enhanced IO capability of current motherboards.

Some motherboards include a SCSI adapter as well, but most people I know prefer the IDE interface as their disk controller. However, the SCSI has additional uses, including support for external scanners, backup systems, and sound card add-on peripherals. The SCSI interface is widely used in Macintosh computers, but the lower cost and easier installation of IDE components makes the IDE system more attractive to most PC users.

Avoid onboard video adapters. The video standard industry is advancing rapidly, and six months sees a new generation of accessories. You need the flexibility to upgrade video performance by spending less than $100 to drop in the latest upgrade. Many software packages spell out a level of video performance required to run the program, and you need the option of easily upgrading to keep up with your future needs.

Sound card options are often added to the motherboard. Once again, if you want to keep up with high-end performance in this department, *do not buy a motherboard with integrated sound.* Sound systems are increasing in capability, yet they require fewer computer resources. Keep this portion of your system open to easy upgrading with a plug-in sound card.

Another built-in feature of the motherboard is the ability to self-test (POST) when you turn on the computer. This POST is one of the many features stored in the BIOS chip. In addition to self-testing, other features are loaded into the BIOS, such as the entire configuration map you create the first time you power up a new system. This configuration information is the only portion of BIOS you can change or modify without a chip or disk from the manufacturer.

Support for larger hard drives and PnP add-on cards is included in newer BIOS. When you purchase a motherboard, look for one with PnP BIOS that supports mode 4 EIDE HDD and DMA-66 protocol. This is necessary to have support for the newest generation of hard drives and the plug and play add-on cards. Fortunately, the BIOS chip is normally installed in a socket, and can be replaced or updated with a file from the manufacturer.

The motherboard manufacturer will be able to upgrade your BIOS by sending you an updated BIOS disk if you request it. You can also update BIOS with files available on the Internet from the manufacturer. As new features are added to the BIOS, you can easily update your motherboard. The newest motherboards support flash BIOS. This is the type of BIOS that can be easily updated with a floppy disk or file provided by the motherboard manufacturer. With this capability, you don't even have to open the case!

When you build a computer and turn it on for the first time, it has to be configured. The system configuration setup program needs information about the hardware present in your system. You input this information the first time, and it is stored and reused every time you turn on the computer. This subject is addressed in detail at the conclusion of Chapter 6.

The configuration information is stored in volatile memory, which is kept alive with a small battery installed on the motherboard. If this battery fails and has to be replaced, you must reconfigure the computer. Keep a record of your CMOS setup in writing, taped somewhere inside the computer case, to prevent real headaches later. A PnP motherboard will always configure the computer automatically the first time you turn it on.

As you can see, the motherboard is the heart of your computer system. A basic upgrade to a faster computer starts here, and many upgrades require only changing the motherboard or CPU. Simple upgrades, like improving video quality, sound support, or increasing memory require only changing add-in modules on the motherboard.

Memory Types

Without memory to store instructions and intermediate results, a computer would be a high-speed typewriter. When a computer compiles data while running a program, portions of the program and data are loaded into RAM.

The CPU accesses the RAM, extracts portions of the data, performs operations on the data and sends it back to the RAM. This interaction may occur thousands of times during the execution of a program. Only after all the processing is completed is the data sent to a more permanent storage device such as your hard disk or floppy. Often, the data is used to display something on the monitor, send information to a printer, or prompt you for more input.

Another type of memory is the ROM, which holds the BIOS information mentioned in the motherboard section of this chapter. This memory is read only, and is utilized on power-up to configure your computer for use.

Most computers have between 64 and 512 MB of RAM installed on the motherboard. The RAM normally consists of integrated circuits mounted on a small 132-pin DIMM. Larger DIMM modules are being utilized, but this is currently the most popular size.

Each DIMM contains between 64 and 512 MB of RAM. The most common type of RAM is synchronous dynamic RAM, called SDRAM. SDRAM must be refreshed often during program execution or the information stored in it will vanish.

Still another type of RAM is SRAM. Static RAM holds data until it is changed, eliminating refresh cycles. RAM is used for temporary storage primarily because each element of information can be accessed and changed as often as necessary. This is what random access means. Random access memory can be modified in part or in whole, depending on the program you are running and its requirements at the time. Any memory location can be addressed, read, or written to independently of all other memory locations.

Data stored on a hard drive or floppy disk, on the other hand, is stored sequentially. It cannot be accessed or changed one byte at a time. This makes access to floppy and hard drive memory a much slower process than RAM access. This is noticeable when you run a large program that runs out of RAM. The computer will use part of your hard drive to temporarily store information normally stored in RAM. You will notice the computer slow down while it searches the hard drive for the temporary results to process. When you hear someone talk about a swap file, they are referring to this process.

There is another reason Pentium machines are faster. Information is stored in RAM in 8-bit increments called bytes. The XT can process one byte of information at a time. The 16-bit 286 can handle 2 bytes. The 32-bit 386 and 486 can process 4 bytes simultaneously. The Pentium, or Athalon, with its 64-bit bus, can handle 8 bytes (which is 64 bits) simultaneously.

Memory utilization is important, particularly for DOS-based programs. DOS, the disk-operating system significantly less prevalent on most current PCs, requires its core programs to live in RAM the entire time you use the computer. DOS, unfortunately, only allows you to use the first 640 KB of memory in your computer. It reserves the next 384 KB for programs you specify in setup files to run in upper memory. Anything above that, unless specially addressed by certain programs, is invisible to DOS. This includes all the additional DIMM memory you can install on the motherboard.

This means large programs will not run fast (if at all) in DOS. Special programs called memory managers allow large DOS-based programs to run. Memory managers give DOS programs the ability to use the additional

memory installed in your computer by allocating portions of it to programs normally resident in DOS, or low memory.

Windows, OS/2, and all Windows XX programs are three operating systems groups that get around the 640-KB limit imposed by DOS. These programs have memory managers, and all three make use of the expanded and extended memory available. Refer to EMM, Expanded Memory, and Extended Memory in Chapter 8 for more details on these subjects.

We talked about DIMM memory earlier and mentioned the common sizes. Now let's talk about configuration on the motherboard. Memory on the motherboard is configured in banks of DIMM. Usually, a motherboard will have between two and four banks of DIMM. The banks are usually numbered from 0 to 3, and loaded sequentially with DIMM, normally from the lowest numbered bank to the highest.

You can load any number of banks with DIMM, but each bank you load must be filled. (Some motherboards auto-detect memory, enabling you to load any bank, instead of the lowest first. All new motherboards support 132-pin DIMM, which comes in both EDO [extended data output] and SDRAM configurations.)

EDO DRAM has arrived in force, and in a fast machine it can be 10 percent faster than conventional memory. EDO RAM also costs about 10 percent more than normal DRAM. Mixing EDO DRAM and regular DRAM is like mixing matter and anti-matter, so don't. If you need speed, buy it. The difference is evident in extremely fast games and complex graphics programs.

Finally, SDRAM is a current evolution from EDO DRAM. With sub-10-nanosecond access speed, it is six times faster than EDO RAM. Don't consider operating an 800 MHz or faster computer without SDRAM.

The next step up is DDR RAM for the Athalon processor, and RDRAM for the Pentium 4 processor. Both architectures are discussed in the next paragraph on RAM selection.

DDR SDRAM is the current state of the art for all Athalon-based computers. It allows for data transfer to occur on both the rising and falling edge of the data clock pulse to the RAM. With this method of data transfer, the effective speed of operation is increased beyond 200 MHz. Note that the bus width is 64 bits on this configuration. This is necessary when comparing its performance to RDRAM, the Rambus offering for Pentium 4 computers.

RDRAM is fast. It can be clocked such that it can achieve an effective 800 MHz of operation. The only drawback is that the architecture is limited to a 16-bit bus. This means that it can only run at 200 MHz, when you compare the bus width with the 64-bit bus of the DDR SDRAM.

Both DDR SDRAM and RDRAM represent a departure from the previous standard of 144-pin SDRAM, so be certain when purchasing a motherboard that you know the number of pins of each RAM slot (144 for SDRAM and 168 for DDR SDRAM, for example). Your motherboard documentation will tell you which types and sizes of RAM it supports. Assume the Pentium 4 motherboards will require RDRAM, and the AMD Athalon motherboards will require DDR SDRAM.

Another price issue: Like the significant difference between the prices of an AMD processor versus the comparable, but slower, Pentium 4 version, DDR SDRAM is much cheaper than RDRAM. For example, today's prices show 512 MB of DDR SDRAM is $75, while the same size in RDRAM is $230. The AMD approach continues to be significantly less expensive than the Pentium 4 equivalent.

Cache memory is one way to speed up a computer. Many times during its execution a program must loop several times through the same steps. The computer uses cache memory—consisting of 256 KB or 512 KB of very fast SRAM memory chips—to store these repetitive operations. Considering that a fast DRAM memory chip runs at 60 NS (nanoseconds), the SRAM processing speed of 7 NS to 10 NS is quite impressive.

Pipeline burst cache was a recent addition to the high-speed improvements for faster machines. It is significantly faster than SRAM cache, and improved the benchmark of a

Pentium 120 by 20 percent. Refer to Chapter 2 to see how much improvement pipeline burst cache made in 32-bit performance as reported by Norton Utilities for Windows 95.

Memory is the easiest upgrade you can perform on a computer. You just find the lowest numbered open bank and fill it with a memory module. Be advised, however, that memory can be the single most expensive item in the computer.

IDE I/O Cards

The IDE hard disk interface and I/O functions are normally paired in a single assembly. This is true whether they share the same add-on card or are incorporated into the motherboard design. The input/output functions normally supported include game controller and printer support. The primary I/O function is support for two serial-controlled devices, the mouse and the modem. Note that the only way to increase the number of CD-ROMs, DVD-ROMs, or hard drives in your computer is by adding an IDE I/O card. Though they used to be an add-in device in all computers, this function is now a normally built-in function. I have a motherboard with a DMA66 controller for enhanced hard drive support, and a standard secondary port that supports two other IDE devices. If I want to add any additional CD-ROM or DVD-ROM devices, such as a DVD recorder or CD-RW drive, I must install one of these cards to accomplish the task.

Most enhanced IDE I/O cards support two floppy disk drives, four IDE hard drives or CD-ROM drives, two serial communication (COM) ports, one parallel printer port, and one game controller port. The non-enhanced versions normally included in purchased computers only support two hard drives or CD-ROM drives. I am currently running two 100 GHz hard drives, a CD-RW, and a DVD-ROM. These are just a few of the types of installable IDE peripherals. We will look at the devices that connect to the I/O portion of your computer later in this chapter. Figure 3-2 shows an enhanced local bus IDE I/O CARD.

Video Cards

The monitor is useless without a video adapter card. This card takes the digital information from your programs and converts it to analog information in a format your monitor can display. Most video adapters have both text and graphics support.

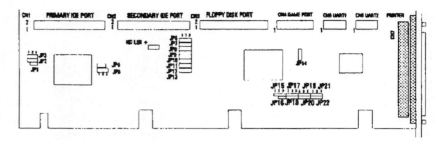

Figure 3-2. An enhanced IDE I/O card.

Figure 3-3. ASUS V8200 GeForce 3, 4X AGP video card.

To display text, the adapter looks up a typed character in its library, then displays it. Video graphics is a bit more complicated, so most video graphics displays are a function of programming. Video adapter software allows the user to put lines, graphs, pictures, and almost any type of image on your computer screen.

Some video cards are referred to as graphics accelerator cards. They perform certain graphics display functions without interrupting the CPU. This is possible because they have special functions built-in and can handle many operations called out by programs without processing data over the bus. Any operation processed without bus interaction is very fast. Certain video cards even have their own built-in microprocessor.

Video cards normally have RAM installed to save having to go through the bus to use the motherboard RAM. Standard video RAM size is 32 MB, which allows you to display 16 million colors at 1,024 * 768 resolution. A better choice is 64 MB of RAM, because you can display 16 million colors at *any* resolution. This is a must for 17 inch and larger monitors.

Most high-quality video cards are available both in PCI and AGO bus types. Figure 3-3 shows a premium video card in AGP bus format. Though 32-MB video cards are available, they typically have limited graphics support and are not generally considered viable purchases for today's computers.

Speed is an important consideration in video processing. Purchasing a 2X or 4X AGP video card will produce a considerable speed improvement over a 32-MB PCI video card. You will notice a significant difference, particularly if you use graphics-intensive games or CAD programs.

To work with an SVGA (super video graphics array) monitor, a video card should have video accelerator functions and 64 MB of memory. Never buy a SVGA monitor without also purchasing an AGP bus video accelerator adapter card. For true colors and depth, a good video card is necessary.

If you have interest in running video graphics from CD-ROM or external video sources, consider an MPEG (motion pictures expert group) video adapter. This adapter supports video compression and decompression, allowing you to capture and display true motion video. Video adapters that support 3-D games and movies are available as well. All video cards that meet MPEG requirements are identified, but I believe most of the current models support this important function.

Hard Disk Drives

The hard drive installed in your computer is the primary storage and retrieval device. Most of the programs you run will be executed from the hard drive. Programs are read into memory, then executed. Data from the programs is stored on the hard drive to be used later. Any permanent data you save is stored on the hard drive in a format that allows you or the program to retrieve it when needed.

The hard drive, when new, is formatted into concentric tracks, which are divided into sectors. Each sector is 512 bytes in length. Since many files are larger than 512 bytes, the system will record as much of a file as will fit in one sector, then look for the next available sector. The remainder of the file will be stored in available sectors as they are located.

During formatting, sectors are grouped into allocation units. No more than one file can be written in the same allocation unit, but a file may span several allocation units. The

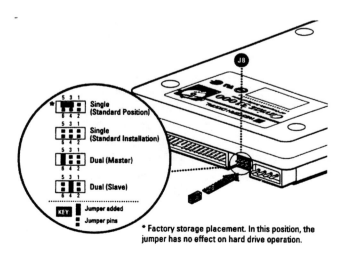

Figure 3-4. Hard drive configuration jumpers.

number of sectors per allocation unit varies with the size of the hard drive. A 200 MB hard drive has allocation units composed of eight sectors, but a 100 MB hard drive allocation unit is only four sectors in size. (You can get more data on a large hard drive if you partition it into several logical drives. This is particularly true if you have lots of small files. More on partitioning hard drives can be found in Chapter 6.)

With all of this data stored on a hard drive, how does the computer find it? A portion of the hard drive is reserved to store a file allocation table, or FAT. The FAT stores the location of each part of every file, and updates itself each time the hard drive is accessed. The computer is smart enough to make a copy of the FAT in case the original is damaged or if you have a disk manager utility program, as mentioned in Chapter 9.

A hard drive may be made of several disk platters, and many heads, to read from and write to the platters. This makes the hard drive fragile and sensitive to rough handling. Hard drives are factory sealed to prevent dust from entering; the smallest dust or cigarette smoke particle can destroy a hard drive by becoming lodged between one of the heads and a platter. If this happens, all data on the affected disk surface will be unreadable and lost.

Care should be exercised when moving your computer or handling a new hard drive prior to installation. The hard drive is also sensitive to motion, especially when the computer is turned on. Avoid moving a computer unless it is turned off.

The two primary specifications used in small computer disk interfaces are EIDE and SCSI. The recently added EIDE specification improves the IDE format to handle larger hard drives and improves the transfer rate of data to 133 MB per second. All IDE hard drives are supported by the EIDE format. There are other formats for disk control, but they are either obsolete or seldom utilized. (DMA33 and DMA66 are two extensions of the IDE data transfer method that allow information to pass faster between the hard drives and, ultimately, the CPU. They have two distinctly different methods on interconnection with the motherboard and cannot be mixed on the same cable. This is an important fact to consider, since a CD-ROM or DVD-ROM cannot share a cable with a DMA66 hard drive.)

IDE hard drives are recommended for several reasons, including ease of configuration and standardization. The IDE control system is inexpensive and is often included on the motherboard. IDE drives can be chained on the same controller, and up to four IDE drives can be easily installed. More are possible, but the installation becomes somewhat complicated. More on configuration in Chapter 6, and refer to Figure 3-4 for a quick look now.

Regarding IDE standardization, some IDE hard drive manufacturers bend the standard a bit. Occasionally different brands of IDE hard drive may not be compatible when installed together. The best approach is to install drives from the same manufacturer.

Who uses SCSI hard drives and why? The primary reason some people move to SCSI hard drives seems to be the capability of installing seven logical devices on one adapter. You can install up to four interface boards, but can only have a maximum of 24 SCSI devices. Each device must be hardware addressed with jumpers to a unique logical unit number, or LUN address.

Other reasons are that some SCSI hard drives are a bit faster than equivalent IDE hard drives, and SCSI hard drives are available in extremely large sizes. A friend of mine recently installed a 180 GB SCSI hard drive! Why eludes me. The safer approach is to spend less on each hard drive and use multiple drives. A hard drive crash is less traumatic if you have multiple drives; you only have to replace a portion of your total storage capacity, and the cost is much lower.

While we're on the subject of hard drives, here's a useful offshoot from the basic hard disk storage system: the removable disk drive system. Several types are available, and each one has its own noteworthy features.

The Peerless drive from Iomega

< www.iomega.com > is a popular choice and among the best removable drives. It is one of the most popular removable drives, in sizes ranging from 5 GB to more than 20 GB. One feature of this drive is its nearly indestructible mechanism. It can be dropped from a height of 6 feet with no internal damage to the drive.

If this drive is the only drive in your system, you can remove your work and store it somewhere safe when you leave your computer. It can also be used in conjunction with an existing hard drive; a common use is as a backup system. It comes in USB format. This drive is only available as an external drive, and is more expensive in that format since you have to pay for the additional hardware and power supply. Expect to spend $200 – $300.

One disadvantage of this system is the lack of access speed. It is slower than newer hard drives. It is a smaller capacity storage medium, much smaller than the 100 GB – 200 GB drives commonly utilized. The clear advantage is the built-in crash protection. The Bernoulli drive has flexible disks, and even if the head comes in contact with the disk, it seldom damages it. If it's properly packaged, you can even send the drive to another user through the mail without concern for damage.

The Iomega zip drive uses a 3.5-inch cartridge. Similar in appearance to a standard 3.5-inch floppy disk, this system can store up to 100 MB on each cartridge. The zip drive is inexpensive at about $100, and the cartridges run about $10. This system could replace your hard drive, but capacity is a limitation. A better use for it is as a backup system.

Another popular removable hard storage medium is the SyQuest drive. SyQuest < www.syquest.com > has a line of removable hard drive cartridges with capacities up to 270 MB uncompressed. Disadvantages include small capacity, slow access speed, and the requirement of a SCSI interface for the drive.

Zone bit recording (ZBR) is the recording method utilized to reach the 270 MB capacity. Each disk is divided into zones. The longer outside tracks are divided into a smaller number of sectors, with a large number of bytes per sector. The inner tracks are divided into a larger number of sectors, but have a smaller number of bytes per sector, which increases the storage capacity significantly. Nearly all other systems stick with 512 bytes per sector.

SyQuest offers both internal and external SCSI drives, and several drives that operate from PCMCIA TYPE III slots. The PCMCIA (Personal Computer Memory Card Industry Association) bus is found in laptop and notebook computers, but this standard occasionally is found in desktop machines. These drives are small in size and capacity. They measure about 1.8 inches across, and the capacities are 60 and 80 MB.

These plug-in drives, mounted on add-on PC cards, can be removed and installed while your computer is running. Some U.S. government offices use this method of storage so that the drives can be removed and locked up for security purposes.

Several companies offer tiny hard drives from 500 MB to more than 2 GB in size. The drives are so small they offer an easy and safe way to secure confidential data and back it up. Look for the greatest advancements in hard drive storage capacity in this type of hard drive.

While SyQuest is still fresh in your mind, consider their parallel port drives. They borrow the computer's parallel printer port or supply an additional connector. The primary use I have seen for this type of hard drive is for backup, but you can use it to secure sensitive data also. If you share data with another computer site, this is a good way to do it. Several other companies use this type of interface.

MO (magneto-optical) hard drives were designed to resist the tendency of hard drives to lose data. Even the best magnetic hard drives will not hold data stored on them magnetically longer than a few years. MO drives store data by using a laser to preheat a small section of the disk immediately prior to data storage. This is performed on a material with a high resistance to being demagnetized. The high heat produced by the laser reduces the material's resistance to being magnetized, enabling you to store data on it. When the area cools down it regains the resistance to being magnetized or demagnetized. This gives your stored data a lifetime five times the life of normally stored data. Common shelf lives exceed 10 years.

These drives have a relatively small storage capacity—normally 120 MB to about 250 MB. Unless you never back up your computer you will not need this level of protection for your data.

Both CD-RW and DVD-RW drives are offshoots of this basic technology, but use laser beams at high frequency to store data on an optically sensitive medium. Typical CD-ROM capacities are 650 MB, and typical DVD-RW capacities for single layer are 4 GB.

The write once, read many times (WORM) drive is an optical storage device similar to a CD-ROM recorder. It typically stores data in the same fashion as current hard drives, with concentric circles of sectors and tracks. The CD-ROM recorder stores data in a single winding track from the center of the CD to the outside.

There are no standards for WORM drives that all manufacturers follow. The size of this system varies from a standard 5.25-inch bay in your computer up to 12-inch desktop models.

Floppy Disk Drives

Your basic resource for installing computer software and transferring data to and from your computer will probably be your floppy drive system.

Floppy drives come in several sizes. The most popular physical size is the 3.5-inch, which will fit in either a 5.25-inch standard bay or the smaller half-height bay in your case. The older and less popular size is the 5.25-inch. Another common drive is the combination drive, which consists of a 5.25-inch and 3.5-inch both driven by the same drive motor. By the time you read this, it might be impossible to find a 5.25-inch drive or the corresponding media.

Instead of a hard drive, the first personal computers had two drive bays that housed one

12-inch floppy disk each. The boot drive was the upper floppy disk, and the bottom disk was the working disk. The only disk I could modify data on was the working disk. The storage capacity of these floppy disks was 150 KB and 300 KB.

Floppy drives have advanced significantly. The first small 5.25-inch drives were single-sided and could only store 140 KB on each disk. The current 5.25-inch drives support media densities of 360 KB and 1.2 MB. The 3.5-inch disk drives support 720 KB and 1.44 MB. There is a 2.88 MB version available, but most people prefer the less expensive 1.44 MB standard.

Since the specifics of data storage on a floppy drive represent a book in itself, let's greatly simplify description of the process as we did in the hard drive section. The recording medium of a floppy drive is different than a hard drive. It is made up of a thin, oxide-coated polyethylene film, hence the name floppy or flexible disk. The 5.25-inch floppies are housed in a flexible case, while the 3.5-inch floppies have a hard plastic case. Unlike most hard drives, the floppy disk medium is removable. The two read-write heads remain in the floppy drive unit mounted in the computer.

The disk surface is written to by magnetizing a small portion of the surface by generating a magnetic pulse in one of the write heads of the disk drive. When the disk is read, that spot causes a magnetic flux to occur in the read head, producing a small electrical signal. This signal is added to other bits and decoded to reassemble the data you stored on the disk. This process occurs thousands of times per second during data storage and recovery.

How does the computer know where the data is stored on the disk? A floppy disk must be formatted. Formatting magnetically divides the disk surface into concentric circular tracks, of which each is divided again into sectors. In a 1.2-MB double-sided high-density floppy drive, there are 80 tracks per side.

It is the same for 1.44-MB 3.5-inch disks. Each track on the 1.2-MB disk is divided into 15 sectors, while each track is 18 sectors for the 1.44-MB disck. Each one of these sectors constitutes an allocation unit. An allocation unit is a spot allocated on the disk for data to be stored. Only single files or parts of a single file can be stored in an allocation unit.

The difference in the number of sectors between the 1.2-MB and 1.44-MB disks is the reason for the difference in capacity. During formatting, a FAT is created on track 0 of the disk. This track is where the index for the disk is stored. Each time a sector is written to, a record of the task is placed in the FAT. This is how the computer knows where data is stored on the floppy disk surface.

The 5.25-inch floppy drive, though obsolete by current standards, is still available. The floppy disk media comes in 360 KB and 1.2 MB. The 1.2-MB disks are labeled double-sided high density.

The 3.5-inch floppy drive is the current standard. The media available for it consists of 720-KB double-sided double-density and 1.44-MB double-sided high-density floppy diskettes, which are readily available and inexpensive.

The 2.88-MB 3.5-inch extended-density drive has been out for several years, but hasn't

FLOPPY DISK CAPACITIES

Disk Size	# Tracks Per Side	# Sectors Per Track	Capacity, Preformat	Used by System	# Available	Max # Dirs
360 KB	40	9	368640	6144	362496	112
1.2 MB	80	15	1228800	14898	1213952	224
720 KB	80	9	737280	12800	724480	224
1.44 MB	80	18	1474560	16896	1457664	224
2.88 MB	80	36	2949120	33792	2915328	240

Figure 3-5. A 64-bit Sound Blaster Live! sound card with 3-D sound.

really caught on. Affordable CD-ROM equipment, with 600+ MB capacity, minimized the importance of the 2.88 MB floppy for program installation. The ED drive is a good concept, but may have been introduced too late. The added expense of a special 1 MB controller may also have influenced its lack of popularity.

In the chart Floppy Disk Capacities, note that the maximum number of root directories is the same for the 1.2-MB, the 720-KB, and the 1.44-MB disks. The limitation is in the DOS file allocation table. To put more directories on a floppy disk, you must create subdirectories beneath the root directories. More information on subdirectories is in Chapter 6.

Sound Cards

To enhance the computing experience and add complex audio to projects, games, and presentations, the multimedia sound card accessory was created. Sound cards often come as part of a multimedia kit, which normally packages a sound card, a CD-ROM, software, and speakers. They usually can be purchased separately for less money. Figure 3-5 shows a Sound Blaster compatible 64-bit sound card with wave table and 3-D audio interface. The Sound Blaster product line is the de-facto standard in sound card performance and standardization. The Yamaha family of sound cards is a good alternative because of the extensive MIDI (musical instrument digital interface) support available and the higher power output they provide. Yamaha-manufactured cards also support Sound Blaster compatible modes.

Most sound cards can record high quality sound from a variety of sources. These include a compact disk, remote stereo, video camera, or any MIDI device connected to your computer. The MIDI built into most sound cards allows you to capture sound bits from keyboards, synthesizers, and a wide variety of input devices.

FM synthesis built into the sound card allows you to accurately reproduce up to 128 MIDI sounds and more than 45 percussion instruments. Some have actual samples of instrument sounds built in and use a wave table for FM synthesis.

Mixer capabilities are a useful addition to sound cards. An audio mixer allows you to control sound levels, bass, and treble in program material you wish to record. A microphone jack is a normal addition to most sound cards, and so is voice recognition software.

Voice recognition software allows you to operate your computer by talking to it after creating a voice-to-text table using samples of your voice reading certain words. After the computer stores your voice, it can recognize commands you dictate through the microphone attached to your sound card.

The sound card is a digital-to-analog interface that converts digitally stored information to analog sounds that speakers and headphones can play. Many sound cards double as an interface for a CD-ROM. If the interface is SCSI, the sound card will also control up to six other devices. The interaction between a CD-ROM and a sound card is digital. The only time the sound card provides analog output is when you are playing something through the speakers or headphones.

The technique sound cards use to record music and voice onto your hard drive is called *digital sampling*. The analog sound is broken into small fragments, and only a portion of these fragments is stored. If the fragments are small enough, and the space between the stored fragments is small enough, the sound can be reliably reproduced.

Most sound cards are at least 32-bit cards. A 32-bit card can break an analog wave into 65,536 (or 64K) fragments. If you use a 44 kHz sample rate to store stereo music, you will need more than 10 MB of disk space to store 1 minute of sound. This is why the average compact disk, with over 650 MB of storage capability, can only store about 1 hour of music, but it is stereo!

When recording high fidelity sound, it is necessary to go well beyond the limits of ordinary hearing. The reason is that mixing sounds outside the range we can hear makes many audible sounds. We would notice if sound cards limited sample rates to the 20 kHz limit of normal hearing; in fact, you must sample at more that twice the normal hearing range upper limit of 20 kHz to obtain good quality reproduction. A 44.1 kHz digital sample produces a 22 kHz analog signal when converted.

The greatest advantage provided by the digital processing of your sound card is the absence of noise; there is no tape hiss or static. Digital processing normally gives a signal-to-noise ratio of -90 dB. At this level, noise is inaudible.

The onboard digital signal processor (DSP) helps reduce any added CPU traffic by keeping most sound-related operations on the sound card. With no bus traffic to and from the processor for sound-related functions, there is less possibility for CPU slowdown when running complex sound and graphics operations.

The obvious advantage the DSP offers is speed, since the processor is not interrupted to handle sound processing. The DSP also handles the music synthesis and specialized digital effects required by many high-end programs. Assembling the many notes for a variety of instruments would be an imposing task for the processor otherwise.

The minimum sound card you should purchase is a 32-bit sound card with a DSP function. Anything else is already obsolete, and will not handle future requirements. Expect to spend around $12 to $15 for basic sound support, and up to $40 for 3-D full-featured wave table 64-bit live sound and 64 MIDI voices.

The Modem

A modem modulates the digital information a computer provides into analog signals the phone system understands. When the analog signal is received on the other end of the communication link, the receiving modem demodulates the signal to digital information the computer understands.

The phone line, being an analog system, is full of noise. This noise affects the quality of transmission to and from the modem. Most modems have error correction functions built in to clean up poor quality communications, and can adjust the communication speed on both ends to optimize response quality.

Baud rate is a measure of the communication speed between modems. Baud rates of 300 means the computers are talking at about 27 characters per second. (To get this number, add the 8 bits that define a character to 1 start bit, 1 stop bit, and the next start bit. Then divide 300 by the total (11) to get about 27 characters per second.)

Two modems, when communicating, must operate at the same baud rate and use the same communication protocol. Fortunately, faster modems are downward compatible with slower ones. Modem speeds can vary from 300 baud to over 56K baud. A 28.8K baud modem transmits at approximately 2,800 characters per second.

One protocol of choice is Zmodem batch, which sends data as a continuous stream. Error checking codes are inserted at certain intervals. If an error is detected, the affected portion of data is sent again.

Other protocols include Kermit, Xmodem, and Ymodem. These three send a block of data with error-checking code attached and await a positive response from the recipient before sending the next block. This...is...very...slow. Since Zmodem batch is a bi-directional protocol, error detection and correction is an ongoing process.

Let's discuss ITU recommended standards. The International Telecommunications Union, previously called the Comite Consultatif Internal de Telegraphique et Telephone (CCITT), was established to standardize worldwide telecommunications. The committee makes recommendations only, and companies can accept or ignore these suggestions.

All suggestions for standardization in small computers have a V or X prefix, for switched or non-switched phone networks respectively. (Most systems are switched.) All revisions or alternate suggestions have either *bis* (for second) or *ter* (for third) following the standard type. An example is V.32bis.

A V.32bis modem can communicate at 14.4K baud, but a V.32 modem can only run at 4,800 or 9,600 bps. The V.32bis standard is a modulation method. The V.34 standard is for the 28.8 K baud modems. The V.42bis standard is a method of combined error checking and compression. Two V.42bis modems can communicate at speeds up to 57.6 K baud.

All modems must use communications software to operate. When you purchase a modem, it normally comes with a stripped-down version of a popular communications package. You may choose to purchase a high performance software package to optimize use of your modem.

Some communications packages worth note are Qmodem by Mustang Software, Procomm Plus by DataStorm, and WinComm Pro by Delrina. There are also numerous shareware packages available, such as Lcom, and BBS software such as Wildcat and WWIV.

Hayes compatibility is an important data requirement for modems. Hayes set the standard and all other manufacturers have established products that adhere to these standards.

There are two types of modems, internal and external, each with its advantages and disadvantages. Both have a speaker to allow you to hear busy signals or ringing. External modems have a switch to turn them off. If you are security conscious, it makes sense to prevent access to your computer by turning your modem off when not in use.

External modems show activity with status LEDs on their front panel so you always know what's going on. The disadvantages of external units are higher cost and the requirement for an external COM port.

Internal modems are the most popular. They are their own communications port when installed and do not require additional desk space. They do not have status indicators and cannot be switched off, however. They also eat up one of the valuable add-on card slots in your computer.

Fax capability is normally included on most modems available today. Any document you create can be faxed to a recipient with a fax modem or conventional fax machine.

CD-ROM Drives

Since the middle 1990s, a CD-ROM has become a necessity. The device that was once a nice option has become a key requirement on nearly everyone's computer. The CD-ROM provides numerous benefits for home computer users, and the host of software available is endless. Figure 3-6 depicts a CD-ROM drive.

The uses of CD-ROM for business are significant, but this book focuses on the home user. Since the price of CD-ROM games and entertainment packages has dropped significantly, people purchase computers with CD-ROMs already installed.

Home entertainment is one of the principal targets for CD-ROM software developers. Games, encyclopedias, music, art, and movies are transformed to CD-ROM software. Educational material is quickly and easily learned from a CD-ROM, and kids are quick to acquire the skills necessary to use the system. Several hundred books, or three hours of compressed video, can be stored on a single CD-ROM.

The total sensory experience of a CD-ROM system seems to make learning easier. With more avenues to the brain, topics can be easily assimilated and retained. School topics become multimedia experiences and learning becomes fun.

The CD-ROM has recently become the de-facto standard convenient medium for software installation, including operating systems, legal programs, medical software, pharmaceutical reference books, and desktop publishing software. The uses for this medium seem to be endless.

Sony and Phillips Corporations first marketed the CD-ROM in the 1980s. Its initial use was playing recorded music without the analog noise common in existing systems. Of course, home units could only play music; the recording system cost at that time was prohibitive.

A CD-ROM disk is made by burning microscopic depressions in the disk material with a miniature laser in response to program data digital logic levels. This creates a pattern of pits and lands. Data is read from the disk by another type of laser. When the read laser is focused on the programmed portion of the disk, the pits do not reflect back as much light as the lands, allowing the read laser to easily distinguish the programmed bits. The digital ones and zeroes represented by the pits and lands are decoded, and the data is recovered.

Data on a laser disk is encoded in one large spiral track winding outward from the disk's center. This single track is divided into about 270,000 sectors, if the laser that programmed the disk is a low-frequency red laser. More than five times that many sectors are available with a green laser, but this technology is not yet commonplace, except in DVD recorders. Each sector in both types is 2,048 bytes. The sectors are numbered in .001 second increments, which allows the data to be easily located.

The rotational speed of a laser disk constantly changes with respect to distance from the disk center. This CLV (constant linear velocity) method allows uniform data acquisition with respect to time, and is similar to the zone bit recording method used in some hard drives.

Like a hard disk, the speed at which a laser disk can transfer data to memory is far slower than direct memory access. The first CD-ROM drives had a data transfer speed less

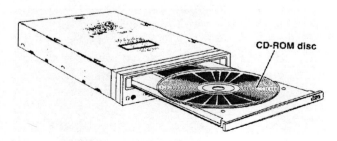

Figure 3-6. The CD-ROM drive

CD-ROM disc

than 100 sectors per second. A sector is 2,048 bytes, or 2 KB, and the first CD-ROMs could transfer 2 KB times 100 sectors, or 200 KB (200 thousand bytes) of data per second. By comparison, current IDE hard drives can transfer between 4 MB (4 million bytes) and 13 MB of data in the same amount of time.

This category of computer accessory has improved substantially. Transfer rates for CD-ROM drives have been the primary performance increase. To put transfer rates in perspective, an old drive was rated about 150 KB per second. A good 4X drive will transfer 600 KB per second. A 6X CD-ROM increases this number to about 900 KB per second.

Access time, the length of time the drive takes to find any sector, is the other measurement of CD-ROM performance. An old drive took 600 milliseconds, or ms, to locate data, and a 6X drive only takes about 100 ms to perform the same operation. Today's drives are 8 – 10 times faster than a 6X CD-ROM drive was.

Remember cache memory? A good CD-ROM drive has a built-in cache buffer. When data is transferred from the CD-ROM drive to the computer, it is temporarily loaded into cache on the drive. The data transfer to the computer can occur much more quickly and smoothly this way. Most inexpensive CD-ROM drives have a 256-KB buffer, but a good drive will have 2 MB.

Several companies offer CD-ROM caching software. These programs set aside memory in your computer to use as a temporary storage cache for use while running programs on CD-ROM. The memory they set aside can be either on your hard disk or on your motherboard. Either way, the access time of the cache memory will be much faster than the CD-ROM access time, so your program will run faster.

There are other differences in CD-ROM drives. The most significant is the internal or external option. An external drive will cost more, but performance should be similar. Stay away from CD-ROM drives with proprietary interfaces, and pick a good IDE or SCSI drive that fits your requirements.

New and faster drives are constantly being designed. Stay at least one speed behind the pack to get the best deals. That $100 60X CD-ROM drive will cost only $50 when the 72X drive becomes commonplace.

The CD-ROM recording system has become inexpensive enough for home use, with CD recorders going for less than $100. Many companies have their paper records scanned and put on CD-ROM, then use the recorder to archive duplicates of the data. With 650 MB (or up to 4 GB of storage capability using compression) you could archive the complete records of a large hospital on a few disks.

CD-ROM recorders are becoming popular as backup systems and for copying systems from one computer to another. Remember that if you purchase software, you normally agree to install the software on only one machine. If you use a CD-ROM recorder to illegally copy or transfer software, you can get into serious trouble for copyright infringement.

Backup Systems

The move to larger hard drives in computers today necessitates a backup system with large capacity. A good tape backup system will save you hours of frustration and yards of gray hair. Tape backups are inexpensive, too.

You can purchase a tape backup system that supports 800 MB of storage on each tape for around $70. A good external drive that puts up to 5 GB on each tape is under $140. The tapes are also constantly coming down in price. A five pack sold recently for about the price of a single tape one year ago. For about $10 you can get 800 MB tapes, and the 5 GB Travan cartridges run $20.

Tape backup systems operate between 15 MB and 25 MB per minute, depending on the hardware. Figure 3-7 shows three backup options currently available.

The best part of a backup system is the ease of use. Most tape drives come with DOS and Windows 9X backup software, which automatically configures the tape system for use. In the event of a massive hard-drive

Figure 3-7: Several systems are available to back up your data.

failure, your tape backup system will save you hours of stressful data recovery.

Consider the three hours required to restore a system crash from backup. If you had to rebuild 100 GB of installed software without a backup system, it might take you several days, if you could accomplish it at all.

A backup system is only good if you use it. Do a full system backup as soon as you install the backup drive. Perform incremental backups weekly if you use the computer daily.

The three backup systems shown in Figure 3-7 are, from left to right, a Hewlett-Packard (HP) 5 GB tape backup system, an IOMEGA 20 GB hard drive-based backup system that runs from a USB port, and a 100 MB IOMEGA zip drive. (The zip drive is best used to back up daily-used data that must be transferred between computers. As a full system backup, it is useless due to small capacity per disk. But it is an excellent method to transfer, for example, the text of this book to my publisher.)

Since the backup system is easy to use, take advantage of it. You will be ecstatic the first time you have to recover data, or must rid your system of a computer virus by reformatting your hard drive.

The Monitor

By now, you know how important a good monitor is. Your monitor will probably outlive everything else in your system, so get exactly what you want. If you will be happier with a larger monitor, get it now. They normally go down in price slowly, unlike other computer accessories.

It is necessary to mention the monitor-sizing scheme. When you buy a 14-inch monitor, you can only use a portion of the 14 inches; there is a border of up to one inch all the way around the monitor screen. This border masks a portion of the monitor deemed unusable due to screen curvature. Even a good 15-inch flat screen monitor has only 13.5 inches of diagonal viewing area.

Size is the most important feature. Get the monitor most comfortable to view, considering your software requirements. If you plan to do any CAD or schematic work, do not get a monitor smaller than 19 inches. Desktop publishing or heavy 3-D gaming requires at minimum a 17-inch monitor. The standard 15-inch monitors are simply inadequate.

What To Watch Out For

Bench test your monitor at a computer retailer before purchase. Check the outside corners for fuzzy display areas or distortion. Ensure that you can set brightness and contrast controls for comfortable viewing without overdriving the screen. (Overdriving is evident as poor focus and excessive glare, and will prematurely age the monitor.) Reflected glare from the monitor face can also be a problem, though many monitors come with an anti-glare screen.

Get a green monitor if possible. A green monitor has circuitry that makes it sleep if left unattended for a period of time. A sleeping monitor consumes very little energy. Since an average monitor can consume 150 – 200 watts of energy, a green monitor can save you money. The EPA Energy Star seal is on each green monitor, identifying it as an energy-conserving computer accessory.

Be sure to get a good quality .28-dot pitch or better SVGA monitor. Many vendors will try to get rid of their obsolete .39 dot pitch monitors, so don't be the next victim. You will notice the difference.

If you spend a lot of time in front of your monitor, consider an LCD monitor. They are flicker and radiation free. If you have been getting headaches during or after a long day in front of the computer, the flicker and radiation from your monitor might be contributing factors. I spend lots of time in front of my new LCD monitor, and since I switched over, the headaches have left the building forever.

The Mouse

In the beginning of personal computing, a mouse was a rarity on a DOS computer; the keyboard was the primary input device. With the advent of sophisticated, graphics-intensive programs, the mouse has replaced the keyboard as the primary input device.

The advent of Windows and Windows-based programs occurred primarily because of the Macintosh success story. If you give someone an easy-to-use computer without a maze of commands to learn, they will learn quickly and enjoy using it. A clean graphic user interface with icons, a mouse, and very little memorization makes for a comfortable computing environment.

When choosing a mouse, consider the fact that a $10 mouse will do most of the things a $100 mouse will. If you have no particular reason to choose one mouse over another, consider saving money and purchasing an inexpensive Microsoft-compatible mouse instead of the high-priced spread.

If you have applications that require a high-resolution mouse, such as engineering, drafting,

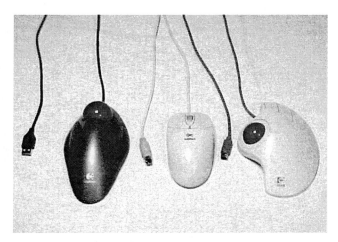

Figure 3-8: USB trackball, USB mouse, and a standard trackball, all types of mice.

or design, you will have to purchase a more expensive alternative. Figure 3-8 shows several mouse alternatives commonly available.

You might spend a few bucks more and buy a stationary trackball. A primary reason is you might have no desk space for a conventional mouse and pad. The other reason is the increased resolution obtained. A trackball is nothing more than an upside-down mouse. The ball is rotated with the thumb and the rest of the mouse just lies there on the table.

The mouse plugs into a serial port on your computer. As you move the mouse, the ball moves two or more wheels. The wheels have holes or indentations, which interrupt a light path to photosensitive diodes or transistors. This creates a data stream, which enters the computer through the serial port. Using the buttons causes additional data bits to enter the data path into the computer. The I/O card or built in function decodes the data stream to know exactly what the mouse pointer is pointing at when you make a selection.

The mouse, like all accessories, must be configured in software to be useful. Windows 9X, Windows 2K, Windows XP, and several other operating systems have embedded PnP software functions to detect and configure your mouse. Other software requires you install a driver for the mouse, and one normally comes with it for that purpose. Mouse drivers are available for all new mice on the Web as well.

When purchasing a mouse, be certain to get a high-resolution mouse if you will be doing high-level design work. If you just want a pointer and don't need the resolution, you can get off inexpensively. Since even the inexpensive type lasts a long time, do not buy a high-end one if you do not need it.

The Keyboard

The keyboard is the most abused part of your computer. You will bang on it when things don't work, spill your drink of choice into it, and fall asleep on it occasionally. It will, however, give you the least trouble of any part of your computer.

Unlike the typewriter, the computer

keyboard has no real standardization. You can blame the independent manufacturers for this. Everyone has his own idea of which keys should be placed where, and how many function keys are necessary.

Newer keyboards are almost micro-computers themselves, with a ROM-based operating system and processor installed on their main boards. They store keystrokes and generate unique codes for each key pressed. They even know when you want to repeat a keystroke.

Many specialized keyboards exist, and you may go crazy trying them out, but try you must. This keypad will be in front of you for a long time. Purchase your keyboard only after trying out many different types. Like the mouse, you can spend $100 or more on a keyboard, or as little as $9. Pick a keyboard you will be happy with many years, since they last a very long time.

Extras

Now for the fun stuff: Have you ever looked at a picture and thought you would like to see it every time you turned on your computer? All you have to do is scan the picture into your computer. Or maybe you'd like to make fliers with text and photos for friends or clients.

The price of a usable single-pass color scanner is in the $50 – $300 range, and it makes an economical and enjoyable addition to your system.

When you look for a scanner, insist on one that is TWAIN-compatible. TWAIN (technology without an interesting name) is an application programming interface, or API specification, that several large corporations jointly developed. This helped standardize the device drivers for the scanners, so you will not have configuration headaches using your scanner in different programming environments. One that works from a USB port is the best choice.

The Printer

To round out the peripheral and accessory section of this book, let's look at printer types. Remember this point, however: printers typically outlast most of your computer accessories, so get one you can live with a long time.

The first color printers were dot-matrix printers with a color kit, which consisted of a ribbon with three-color bands and a black band. Special software was necessary to drive the print head up and down the ribbon to produce color images.

The advantage of current dot-matrix printers is cost. The lower initial cost is added to the lower cost per page of printed material. A good dot-matrix printer can be purchased for around $40 with the color ribbon and software. Dot-matrix printers come in narrow and wide styles. The wide style can handle the 11x14-inch paper commonly used to print ledgers and spreadsheets. Most dot-matrix printers use fanfold continuous feed paper.

Disadvantages of this type of printer include lower print quality than other types of printers and extremely slow color printing. The noise from a dot matrix printer is often very uncomfortable. They have a very small print buffer and are generally without scaleable fonts. (Scaleable fonts are text styles that can be made larger or smaller by newer printers.)

Ink-jet printers normally cost from $90 to $600, and are a quantum leap from the dot-matrix printer. HP invented the ink-jet printer, and holds a vast portion of the current market share. A color ink-jet printer from HP will cost about $200 with the color kit included. A competitor, Digital Equipment Corporation (DEC), often advertises their color ink jet printer for about $180 and includes a $40 mail-in rebate.

Several ink jet printer manufacturers include a fax machine in their printers. They can be used as a copier or printer. HP and Ricoh both make these machines.

Laser printers do premium black and white printing. They normally have resolution of 300 to 600 dpi (dots per inch). The common resolution for a low-cost ink-jet printer is also 300 to 600 dpi, but the laser image always looks better. Today's laser printers are available for $150 and up.

Laser printers, at four to 50 pages per minute, are the fastest printers available for home computing. The technology behind the laser printer is a book in itself, but this description fits most of them: A laser printer utilizes complex optics and mirrors to write text and graphics onto a photosensitive rotating drum assembly. The laser beam is swept across the drum, pulsing in intensity to identify light and dark areas. The laser beams onto the drum, sensitizing the dark areas, where printable material is encoded. As the drum rotates through the toner material, the sensitized areas pick up the carbon toner. Paper is pressed against the drum, picking up the toner. The paper is heated, fusing the toner to the paper. Except for the laser, this system is similar to a standard copy machine. Copy machines are just beginning to use this lower-cost method as well.

The prices range from about $150 for a good 15 page per minute 600 dpi unit to around $2,500 for a 50+ page per minute unit with 1,200 dpi quality. They can't commonly do color at an affordable price. If you wish to spend $1,000 to $10,000, you can have a Xerox, Tektronix, or QMS laser color printer. This price is 10 times the cost of a good color ink jet printer.

Laser printers can use lower quality paper easily, but some paper will eventually clog up the printer. The high level of solid particulate material associated with cheap paper eventually impairs the workings of the laser printer, so clean the paper path often if you use cheap paper.

Laser printers format data before printing, so a print buffer of 4 to 16 MB is a necessity. Most laser printers have built in scaleable fonts for more flexibility in printing. These two options add to the printing speed.

A typical laser printer will get 2,000 – 4,000 pages or more from a toner cartridge. Most ink-jet printers can only print about 300 – 600 pages per ink cartridge. The average price for a laser toner cartridge is between $40 and $100, while color ink jet cartridges cost $20 – $40. Expect to spend more time maintaining an ink-jet printer than the average

laser printer because of the difference in toner and ink capacities.

In summary, if you only print an occasional letter, get an inexpensive dot-matrix printer. If you often print in color but don't need laser quality resolution, get a good ink-jet printer. If you print tons of high quality black and white letter-quality documents, get a laser printer. The most versatile setup is to have a 600 dpi laser printer and a color ink-jet printer.

Power and Line Voltage Conditioning

Nearly everyone has experienced a power blackout or brownout. These interruptions in power can be harmful or destructive to your computer. If you live where lightning strikes are commonplace, you know the amount of damage they can cause.

Plan on purchasing a power strip with surge protection for your computer. Power surges, caused by line voltage fluctuation, often damage or destroy home electronics. Lightning strikes, power pole damage, or any sudden load on the power grid in your area can cause them. You will be adding $30 to the price of your system, but this is an inexpensive insurance policy, considering the investment.

An uninterruptible power supply, or UPS, is a necessary purchase if you live in an electrically challenged area. A computer plugged into a UPS largely ignores blackouts, brownouts, and electrical storms. A UPS is a stand-alone power source that converts direct current voltage from a set of internal batteries into 60-cycle 120 VAC. The UPS is plugged into the wall socket, and the computer draws power through the UPS from the wall socket. If power is interrupted for any reason, the UPS starts up immediately and supplies power to anything plugged into it without any interruption in service.

When choosing a power-conditioning device, be certain that you assess your needs honestly. Trying to save a few dollars now can cost you hundreds later.

We have looked at truth in advertising in the computer store, studied types of systems, and examined in reasonable detail the components of a computer system. We have reviewed peripherals and accessories. With the information presented up to now, you can make intelligent choices regarding the specific components you want in your system. When you decide on your components, you will have created an integrated working computer model. This model will serve as your dream machine for comparison with store-bought systems.

Put together on paper the system you desire. Compare your dream system to actual hardware on sale at a retail vendor. Try out a system that closely matches your model, and be certain your plan has omitted nothing important. When you finish this exercise, you have removed all doubt that you will be satisfied with your system.

4

Designing Your Computer and System

PRICES OF COMPUTER COMPONENTS RELATIVE TO THE WHOLE COMPUTER'S COST

Component	Price*	Percentage of Whole
Motherboard, Pentium 4	$159	11.60
Case, mid-tower	$29	2.07
Microprocessor, P4	$449	32.81
Ram, 256 MB RDRAM	$102	7.44
Video card, GeForce Pro 32	$79	5.76
Hard disk, 80 GB	$210	15.31
Floppy disk, 1.44 MB, 2 each	$25	1.82
Keyboard, 101 style	$12	0.88
Mouse, three-button	$7	0.51
Monitor, 19 inch, .26 dpi, flat screen	$299	21.8

*Your prices will be lower, but this is representative of the ratios you will find at any time. A comparable pre-built system costs $2,299, but this one is $1,371. Build it yourself and save money!

The prices above are for a typical Pentium 4, 2 GHz system with 256 MB of RDRAM and a good quality AGP video card with 32 MB of VRAM. A Western Digital 80 GB hard drive and two 3.5-inch floppy drives are included.

The rest of this chapter will show you how to select

the components for your computer. You will be shown how to make your shopping list and given the information to allow you to intelligently select the accessories you need.

When you finish this chapter, you will have a list of the components to build exactly the computer you want.

One necessary consideration is your software requirement. After selecting your software, be certain that the computer you are building will support the software you plan to use. Failing to do so is a common mistake that people who buy packaged systems often make. The system looks good enough but unless the buyer has done his homework, he goes home with a system that does not fit his needs.

Keep your current and future software requirements in mind as you select your components and you will not be disappointed or unpleasantly surprised.

MAKING YOUR SHOPPING LIST

I have never seen any book or periodical that gives you information on exactly what to buy to make a computer; other books discuss some features of a few necessary components and leave the rest as guesswork. This book is the exception. My objective in this chapter is to eliminate any doubt in your mind that you are buying exactly what you want and need. If you follow my instructions, you will wind up with the best possible computer for your requirements and have more money in your pocket than you expected.

As detailed in Chapter 1, the minimum components required to build a computer are the case, a motherboard, the microprocessor, the RAM, a video card, either onboard IDE I/O or an IDE I/O card, a hard disk, a floppy disk, a keyboard, a mouse, and a monitor.

The Motherboard

Start with the motherboard. The motherboard determines the required characteristics of the rest of the components. Figure 4-1 shows an Athalon motherboard with the PCI bus. The PCI slots are the short slots next to the AGP connector in the middle.

The motherboards readily available today are, from slowest to fastest, the Celeron PCI, the AMD Duron PCI, the Pentium 3 and 4, and the AMD Athalon XP. Pricing is approximate, but here are some guidelines.

Expect to procure an upgradable Pentium 3/Celeron motherboard for $70 to $100. It has onboard EIDE I/O and onboard sound card support.

A faster Pentium 4 PCI motherboard with pipeline burst cache and onboard EIDE I/O will run you about $105 without the processor but remember, it supports faster RDRAM.

Now, hold onto your pocketbook. The Intel motherboard that supports the Pentium 4, 2 GHz microprocessor runs about $185 *without* the processor, which is about $400. This motherboard has full support for RDRAM, sound, onboard network card, and a modem riser card. These prices will generally fall with time and serve as references only.

The hottest processors on the market today are Intel's Pentium 4 and AMD Athalon models. The CPU assembly looks more like an add-on card than a CPU, and the motherboard is unique, costing about $150. The processors range in price from $150 to $500, at frequencies from 1 GHz to beyond 2 GHz.

Someone asked me about quality and mechanical configuration issues recently, so they will be addressed now. Quality between different manufacturers is very similar. The primary reason is component vendors have no sense of humor when it comes to returned items, and they will not tolerate any manufacturer who does not conform to their standards. The quality issue is resolved before the customer gets involved. It is necessary, when doing large volumes of business, to start and maintain a good quality-control system.

Motherboards determine the ultimate use and performance of your computer. Choose the motherboard that supports your processor of choice and select the fastest RAM available in the configuration you choose. Ensure the motherboard supports the fastest RAM for the processor in question. Know and understand that RDRAM for the Pentium 4 processors and DDR RAM for the Athalon-based processors

Figure 4-1. AMD Athalon motherboard for the 1.4GHz Processor and DDR

are the current state of the art. Note that if you are not building an extremely fast machine that these choices in RAM might be a little steep, particularly in the RDRAM category.

The motherboard in Figure 4-1 is an example of a good, reliable, fast Athalon-based motherboard with support for DDR RAM. It includes sockets for extended modem capability with voice, and a 4X AGP slot, the premium setup for extremely fast graphics and game support.

This should be enough information to pick a motherboard to fit your needs and budget.

Configuration between different manufacturers of motherboards and components is tightly controlled by the standards to which each component has to adhere. Without going into extensive detail, let it suffice to say that the components that are used to make an IBM-compatible PC are, for the most part, completely interchangeable within the families.

The Case

Get the case that suits your future needs. If you want a desktop case, you are somewhat limited in what can be put inside. Remember also that the primary reason for moving from the desktop case is your health. A monitor placed on a desktop case is too high to view without neck and back strain.

The medium-tower case is a good buy and

is suitable for adding extra goodies later. It has a larger power supply, more connectors, a larger fan, and more room for tape drives, CD-ROMs, extra hard drives, and additional floppy drives.

Mini-towers are generally the best buy, and around $20 to $25 will buy a good one. If you do not plan on the combination of a DVD-ROM, two floppy drives, an internal tape drive, and a CD-ROM, a mini tower will suffice. Figure 4-2 shows a mini-tower case.

This case is suitable for the majority of computers, but the larger medium tower allows an additional bay for an internal tape drive.

There are so many types and styles of cases that it would take hours to describe them all. Since it is one of the most visible parts of your computer, make your choice carefully. The case will generally outlive upgradable items such as the motherboard and all internal components, so get a case you are comfortable with, one that will serve your current and future requirements.

When you evaluate your need for a computer case, consider future expansion. Though most people select a mini-tower case and most purchased computers come with one, you may decide to add enough peripheral equipment to make a mini-tower useless.

Add up the equipment you will be installing in your computer and are planning to purchase over the next several months before you firm up a decision on your case requirements.

For example, if you decide to install two hard drives, a tape backup system, a CD-ROM drive, and two floppy drives, you have one more device than you have drive bays. A medium tower is your most viable choice with these peripherals.

Most vendors have a good selection of cases. Ask for the advantages and disadvantages of each case you are interested in before you make your decision to buy. Buy enough case for your predicted future requirements and be certain to look at a sample case to confirm it will actually suit your needs before making the purchase.

The mini-tower and full tower cases have

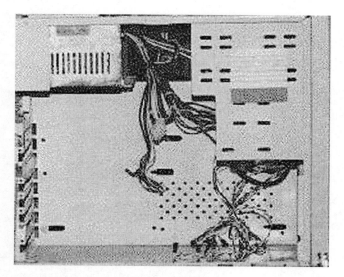

Figure 4-2. A mini-tower case.

the same configuration. The difference is the medium tower has an additional 5.25-inch bay. The mini tower will support two hard drives, 3.5-inch drives and 5.25-inch drives. The medium tower adds the third 5.25-inch bay.

RAM

The type of motherboard you purchase will determine the RAM you buy. You may have banks for 72-pin SIMM only, 72-pin SIMM and 168-pin DIMM, or 168-pin DIMM only. DIMM are primarily utilized on Pentium Celeron and Athalon Duron motherboards for SDRAM.

The fastest computers use DDR RAM or Rambus-manufactured DRAM. The AMD processors lean toward DDR RAM, and Pentium 4 utilizes the RDRAM. Both are extremely fast architectures. DDR RAM utilizes a "dual pumped" technique for increased performance, which allows data to be clocked both on the rising and falling edge of a clock pulse. (The clock pulses are nothing but a way for the microprocessor to tell the RAM when to move data.) This symbol (|_|) represents a falling clock edge followed by a rising clock edge. Normal RAM would pass one set of data, while DDR RAM would pass two sets of data, making it twice as fast per clock pulse.

RDRAM utilizes a different architecture,

developed around a 16-bit bus instead of the standard 64-bit bus. It runs at only 800 MHz, but with a 16-bit bus that is equivalent to the 200 MHz speed of DDR RAM. DDR RAM uses a 64-bit bus. The equivalent data rates are the same (800 divided by 4 is equal to 200 MHz).

You need 64 MB of RAM to run most 32-bit applications, including Windows 9X and Windows NT, with any degree of speed. You need at least 24 additional megabytes of RAM to run most office and desktop suites, and 32 MB is better. That means it is a good idea to plan on at least 128 MB of RAM to allow Windows 98, 2000, NT, or XP to properly perform multitasking, for which all of these operating systems were designed. The most common memory capacity today is 128 MB. Soon, due to 32-bit applications, the most common size will be 256 MB. Get 256 MB now and you will be glad you did.

Plan on buying SDRAM if you are making an AMD Duron or Intel Celeron machine. Plan on expensive RDRAM for a Pentium 4, and cost-effective DDR RAM for use with an Athalon or Athalon XP-based computer.

You now have the case, motherboard, CPU, and RAM specified for your system. The next thing to look at is the video adapter card.

Video Adapter

Remember, the video adapter is an add-on card that converts digital information from your computer into signals used to display information on your monitor. The range in video performance for a computer is staggering.

You can purchase a basic PCI video card for as little as $22 – $35. This card will have 32 MB of video RAM, but no bells and whistles. The next step up is a 2X AGP video card with 32 or 64 MB of RAM. These cards will be priced in the $44 – $75 dollar range.

The next jump is a 64 MB 4X AGP video card with TV outputs and significant 3-D and virtual reality support. Plan on releasing up to $300 for this baby. This is not the best choice for a generic home computer unless you have programs like AutoCad or the latest video games installed.

AGP Video Cards

The Diamond Fire Gl 1000 series dominated this category at one time, introducing accelerated graphics port (AGP) capability. Now nearly every motherboard has a 2X or 4X AGP port and all video card manufacturers offer several products to fit this enhanced IO bus.

There are dozens of game video adapters available. Beware of a video adapter that supports only one or two 3-D games—it will be expensive and perhaps not compatible with forthcoming software packages.

The average Duron or Celeron user should purchase a 2X AGP video card with 32 MB of RAM. If you are building the fastest machine in either the Pentium 4 or Athalon category, go ahead and spill your wallet for a 4X AGP video card with 64 MB of RAM. To do otherwise will definitely show up in performance.

Why spend more money for a better video adapter? The reasons vary, but support for graphics-intensive programs is the primary reason. The speed of an AGP video adapter is significant in high-end 3-D applications like solids modeling and CAD programs.

The other primary user of high-end graphics adapters is the extreme game player. The new 32- and 64-bit video games use MPEG video compression to store embedded video clips in computer games. Only the best video adapters can display the video clips smoothly. If your requirements fit in these categories, consider a high-end video adapter a necessity.

The Hard Disk

Hard disks come in all shapes and sizes, in capacities from 10 GB to more than 180 GB in IDE format, and well beyond 200 GB in SCSI format.

What do you need and why? If your intended applications are considerable, your hard-disk capacity requirements will match. Consider the software you will be installing and get a hard disk with a minimum capacity of twice or three times that much.

Access times are similar for most hard disks today, so this factor is not significant in

selection. You will find the prices are pretty similar, too.

The most popular hard drives today are high-capacity IDE hard drives. Conner, Maxtor, Quantum, Seagate, and Western Digital all make hard drives in excess of 100 GB. Conner, Maxtor, and Western Digital make drives in the 180-GB range and beyond.

Both Conner and Seagate make large capacity hard drives in SCSI format. If you are planning on installing a SCSI adapter for any reason, consider one of these.

What to Buy...

If I were assembling a budget computer, I would purchase a smaller IDE hard drive, such as the 20- to 40-GB IDE hard drives available for about $70. If I were making a fast Pentium or clone machine I would double up a pair of Western Digital 100-GB hard drives for about $200 to $220 each. There are many variations in size and price between these two extremes, and also 200-GB hard disks and beyond. Just look at everything available before you decide, and remember that the newest hard disks are overpriced in comparison with drives a few months older.

Floppy Drives

Most people will buy only one 3.5-inch floppy drive for a first time computer. The only people who should even consider a 5.25-inch floppy drive are owners of older computer with data or software on 5.25-inch disks. Some people, like myself, have to duplicate data disks often for clients, and a pair of 3.5-inch floppies makes this easy. (The DOS Diskcopy program supports dual identical drives and makes exact duplicates of a disk in one pass.)

Important things to consider when buying a floppy drive are price and adaptability. Though floppy drives once cost hundreds of dollars, today's prices for floppy drives range from $10 to $15. *Never* pay more than $15 for a Sony or Teac 3.5 inch 1.44 MB floppy drive. For adaptability, the floppy drive should include a 5.25-inch mounting kit so you can install the drive in either 3.5-inch or 5.25-inch bays in your case. Since floppy drives are so similar in all other respects, including longevity and quality, these are the two primary issues to keep in mind.

Keyboard and Mouse

Like your pillow and mattress, your mouse and keyboard are individual and personal. *Nobody* touches my mouse without my permission! Since most of the operations you perform on a computer require one of both of them, you should purchase wisely.

There are numerous designs, types, and configurations of the keyboard. Ergonomic keyboards suit the power user because they conform to the individual requirements of someone who spends hours on a computer. A casual user may be happy with a $12 keyboard conforming to the AT specification. The best place to test drive keyboards is a computer store, or even a large department store. They will have a selection of computers available with a wide variety of peripherals from which to choose.

There are as many types of mice as keyboards, and I recommend trying several out before purchasing. Try the stationary trackball mouse as well. If you have limited desk space, a trackball is a good choice. Remember to evaluate both two-button and three-button mice. A three-button mouse allows you to program the middle button in certain applications and can save you hours of typing.

Pricing for mice and keyboards varies widely from store to store. I purchase inexpensive ones for people I build for, because I know they will be the first things the new owner replaces to suit his own personal taste.

For $20 you can buy a keyboard and three-button Microsoft-compatible mouse. You can also spend $75 for a Logitech trackball and upward of $100 for an ergonomic keyboard, if you wish.

IDE I/O

The only time you will be interested in this add-in card is if you plan on installing multiple CD-ROMs or DVD-ROMs in a case that already has at least one DMA-66 hard drive.

Figure 4-3 shows an EIDE I/O card, which supports four hard drives or CD-ROMS or DVD-ROMs, two floppy drives, and I/O functions, such as a parallel printer port, a game adapter port for a joystick or flight controller, and two serial data ports.

In current versions, this card has Ethernet capability as well. This component speeds up Internet data transmission, particularly through a cable modem.

Obviously a motherboard with these built-in functions reduces the need for an add-on card in all but the most extensively loaded systems, but if the built-in function fails on a motherboard, provisions on the motherboard allow you to add a card like this to restore the function.

The Monitor

You must try out all types of monitors before you consider a purchase in this department. The monitor you like may not work for anyone else. Everyone looks at monitors differently; that's why there are so many different types available. The monitor features most computers users are concerned with are the size of the screen, whether it is interlaced or non-interlaced, and if it is digital.

The largest screen is not necessarily the

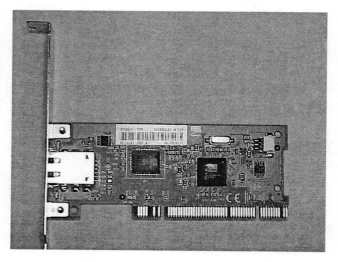

Figure 4-3. An I/O and Ethernet add-in card.

best. I tried a 21-inch monitor for about a week, then came back to a good digital Shamrock 17-inch non-interlaced SVGA monitor. The 21-inch monitor was ghosting on some of my faster moving applications and giving me a headache. A 15-inch monitor will probably give you a headache, too, because the image is so small. If you use your computer more than twice a week, do yourself a favor and get at least a 17-inch monitor or a 15-inch LCD monitor.

Most people prefer a 17-inch digital non-interlaced SVGA monitor. It combines all the good features in an affordable package. If you have high-definition graphics, such as Autocad drawings, multiple layer schematics, or PCB layout applications, a 19-inch or larger monitor is necessary. Most other applications run very well on a good 17-inch monitor. Disregard 15-inch monitors, except in LCD format. (A 15-inch LCD monitor has nearly the same viewable measurements as a 17-inch picture tube monitor. This is because the measurement scheme of a picture tube monitor includes a portion of the monitor that is not viewable because of the bezel surrounding the picture tube.)

Now let's discuss non-interlaced monitors. A non-interlaced monitor writes the screen with data in one pass. An interlaced monitor, like a television, writes the even numbered lines in one pass and the odd numbered lines in the next, meaning it takes two passes to display one screen. Doing this causes a visible flicker on the screen, which often results in eye fatigue. Get the non-interlaced monitor. (There is no flicker on a LCD monitor due to the technology behind the display.)

A digital monitor can be preset to a number of different display control settings, any one of which can be automatically recalled with the push of a button. This is important if several people use the computer because each can customize the display to his liking. You may like different brightness, contrast, and screen sizes in different programs, and can set the monitor to display your preferences at will. Most digital monitors can be controlled by software as well.

Green monitors have an energy-saving feature that allows you to set a timer to shut them down when not in use. This is an EPA plus often ignored by computer buyers that can save you money in utility bills, particularly if you occasionally leave your computer unattended and turned on.

Monitor prices vary by manufacturer. A 15-inch monitor should cost around $100 if it is digital, non-interlaced, and SVGA. The .28-dot pitch is mandatory. A 17-inch with similar specifications should run around $125. Expect to pay about $400 for a digital 21-inch monitor. Remember, most computers sold in stores come with a small 15-inch monitor; when comparing system prices, plan to replace it. A 15-inch LCD monitor will cost you around $250.

These items and prices give you an idea of what it costs to build a basic computer. You have noticed it is much less than a packaged system. Now that you have prices for the basic computer, it is time to look at the add-on stuff you will include to make this system your own personal computer.

Personalizing Your Computer

Most computer users have unique operational needs. These may include requirements for adding pictures to presentations, faxing from within documents, and surfing the 'Net. The proper combination of hardware and software allows you, the user, to perform virtually any task from your computer. What follows now is a brief look at the options available.

Talking to Other Computers

In a business environment where seemingly everyone in the company has a computer, local area networks (LAN) provide the link between users. A LAN can be wired or wireless, depending on the needs of the company. Most home computer users have little interest in networking unless they have more than one computer.

For this user, the ability to connect computers directly by cable is supported in Windows 9X, 2K, and NT. There are also third-party programs that provide more enhanced networking functionality through direct cable connection than these programs.

The Modem

Most home computers communicate via modem. This requires support software. If you purchase a modem, it should come with all the software that allows you to use it as a fax machine, an Internet access device, and a full-featured modem.

A basic 56K internal fax/modem can cost from $10 to $20, depending on the brand. The external version of 56K modems is priced between $35 and $45.

An external modem, like the one in Figure 4-4, lets you monitor what the modem is doing. The lights on the front panel show communication occurring. Another good thing about external modems is you can turn them off instantly. The additional cost is due to packaging and power supply requirements.

For those looking for faster communication over the phone lines, the ISDN (integrated services digital network) connection is another low-cost option. The system was designed to replace standard analog phone lines with faster digital lines. Compare the 1 megabit per second transfer rate to the 33,600 bit per second rate for a good modem and you can see why it is preferable. Other advantages of ISDN are clean digital voice, fax, and even high-quality video transmission. ISDN modems are priced between $100 and $300, but expect prices to fall. Installation costs about $160. The service itself is $28 to $34 monthly, not unlike standard phone service.

Cable modem service, available from your cable supplier, is 10 times faster, however, and readily available. The cost ranges from $30 to $60, depending on your existing cable subscription. Unlike modem surfing, you are always logged on, so you never get a busy signal.

Another method of communication is DSL. It uses existing phone line twisted pair so it is not as clean as a cable modem, but in many instances it is faster. A cable modem slows down considerably with each user that signs

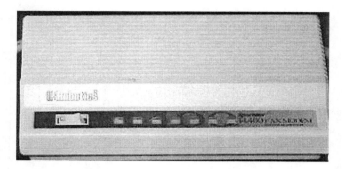

Figure 4-4. An external modem.

on but DSL remains consistent both upstream and downstream. There is more on cable modems and DSL later in this chapter.

CD-ROM

A CD-ROM drive is no longer an option; it has become a necessity for anyone who prefers easy software installation or enjoys computer multimedia entertainment. Forget dumping 10 to 30 floppy disks into your computer to load a software package. One CD holds the storage equivalent of 400 to 500 floppies.

The principal use of a CD-ROM drive today is running large multimedia packages. One or two of these programs loaded onto a hard disk could fill up 1.2 GB of hard drive space completely. Most educational and reference material comes on CD-ROM now.

There are even CD-ROM drives available that can record in multi-speeds. They are

Figure 4-5. A CD-ROM drive, one of two in this computer.

designed to fit in the same space a normal CD-ROM drive occupies. Some people use a CD-R drive to archive large amounts of data. This is a good idea, particularly if the data is in the form of video clips or other memory-hungry applications, because large volumes of data—up to 650 MB—can be stored on one disk. Companies that store data for long periods of time, including hospitals and legal practices, can benefit from the durable nature of a recordable CD-ROM disk. Figure 4-5 shows an internal CD-ROM drive made to fit a 5.25-inch bay in your computer. It is a CD-RW and can write the same disk repeatedly.

Prices for CD-ROM drives are pretty consistent. The 48X IDE CD-ROM is available for about $20, 52X drives are going for $30 or less, and the 16X DVD drives bring in about $55 to $75, depending on brand name. What's in a name? Check the features. The more expensive CD-ROM drives by NEC have a large cache buffer, which allows the drive to transfer data to your computer faster.

Ask around and get the CD-ROM drive that fits your budget and requirements. (The 52X, 48X, and 16X mentioned are speeds. A 4X CD-ROM is four times faster than a single speed. See Chapter 3 for a review on CD-ROM speeds and more information.)

Another way to acquire a CD-ROM is purchase a multimedia package. The package will normally include a CD-ROM drive, a sound card, speakers, and several software titles bundled with the hardware. Multimedia packages can vary widely in price, due primarily to the differences in the individual components. (Unless the software titles particularly appeal to you, I suggest buying the individual components. You will save money.)

Multimedia Packages Without Software

Multimedia packages that do not include software titles are composed of the CD-ROM drive, a 32-bit sound card with amplified speakers, and an AC adapter for the speakers. They have installation software included, plus all required cables and instructions.

A package with a 52X IDE CD-ROM drive costs less than $75 and the same package with a 16X DVD drive is less than $100. A packaged system is a good idea for the person who does not want to customize his sound card or speakers, and is a great idea for anyone who fears a complicated installation. Remember, however, that you can probably save between $25 and $30 by buying these items separately.

Multimedia systems have become commonplace in computers sold today. Unfortunately, the clone business is invading these systems. The clones in some "fast-food" computers often have compatibility problems with some programs, leading to headaches later on. These show up when new software stretches the capabilities of the clone cards. The most affected clone card in this area is a sound card claiming to be "Sound-Blaster compatible." I found out the hard way that there is no substitute for the real thing when it comes to sound cards.

Sound Cards

Many sound cards exist, and most *are* Sound-Blaster compatible. But since all sound cards have to emulate Sound Blaster characteristics to be compatible with the largest variety of software, just buy a Sound Blaster card. Then you will not have to be concerned about any compatibility problems between your programs and sound card.

Prices for sound cards oscillate around the Sound-Blaster prices, so I will give you prices for the Sound-Blaster family. Again, these prices are approximations; everything changes fast in the computer world. These are a few common Sound-Blaster cards and serve as representative performance levels of all sound cards available.

A 32-bit Sound Blaster Pro will cost around $29. The next step up is the surround-sound version, at $35 or so. A jump to 64-voice performance costs around $50, and is called the Sound Blaster Live! Audigy. The platinum version is more than $100. Advantages of the more expensive cards are discussed in Chapter 3.

Figure 4-6 shows a standard 64-bit Sound Blaster Live! sound card. This generic sound card is the most commonly available, and is

Figure 4-6. A Sound Blaster Live! sound card being installed.

primarily used by superstores in their fast-food systems. It has some of the features available on the real thing, but lacks many of the more sophisticated features.

Printers

I have found recently that the printer market is shifting toward the inexpensive color ink-jet home printer. This family of printers has, in the last two years, dropped in price by several hundreds of dollars.

I bought an HP color ink-jet printer about two years ago. I thought I paid an unbeatable price. I was wrong! The average price for a color ink-jet printer with at least 300 dpi resolution is under $150. This makes obsolete everything except a good laser printer.

I feel the two choices for home printers are a good ink-jet printer or a high-quality laser printer. The amount of black and white printing you do should influence your decision. If you do mostly high-quality black-and-white printing, get a laser printer. The speed of a laser printer is up to 10 times faster than an ink jet and the print quality is at least four times better.

Consider price per copy when evaluating your printer needs. For black-and-white printing, a laser printer is much cheaper to operate. A toner cartridge will outlast several ink-jet cartridges and the cost per copy on an ink-jet printer for identical copies is five to six times more expensive than with a laser printer.

The best reason to get an ink-jet printer is color printing. If you have kids, get an ink jet. If you need presentation-quality color printing for work or home use, the ink jet is the only way to go. Many ink-jet printers will do near-photographic quality printing.

And don't forget price. The ink-jet printers are cheap. The Epson Stylus color ink-jet printer costs less than $100 today. The average HP laser printer, on the other hand, lists in the same catalog for $199. Both are near the lower end of the price range in their respective disciplines, though it is not uncommon for laser printer manufacturers to run sale prices down to the $150 range. You should purchase the printer that suits your long-term needs, since printers typically last a long time and are relatively expensive to replace.

Scanners

The family of optical character readers, commonly called scanners, is being expanded daily. As scanners become more popular, they also become more affordable. When scanners first became available to the masses, they cost upward of $6,000. Today's full-page color scanners can be purchased for less than $100. Hand-held scanners are even more affordable. You can purchase a monochrome, hand-held scanner for around $15 and the color version for $35.

The most important thing to know about scanners is the difference between true and interpolated resolution. Many inexpensive scanners use interpolation software to fill in the dots and advertise an interpolated resolution much higher that their actual performance. These scanners have true resolutions of 300 to 400 dpi, but report resolutions of up to 2,400 dpi!

Most scanners come with optical character recognition software. OCR allows a scanner to recognize each character of a document you scan and import the text into your computer for processing. You can then edit or fax the document as required. Obviously, anything you scan into your computer can be added to a prepared document, including pictures. This fact makes a scanner a very useful tool for the home office.

YOUR COMPUTER'S PROTECTION

Here are some of the issues you must address in order to ensure a safe environment for your computer and peripheral equipment.

Software Safety

If you have ever experienced a hard disk crash but had not backed up your system, you know exactly what true horror is. You get to expend many hours trying to get back to where you were before the crash.

Another thing to think about when considering such unspeakable disasters is the possibility of a computer virus invading your otherwise perfect system. Every time you go online or insert a disk into your system you risk infection.

The solution to either of these problems is having a recent tape backup of everything on your system. With large disk capacities, the safest and most cost-effective way to keep an exact duplicate of everything on your system is tape. Figure 4-7 shows an external tape backup system and two disk-type backup systems. These are my backup systems of choice. The tape drive is for long-term backups, and puts 5 GB on each tape.

The disk-type backup systems are both from IOMEGA. The vertically mounted Peerless drive will put 40 GB on a cartridge, while the Zip drive alongside only holds 100 MB. I use the Zip to shuttle copies of this and other books to and from the publisher while I use the Peerless drive to back up the entire computer on a weekly basis.

Tape drives are available in internal and external types. The internal drives are much less expensive at $40 to $80 less than the external version. An HP tape drive will put up to 5 GB on one cartridge if the data on your hard drive can be software compressed 2:1. The average capacity is closer to 4.2 GB per tape.

What is software compression? There are several types of software compression used in backup systems. Each compresses data by eliminating the unused space in data packets. If, in addition, you use coding to replace repetitive terms, you can approach 50 percent compression.

In addition to removing the white space or blank portions in text files, data compression software searches for repetitive strings. During compression, each string is replaced by a single character, or token. When a program needs a portion of the compressed data, the compression software decompresses the data. Software compression is how most tape drives get 200-MB capacity from a 120-MB DC2120 tape cartridge.

For about $130 you can have an HP T5000 Travan tape drive, with up to 5 GB of storage per tape. As you may have guessed, the average storage capacity is somewhat less, and to get this capacity you must use longer Travan tapes.

The external versions of these tape drives are normally $40 to $80 more expensive. The reason is simple. The tape drive must interface to your system in some manner. An internal tape drive shares resources with one of your floppy drives, and even shares a control cable with the drive. An external drive, on the other hand, must have its own power supply and enclosure. It must also have an interface compatible with either your printer port or

Figure 4-7. Several backup systems commonly used today.

one of your serial ports, or have its own add-in card. What you are buying with an external drive is more hardware and portability to other computers.

Protection from the Elements

Review Chapter 3 to determine what type of power protection you require. The minimum should be a good surge suppression power strip. A good strip always comes with an equipment replacement guarantee. If your area has power problems, consider an UPS. These topics are covered at length in Chapter 1.

Toys

Toys are nice things to have, but some toys become essential parts of your computer and can both generate enjoyment and facilitate the work you perform. For example, I have a color scanner and use it to enhance documents I create by adding color pictures to them. I also have two game controllers and a host of small accessories too numerous to mention. Some accessories, such as microphones, allow you to interact with your computer in exciting ways. More than toys, my digital camera, memory stick reader, and digital video camera interface have become invaluable tools in my occasional book-writing experiences.

New toys—digital movie cameras, golf trainers, flight simulators, and more—are coming out all the time. For every new game there is a new function added to existing game controllers. Examine options for playing on your computer, because all work and no play will make any computer user less efficient.

You will be amazed when you compare your new computer's performance to the fast-food variety with larger price tags. What will amaze you more, perhaps, is your newfound willingness and ability to jump in and modify your computer as new options become available.

You now have the list of the parts you need and an idea of the prices to look for. Now let's look at the tools required to build a computer. You will find these tools in nearly every household today and, if not, they are inexpensive to purchase.

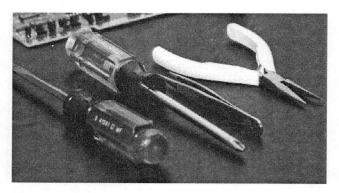

Figure 4-8. The tools of the trade.

Looks like this is going to be easier than I thought, the novice computer builder thinks.

What to Watch Out For

When purchasing computer components, there are a few pitfalls to look out for.

When you first scope out a prospective source for parts, examine how things are packaged. Add-on cards, motherboards, memory, and hard disk drives all have CMOS parts installed on them, which are extremely sensitive to electrostatic damage (ESD). Components of this type should be packaged in static-suppression packaging, such as sealed dark gray, black, or pink polyethylene bags labeled "Attention: Contents static sensitive." The motherboard and add-on cards should also be packaged inside a box.

The primary reason computer components are DOA or die within the first month is attributable to poor handling of some kind, usually the result of electrostatic damage.

Beware of missing or incorrect manuals or documentation. Check the manual against the parts to be certain you have all the proper hardware, software, and documentation. The motherboard, hard disk, CD-ROM, and monitor each will come with a book. Other items may come with a one or two page handout. The modem will come with software and several other documents, such as a manual for the software and quick setup guides. The CD-ROM will come with driver software and a cable. The sound card will have a book, two cables, and software. Exactly what comes with each item you purchase varies widely, so be certain you open everything and check the packing list for omissions.

Beware of places offering more than a 3 percent cash discount—the amount normally charged a supplier if he accepts a charge card. (Some get away with 2 percent.) Charge it if you can do it without incurring an additional cost, as you'll have more flexibility on returns or exchanges.

Judge quality in the products you purchase by completeness of documentation, proper packaging, and good ESD protection and packaging practices.

One of my greatest fears is buying something that I will have to send away for service. Make it mandatory that the stores where you buy components or systems have a service center. If not, you may not be able to easily exchange a defective item.

These are the things I look out for. If you purchase from a catalog, see the cautions I list for catalog ordering later in this book. The cautions follow the extensive list of computer magazines and literature, since this is where you will select the magazines from which you make your purchases.

High-Performance Parts

Several components enhance your computer's performance. The most significant is fast RAM. DDR RAM and RDRAM for the Pentium 4 systems are significant performance enhancers. In addition to this, a fast video card will make itself evident in a Pentium 4 or Athalon XP system.

Of course, many clone chips are available in the microprocessor department. Expect the AMD Duron processors to be much faster than the Intel Celeron processors and the Athalon processors to outgun the Pentium 4 devices in non-floating point applications.

Those tips will wring out some additional speed for enthusiasts who want to live on the edge.

Static Handling

When you get your computer parts home, do not handle them carelessly. The time to open the bags is while installing the components, and not before.

When this time arrives, handle all PC cards by the edges only and, before you touch any of the components, touch the bare metal part of your case to discharge any electrostatic voltage.

Electrostatic damage is not immediately terminal. Tiny junctions within an electronic component can be damaged enough that, over time, the part degrades sufficiently to finally fail.

The spark you receive from a metallic surface after walking on carpet is enough to destroy or damage many electrical parts in your computer. The damage may be slight, but a failure can occur up to six months from the initial damaging spark.

I have an ESD-safe work area because I build so many computers. You will not damage anything in your computer if you follow the simple guidelines above. The documentation for your components may have additional advice, so follow all static control instructions you receive.

5

Software Selection

Software is the principal reason people buy computers. Without software, a computer is merely a box with hardware inside. Nothing ever accomplished with a computer happened without software programs running things. At today's prices, the software you purchase can cost more than your computer but, unless you have software in your computer, the only thing you have to show for your expenditure is a high-speed moron.

Just a quick interjection: software consists of lists of instructions written in computer language that tell the hardware in your computer what you want it to do. The firmware instruction sets written into your system BIOS as permanent memory configure the hardware to operate properly, but you must install programs to exercise any control over your hardware.

Thousands of software companies are hungry for your money and support. There are so many programs out there you could never install all of them in a single computer; you must choose the programs that support what you want to do. This chapter will help you do that and, in the process, save hundreds or even thousands of dollars.

Computer software is categorized according to basic functions. There are word processing programs (like the one that built this book), database programs, Windows programs and utilities, non-Windows programs and utilities, games, and the list goes on. We will take a detailed look at many common categories later in this chapter.

Prices for software will vary significantly depending

primarily on where you purchase it. There are also discounts for upgrades if you already have (or can buy) a previous version of the software installed on your computer. You will find that good software packages often cost more than your computer, but never buy software until you get several price quotes.

WANT TO SAVE LOTS OF MONEY? GIVE THIS TRICK A TRY

I read about and then tried a neat trick to reduce my software expenditures. Several local vendors in my area make a good business of buying outdated software from retail vendors. They pay pennies on the dollar. Then, they offer the software at substantially reduced prices to people who are not interested in the latest and greatest.

Here's the trick. You can qualify to receive substantial discounts on great software packages if you have older versions of either the same software or a competitor's version.

Step by Step

Find a vendor of obsolete software. If you can't find one, contact **Surplus Software** < www.surplusdirect.com >, a legitimate and very helpful company that can send you a catalog of older software.

Then identify the software packages you want. Look for software that offers either a competitive upgrade or special price for upgrades. For example, I bought an old version of Microsoft Visual Basic for $30. Instead of installing it, I ran over to Egghead Software with the unopened box and purchased the new Visual Basic 5.0 professional version for $94. The regular price for this software is $498.

I am writing this book with Microsoft Office Suite for Windows 2000. How did I get it? I bought Word 2 for Windows at $29.95 and went to a local computer warehouse. I paid $199 for a $540 software package.

By the time I was finished I had saved more than $1,500 by either purchasing outdated competitor's software or buying older versions, then upgrading. I also had a cache of older software, unopened and unregistered, that I could give to friends who might be less upgrade-conscious. I kept the old stuff, just in case... Where do I buy software? I live in a very competitive area for computer products, so my possibilities are endless. I use various computer stores, depending on who offers the best upgrade discount. Other good sources I use are the many catalogs available. Here's a brief list:

Computer Discount Warehouse	www.cdw.com
Computer World	www.computerworld.com
Dell	www.dell.com
Desktop Publishing	www.publishingperfection.com
Egghead Software	www.egghead.com
Global Software	www.glbsoft.com
Image Club	www.imageclub.com
Insight	www.insight.com
Micro Warehouse	www2.warehouse.com
MAC and PC Connections	www.pcconnection.com
PC Zone	www.pczone.com
Shareware Express	www.filelibrary.com
Tiger Software	www.tigersoft.com

I mentioned several types of software that are available. Now, let's take a closer look.

Every computer uses an operating system of some type. Many systems have more than one. DOS, Windows 9X, Windows 2K, XP, NT, and OS-2, are the systems commonly used on the IBM-compatible family of computers.

Utilities are programs used as tools to correct problems or tune your computer from a software standpoint. SpinRite, Norton Utilities, Checkit Pro Analyst, and PC Tools are examples.

Word processors, spreadsheets, database programs, and drawing programs are necessary to most computer users. I will go into detail on some of these later in this chapter. Suites are combinations of the above-mentioned programs built into one large program. More on these later, too. Figure 5-1 shows a sample of the programs used by a typical desktop publisher.

A desktop publisher often must utilize several programs to achieve a given task, and

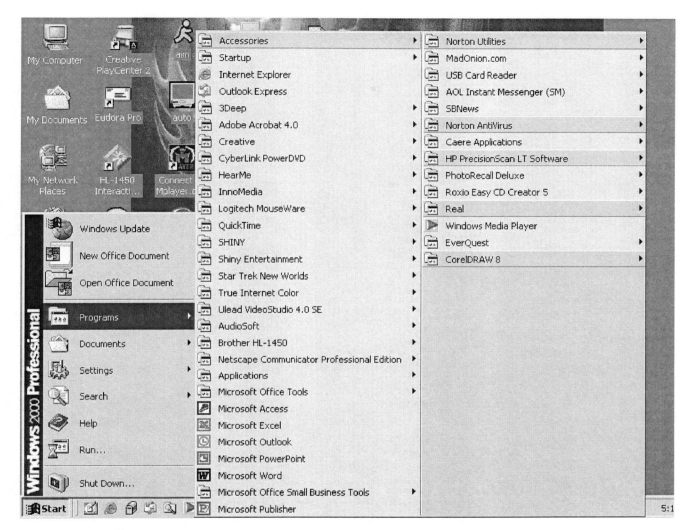

Figure 5-1. A good Windows 2000 environment.

will purchase many more programs than the average user. Of course, he will have Windows 95 or NT. Figure 5-2 shows a Windows 2K opening screen.

We have looked at several aspects of software, including where to buy and tricks to get better prices. Now let's take a detailed look at the software types and programs within each common type.

Remember that there are more programs than we could possibly talk about. The ones I discuss are the most often utilized programs, according to the sales personnel I know.

The best approach to deciding on the software you will be purchasing is the try-before-you-buy technique. Several options are available to you. The best option is finding a computer in a store with the software you might be interested in purchasing. Obviously, you will have to try several different stores, to get a good sample of software types, but it is worth your time. Many software titles fall short of your expectations, and software is very difficult to return to the store.

Try it before you buy it!

OPERATING SYSTEMS

DOS

I always start discussions of operating systems by talking about DOS, the disk operating system used by the industry for

Figure 5-2. Windows 2000 opening screen.

many years. Many people learned DOS long before Windows and other operating systems were developed. My DOS operating system has over 70 commands but, like most people, I use only a few of them.

I recommend installing DOS regardless of the operating system you prefer. DOS is excellent for repairing problems in other systems, especially if you cannot properly initialize Windows 9X or Windows 2K. The editing features of DOS allow you to edit the initialization files WIN.INI and SYSTEM.INI and fix many problems caused by improper installation of Windows.

DOS is an excellent tool for emergency backups if you have a tape drive. (And you will have one, if you follow my recommendations!) In the event of a destructive crash that forces you to format or replace your hard drive, you need only install DOS and the tape backup software to recover. DOS plus your tape software will finish the reinstallation of your software and restore your old configuration.

If you install Win 9X, be sure to keep DOS running under it. Win 9X allows you to restart in DOS mode, if you have to. Some older programs do not properly run in a Windows environment. (Windows ME and Windows 2K allow you to enter a CMD mode. It is a DOS clone that allows you to perform the same actions.)

Windows 3.1

Though obsolete, this program will die hard; many people refuse to make the jump to Windows 95. Windows 3.1 is a fairly stable environment with which many people are very comfortable, so it will be around for a long time. It is a 16-bit operating system, however, so it is inherently slower than Win 95. It is only for people that will never buy another software program in their life.

Windows 98 and Windows ME

This upgrade from Windows 95 is a hybrid system with both 16-bit code and 32-bit code. It is measurably faster than Windows 3.1 and even more stable, especially running older DOS programs. The memory management is superior to any other operating system, and multitasking is easier also. You will find it easier to use, and upgrades are much simpler under Windows 98 or ME. Both hardware and software installations move much more smoothly. Windows 98 has its own programs, and 32-bit upgrades for most Windows software are now available. I outfitted my Windows 2K system with upgrades for Microsoft Office, Visual Basic, Microsoft Works, and Microsoft Publisher. Of course, I got them for a fraction of the new list price by using the competitive upgrade technique mentioned earlier in this chapter.

OS/2 WARP

This true 32-bit operating system includes multitasking, full DOS program support, full support for programs written for Windows, and large memory addressing. It is a good alternative to Windows 2K, but takes getting used to. It has a bit less functionality than Win

2K, but runs on less of a computer, and with a smaller RAM requirement. A 286-16 with 4 MB of RAM (there's one in the Smithsonian!) will run this software.

Windows NT and Windows 2000

Look for a Windows NT variant to be the operating system of the future. It will run very fast on the RISC machines mentioned in Chapters 2 and 3. Though it is designed for high-end users and workstation environments, it will soon be in the home as Windows 2000 Professional. Advancements by Microsoft will focus on Windows NT, Windows 2000, and Windows XP, all 32-bit variants of the same basic program type.

Why? It works on both CISC and RISC machines equally well. It is a true 32-bit operating system, with all the functionality of Windows 98 and much more. New software written with a Windows NT variant in mind will be streamlined and fast, and the NT front end is very easy and comfortable to use. It is also the most stable operating system in use today.

Windows XP, the current state of the Windows architecture, is strongly focused on document design tools and voice recognition functionality, and is geared toward networking and Internet functionality. It has software to improve Web-based sourcing, and will be the software of choice in all new Intel-based machines. (It also unleashes tremendous power in all Athalon-based machines with the XP processor.)

Now let's look at some useful program types other than operating systems.

UTILITIES

Utility programs are your personal in-computer toolbox. They do everything from clean out and organize your file system to repair damage to your hard disk.

SpinRite, from Gibson Research < www.grc.com >, is the first disk repair utility I used. The original version for MFM and RLL hard drives could repair bad portions of your hard drive. MFM and RLL are two obsolete hard-drive technologies. Due to changes in hard-drive architecture (such as sector translation), SpinRite is limited to recovering data and moving it to a safe part of your hard drive. Sector translation is one way of fooling DOS and older computer BIOS into recognizing very large hard drives.

Symantec's < www.symantec.com > **Norton Utilities** and **SystemWorks 2001** encompass a large set of unique capabilities. Norton can repair damaged or lost files, recover recently erased files and directories, back up your computer, and run in the background. By running as a background process, Norton allows you to continue using your computer while it does its work.

The Windows 9X, 2K, ME, and NT version includes a protected recycle bin, which means even when you empty the trash you still can recover most deleted files. Both include a feature called *image*, which creates a mirror image of your file archive table and stores it safely. If you lose your original FAT, you have a backup. Remember that the FAT is an index to all the files in your computer.

Norton Utilities has the ability to automatically correct problems as they happen. You are prompted for this option when you install it. This is a valuable option, as it keeps your computer in top tune.

Another utilities program is **PC Tools**, also by Symantec, which has embedded anti-virus tools, backup support, a shell program, and data recovery capabilities.

Checkit Pro, from **TouchStone Software** < www.touchstonesoftware.com >, is an analysis program designed to keep you updated on your computer's configuration. It can test performance and benchmark your system as well.

Virtual Drive, from Farstone Tech, emulates a CD drive, allowing you to create up to 23 virtual CD-ROM drives.

Partition Commander 6.0, from V Communications, will allow you to repartition your hard drive, prep a new drive, and makes drive maintenance significantly easier than before.

You will notice a lot of functionality overlap in the utility programs. It is not necessary to own more than one of these specialized tools. Personally, I prefer the Norton package. It has the most functionality in one program for my personal requirements.

VIRUS DETECTION AND PROTECTION

This is a good time to mention computer viruses. A virus is a program—designed by jerks that know quite a bit about computers and software—to corrupt some aspect of your computer's performance. The virus is placed on a public access domain such as the Internet or an online service such as Prodigy. When you access the infected file, the virus can be transferred into your computer.

Some viruses have completely shut down military defense systems, automatic payroll systems, and computerized phone systems all over the country. A virus in a company computer can wreak all kinds of havoc. In your home computer, a virus can format your hard drive, erase some or all of your data, modify the way some programs run, print obscene messages on your screen, or just make your speaker go off at unusual times.

Viruses can be tricky, and it takes special programs to get rid of them. Symantec offers a great anti-virus program in **Norton AntiVirus 2001**. Another to check out is **F-Prot** from **Command Software Systems** < www.commandcom.com >, a shareware program that can find as-yet-unknown viruses by looking for their characteristics.

McAffee < www.mcaffee.com > is a pioneer in anti-virus programs, and constantly updates their programs as new viruses arrive. Finally, try **Invircible** from **NetZ Computing** < www.invircible.co.il >. This program scans for polymorphic (moving) viruses by cleaning main and video memory, then searching quickly through all files by checking them against their signature. If a virus is hitchhiking on any of your programs, this program will find it.

Other programs have anti-virus routines embedded in their program set. The boot block virus checker in most motherboard BIOS is an example.

Note: To be effective, an anti-virus program must be updated regularly. Be certain you have a program newer than 1 month old.

HOME OFFICE PROGRAMS

Suites

If you're going to buy a publishing program, a database or spreadsheet program, and a graphics package I recommend purchasing a suite. A suite "packages" several useful functions, or programs, in one package and delivers a better bundle price than the individual elements. A suite includes a common interface between the packages, making it simple to move tables, graphs, and pictures from one document to another.

The **Lotus SmartSuite** includes the latest Lotus 1-2-3 spreadsheet, the Word Pro Approach publisher, Freelance Graphics, and Organizer programs. It also includes a SmartMaster template and Lotus Assistants to merge the separate programs into a seamless system.

Separately, the programs would be very expensive, but you can find this package for under $400. Or, if you can find an older version, you can walk away with the upgrade for less than $170. This is less than any one of the included programs would cost.

The **Microsoft OfficeXP Professional Upgrade** is available in Windows XP and 2000/NT versions. It combines Microsoft Word, Excel, Powerpoint, Scheduler, and Access into one seamless system. The Windows 2K version is 32 bit, and at least twice as fast as the Windows 9X program.

To purchase Word, Excel, and Access separately, you would have to pay $900. The five-program package retails for $329, but the upgrade price is only $250. (Less if on sale.)

Obviously, if you need any two of the programs, it's cheaper to buy the suite. Purchasing the suite also buys you the seamless interactivity of the Office program, with its many wizard programs. These page wizards will auto-format any type of presentation document you wish. There is even the capability of placing moving pictures and sound in your presentation.

Since Corel and WordPerfect have become synonymous, the **Corel PerfectOffice** suite was born. This suite encloses WordPerfect 2002, Quattro Pro, Presentations, InfoCentral, GroupWise, and Envoy in a single system.

Envoy is a publishing program, GroupWise is an e-mail, scheduling, and task manager. Presentations, like the Office program's PowerPoint, is a presentation designer. Quattro Pro, like Lotus 1-2-3, is an excellent spreadsheet, and WordPerfect is an excellent word processor.

Since the acquisition of Ventura Publisher, Corel created a suite of its own. CorelDRAW incorporates CorelDRAW, Ventura Publisher, photos, fonts, and clip art. Though not as comprehensive as the other suites, it's a good start.

Another basic suite is **Microsoft Works**, one of the many "freebie" programs normally bundled in the "software package valued at $1,000" included with a fast-food computer system. At less than $80 retail, it represents a good start for a budget-minded user. We should now go into depth on several of the programs that build a suite. Some people may not wish to buy all the programs in a suite, but rather own just one. Most programs in a suite are available individually.

Example: Microsoft Office includes Microsoft Word, Excel, and PowerPoint. If you only need Microsoft Word, just buy it and save hundreds of dollars.

The following programs are suite elements broken out separately:

Spreadsheets

Business applications often require a method to display and manipulate large amounts of related numeric data. Programs designed for this purpose are called spreadsheets. They have the ability to handle accounting tasks, expenses, provide forecasting, display and change inventory numbers, and create presentations of the results. Most spreadsheets will automatically perform math operations on large databases, as you require. Most will display data in graphic format if you request it. If you are like me, and your work sometimes follows you home, a spreadsheet program is critical.

Examples of feature-filled spreadsheets are Microsoft Excel, Novel Quattro Pro, and Lotus 1-2-3. Lotus is the original spreadsheet of choice for the PC, functioning as a spreadsheet, graphics package, and database. Microsoft Excel doubles as a database and provides easy to use menus for the inexperienced user.

Borland's Quattro Pro looks and works like Lotus 1-2-3, so much so that Lotus attempted (and failed) to sue Borland. The Borland package has several features that make it unique. Like Excel, Quattro Pro has pull-down menus, but unlike Lotus, Quattro Pro can print sideways. It can, however, manipulate Lotus spreadsheets.

Database Programs

Like spreadsheet programs, database programs are designed for the office environment. Most people will not need this at home unless the Work Fairy loads their trunk with something special to take home with them. Like a spreadsheet program, a database can store and manipulate large amounts of data. Most have built-in search and sort functions. Database programs store information, allow you to perform calculations on it, sort it, and create reports from the data.

Microsoft Access allows you to work with a replicated copy of database files. It will then synchronize the changes with the master document. You can grab flat file data from a wide variety of different formats and create a relational database from the data. Application performance can be monitored and improved with the onboard performance analyzer wizard. This menu-driven application allows you to optimize spreadsheet manipulation. If this means nothing to you, do NOT buy this program—you don't need it.

I tried the DOS version of dBASE years ago and abandoned it. The Windows version is much more user-friendly and an extremely powerful program. The onboard tutorials and help menus enable you to quickly learn the program, a real plus in today's stress-filled office environment. It's easy to click and drag forms, and reports are much simpler to create.

People that use **Borland Paradox** claim it has features that make it uniquely easy to use and learn. The main menu is full featured, and each menu item opens up subtopics associated with the item, a great feature for the novice and casual user.

Word Processing

Processing data and thoughts into readable documents and manipulating text are the primary reasons computers are used today. That means word processing software is the most used software currently available. More than 30 word-processing software packages are available in a variety of languages.

Spelling and thesaurus subprograms are useful. Multiple formats are a necessity, including page layout, outline, and full-page views. The ability to easily import graphics, text, and pictures is essential in today's desktop publishing environment. Let's look at some programs.

Microsoft Word is the program that stole me away from WordPerfect 5.1. Why? First, I already used Word for Windows at work. The first thing I found out is you can use WordPerfect commands in Word. I thought, if they made things this easy for a WP nut like me, how hard could the program be to learn? I decided to try it at home where I had the luxury to learn at a leisurely pace.

I never even opened the book. Each time I needed to determine what action an icon performed, I placed the mouse pointer on the icon and the computer told me the function. After I wrote my first report, I tried the auto-format function and achieved automatic and great results.

I erased WordPerfect from my hard drive the next day and upgraded to Microsoft Office.

Briefly, Microsoft Word for Windows 9X and XP pro both have drag and drop for adding charts, graphs, and pictures to documents, and a full find-and-replace routine, spell check, thesaurus, and the capability to print or fax within the program.

I hate to admit it, but I haven't been back

to the WordPerfect environment since version 5.1. It has the ability to do most of the functions of Microsoft Word. The interface has always been an easy one to learn, and the ease of importing text and graphics is wonderful.

Since the merge with Corel, I'm certain WordPerfect will become one of the top contenders for the desktop publishing and word processing marketplace. Tremendous improvements have already occurred. Power users of the Windows version or WordPerfect insist that the program is more comfortable to use than any other desktop publishing program.

One of the first word processors was WordStar. I wrote my first novel on it. It still resides on my old XT, and is the only word processor this machine will support today. I still use it sometimes when my other machines are tied up.

Special note: I recently read that WordStar has one of the most full featured dictionaries available, so don't expect me to get rid of this very special program. Though WordStar has fallen behind the others in the bells and whistles category, I believe it is one of the easiest programs to learn and use for basic publishing.

Now, let's stray from the office environment, and look at some good software for home use.

Home Accounting

Home accounting is an important part of daily life, and programmers recognize this.

Peachtree Accounting's Windows version is the multi-user solution. It is a popular home-accounting solution that is network-ready upon installation. It handles invoicing, general ledger, budgeting, receivables, and numerous other operations. It costs less than $120, making it a realistically priced package for your home office.

Microsoft Money, a freebie with Windows 9X, is a more basic program catering to the casual home user. You can schedule, manage, and pay bills with this program. You can even print your own checks. It has a retirement planner built in. If you have to pay for the program, it is less than $15 for the Win 3.1 version and under $30 for Win 95. Be

certain you give it a try, especially if you can acquire it free.

Quicken, from the co-op created by the merger of Intuit and Chipsoft, is a full-featured home and office accounting package. Properly kept records will merge with Turbotax at tax time, and create a complete tax return with minimal input from you. Your primary contribution will be the signature at the end of the tax form.

Quicken offers full-featured interaction with your banking institution. With a modem, you can perform most banking tasks through the phone lines. Quicken has investment advice, home inventory, and a full video tour, all in one package.

A quick note on the subject of banking over the Internet: You can be certain that someone is watching every aspect of any transaction you make. Keep your banking transactions private by using a modem along with the phone number supplied by your banking institution. Do not use the Internet. Also, keep in mind the lack of security on the Internet when you are tempted to give out your charge card number. Many people have had their number stolen needlessly.

Now, step into my office. These are the two programs I use the most.

Programming and Development Tools

Microsoft Visual Basic 6 revolutionized the programming environment of Basic. The interactive tutorial is a modular, completely interactive course with flexible search routines, good notes, and sample code. This program is the fastest way I have seen to create clean, good code and state-of-the-art solutions to programming issues.

Microsoft Visual C++ version 6 is for C programming what Visual Basic is for Basic programming. Version 6 introduces the Component gallery, a one-step storage area for reusable objects. The Microsoft Foundation Class Library, or MFC, contains more than 120,000 lines of code in 150+ classes. This proven and tested code enables you to get online quickly. The application wizards you can create easily will double your throughput.

Print Shop Programs

There are quite a few graphics programs that allow you to design and print color cards, posters, and envelopes. Here are some examples.

The **Print Shop Deluxe CD Ensemble** from Broderbund Software comes on one CD-ROM or a large handful of 3.5-inch floppies. You can pick the project you wish, then choose graphics from a long list of candidates. This program supports greeting cards, labels, signs, calendars, custom-designed envelopes, and more. With more than 4,500 graphic images to choose from, you may never use the same one twice. It runs in Windows and Windows 95.

The special option that **Announcements**, from Parson's Technology, offers is the capability of making large-format posters. The program divides the poster into 8 1/2x11-inch modules and configures your color printer to print each module separately. You can attach the pages together to make a large banner if you wish. Thus, you can make great announcements and large banners with relative ease. It is available in CD-ROM format, or on 3.5-inch floppy disks for Windows 9X and 2K iterations.

Studio M is a program that allows you to introduce multimedia to your presentations. You can create speaking greeting cards and moving e-mail. It has an easy-to-use interface, so learning the program is simple. You can personalize sounds and morph between two different photos. Available in 3.5-inch floppies.

RANDOM ACTS OF PROGRAMMING

There are so many programs out there! Here are just a few that caught my eye.

Anything that can create a television image can be captured in your computer with **Snappy for Windows**. Images from camcorders, VCRs, and laser disks are available for your computer enjoyment. A morph program is included to further manipulate the images. Stills can be created from any of the sources listed above, and more.

Easy-to-use movie file editing, more than 70 filter effects, and a multiple-document interface makes **Corel Photo Paint** an excellent addition to your computer. Though this is a full-featured paint and edit program, you will find it easy and convenient to use.

Autodesk Animator Studio has the ability to create animated images for games, Web-site logos, and audio-visual presentations. The true-color environment enhances the full motion and sound creations you generate. This program requires a CD-ROM.

See the human anatomy as you have never seen it before with rotating 3-D representations that allow you to zoom in and out. **BodyWorks** is probably the best reference module of its kind. You will need a CD-ROM running at 24X or faster to get full benefit of the solid model rotation capability of this program.

The **Microsoft Encarta** encyclopedia is extremely easy to use. It has pull-down menus, full-color video presentations, and stereo sound. Microsoft Encarta is available exclusively on CD-ROM.

More than six hours of multimedia entertainment is available with **Grolier Encyclopedia**. Full narration on complex topics is included. This program is available on CD-ROM only.

You will spend hours just viewing the many options available on the **After Dark** screen saver. This heavily endowed and well-animated multimedia screen saver is a favorite. It can be found on 3.5-inch disks or CD-ROM. Several packages are available for this screen saver, including the "Outer Space" and "Sierra Club" collections. With **Microsoft Scenes**, you can customize your own screen saver using pictures you choose. I have included several dozen scanned photographs in my collection. Available on 3.5-inch disks.

A must if you have Quicken, **TurboTax** is an easy way to handle even fairly complicated tax preparation. I have legitimately saved many thousands of dollars on my taxes using TurboTax, and can recommend no better program for doing personal taxes.

Like BodyWorks, **It's Legal** comes to us from Parson's Technology. It's Legal is an excellent source for legal documents of all types. I have saved many hours of a lawyer's time using this program.

Parsons Technology has a great **PDR** also. This prescription drug reference is a necessary product to have, particularly if you have small children.

While on the subject of Parsons software, I want to mention their tax software. Their **Personal Tax Edge** program is less costly than TurboTax, and will suit many individual tax preparers just as well.

If you have kids in school, consider **Mathcad**. You can make full graphic representations of math equations, enabling you to get an easy grasp of complex problems. Inserting math equations and graphs into existing documents is easy with Mathcad.

Though the Internet is a library in itself, perhaps the best way to surf the 'Net is **Netscape Navigator**. Available for Win 9X, 2K and NT, this program is full of single-click options. Get the **PowerPack** for additional functionality.

There are so many programs available this chapter barely scratches the surface. There's software for just about anything you want to do with a computer. Read the reviews, literature, or box carefully before you make your purchases. Check for functionality overlap between software packages. It is expensive to buy two packages that provide the same functions.

One more thing about software: I like to try before I buy. In most cases, this is impossible, unless your friend has the program or a computer salesman gives you a demonstration of the program.

The **Software Dispatch Company** < www.cdw.com > will send you a CD-ROM with programs on it. You can try them out with a software key for a limited time. A software key is a program that allows you to use the programs you might like to purchase. If you like them, you buy them and the company "unlocks" the programs so you can install them on your computer. This is one CD-ROM that the manufacturer encourages you to pass around to your friends.

When you want to buy a program, they give you a password over the phone that allows you to install the program. The package they offer is expansive, but not expensive, and you may find many of the programs that you want are on the disk.

INTERNET-BASED DISTRIBUTORS

Let's take a brief look at typical software from an Internet-based distributor.

Business and Office

Microsoft Office XP Professional Upgrade: $249. Features: Document design tools, voice recognition capability, network and Internet Web-based sourcing.

WordPerfect Office 2002 Professional Upgrade: $249. Features: Advanced word processing, spreadsheets, presentations, e-mail client, and address book. Speech recognition and database management.

Electronic Acrobatics: $239.99. Features: Share, review, and edit documents across broad networks. Converts office files and documents to PDF (portable document format).

Business Plan Pro: $79.99. Features: A 17-question query providing financial help to get your venture seeded. Custom business plan outlines.

Microsoft Money: $34.99. Features: A good and easy way to keep track of expenditures for home or office.

Omnipage Pro: $499.99. Features: OCR (optical character recognition) scan software allows you to scan text and graphics into an application for editing. This is the one program that will allow you to scan nearly any format and type of document, including photos with text, and allow editing from another unrelated program.

Word Processing

Corel WordPerfect Family Pack: $69.99. Features: Desktop publishing and document formatting for home or school. Easy to learn and use.

Microsoft Word 2002 Upgrade: $69.99. Features: Desktop publishing. Converters from most other publishing programs to RTF word documents. Easy picture editing and insertion.

For the Kids
LEGO Island: $24.99. Features: Thinking game using animated characters to solve situational puzzles.

Spy Fox: $19.99. Features: Save the world against Ozone threat.

Let's Get Physics: $19.99. Features: Save the world with physics.

Communication
QuickLink Mobile: $79.99. Features: Use your laptop and a wireless phone to work from anywhere.

Procomm Plus: $132.99. Features: Supports 30 different terminal types. Data integrity confirmation.

Education
Standardized Test Prep for Preppies: $39.99. Features: More than 2,700 sample tests and information on selecting college, applying for scholarships, and improving study skills. A must for anyone that wishes to move ahead.

Study Works Science Deluxe: $39.99. Features: Extra help for the beginning science student.

This is just a sample of the tremendous amount of software available. I often use Amazon.com to evaluate my software needs. These programs, and many others, are available online from Amazon.

Now is a good time to shut the door on software and move on to Chapter 6, where we will begin the experience of building a new computer. But first, take a look at one of my early newsletters that defines a problem with older computers. If you have one lying around gathering dust, you might have some interest in this information.

With each innovation in computers today, problems tend to crop up. It is up to the software designers and code writers to reduce or eliminate the hardware issues and incompatibilities that occur. This article describes the problem and shows what the software people had to do to implement a durable fix.

SHADOW'S RULES

FAT32 AND WHAT IT MEANS TO YOU

Imagine buying a second computer with the intention of sharing resources between the two and finding out, through experimentation, that it is impossible. What has happened and why? This article attempts to answer your questions.

A Little History

The FAT, or file allocation table, was invented as a means to store and retrieve data to and from both floppy and hard disk assemblies. Very few improvements in the technology of the FAT structure have been implemented, at least up to now.

The only major improvements in file allocation of note have been to modify the FAT to allow use of larger hard disk assemblies. From its invention for use on floppy disks through the adaptation that supports 2-GB hard disks, support for larger hard drives has been the principal concern. That is, until now.

Microsoft, in its infinite wisdom, broke the FAT16 barrier by introducing FAT32 in its newest release of Windows 95, a version available to the home user ONLY if purchased on a new computer. (This version is available only to OEM suppliers, and cannot be independently purchased.) This introduction has its good and bad points, and we will examine them now.

The Good

Many new computers come with 2.5 GB and larger hard drives, which must be partitioned into two or more virtual drives to make use of any space beyond 2.0 GB. I have built computers with 9.1-GB hard drives and had to make a bunch of 2-GB partitions to use the drive. FAT32 increases the allowable hard disk size to 2,000 GB.

Now the answer to, "Why does my 1.6-GB hard drive only hold 1.1 GB of data?" For the answer, I contacted Western Digital, a hard disk manufacturer.

Cluster size is the answer. Each file stored on a hard disk must take up at least one cluster, or allocation unit. An allocation unit is the smallest amount of room a file can occupy on your hard disk. Cluster size increases with the size of your hard disk partition. The following table gives more information.

DISK OR PARTITION SIZE	CLUSTER SIZE
0 – 127 MB	2 KB
128 – 255 MB	4 KB
256 – 511 MB	8 KB
512 – 1,023 MB	16 KB
1,024 – 2,047 MB	32 KB

WHAT DOES THIS MEAN?

This means if you have a 2-GB hard disk and it is not partitioned, each file, no matter how small, will occupy at least 32 KB of hard-disk space. A small batch file that is only 100 bytes will waste 30,000 bytes of your valuable hard-disk space!

FAT32, as you must have guessed, gets rid of this problem, too. The user can configure FAT32 to set cluster size at 4 KB, allowing the user to increase usable disk space by 15 – 30 percent.

Other improvements include the ability to eliminate the current limitation on the number of directories you can create in the root directory. Since FAT32 treats the root directory as just another cluster chain, it can be any size and located anywhere on the hard disk. You can eliminate the annoying need to run FDISK and destroy all your hard disk's data when resizing partitions, too. Sounds too good to be true? Let's look further.

The Bad

Everything in life has advantages and disadvantages. FAT32 is no exception. Microsoft does not intend to test FAT32 on older hardware, so no guarantees of compatibility will be implied or stated.

At this time, nobody has released utilities that will convert your existing hard disk to a FAT32-compatible hard disk, and Microsoft will not assume that responsibility.

Even on new computers with pre-installed FAT32-compatible systems, problems can occur. As of now, no other operating systems, including Win 3.1 and Win NT, are guaranteed to work. Forget using your dual-boot machine with FAT32.

Legacy hardware and software may be incompatible. If you have older external hard disks, backup systems with accelerator cards, zip drives, or other external peripherals that read and write to the hard disk, you may be out of luck.

Existing drive space and Microsoft Plus applications are out. You cannot compress file systems formatted with FAT32. According to what I have read, it seems that disk maintenance features will be supported by updated versions of FDISK, FORMAT, DEFRAG and ScanDisk.

I suggest using FAT32 only if your new computer comes with it. *Never* hook up any older peripherals to the new system.

6

Getting It Together

The first time I assembled a computer I built it on a fine dining room table. The next time I came home with boxes of parts I found that my wife, in her infinite wisdom, had purchased a small card table with a soft vinyl cover. This was her way of convincing me the dining room table was inappropriate for use as a secondary computer-testing site. I totally agree. For a few dollars, she gave me a spot of vinyl to call my own.

Choose your assembly site carefully. Make certain there is enough room to safely put your computer together and that there is power available for operational tests. Ensure in advance the table can support the combined weight of the computer components and that it is a stable workstation.

You have come a long way to get to this point in the project. You have a considerable pile of computer parts and accessories before you, but you are going to make sense of it all. Look at Figure 6-1 to see the pile of parts Lisa turned into a computer.

When you finish this chapter, you will be able to confidently and efficiently build your computer. The real benefits come when you put your computer to use, the whole time realizing you created that wonderful machine. I still get goose bumps when I think of the money I have saved through the years by building and upgrading my own systems.

Read on. The process goes quickly from here.

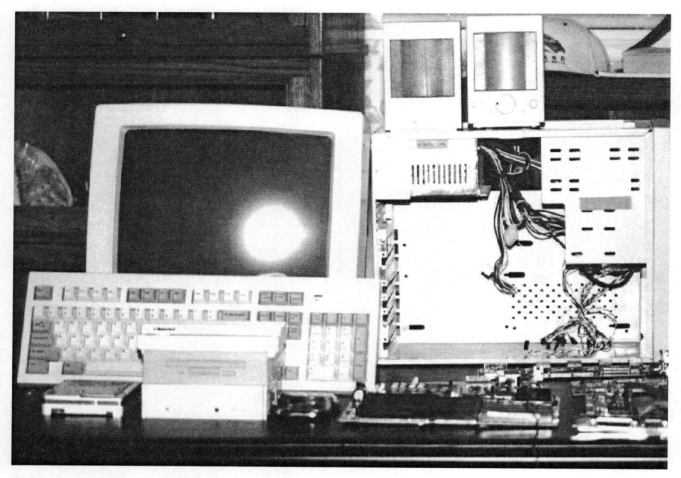

Figure 6-1: The components of a computer.

ASSEMBLING YOUR NEW COMPUTER

The first step is inspection. Confirm you have everything you need. Inspect all components for damage and completeness of assembly documentation, and be certain you have all the interconnecting cables. Connect all cables to the add-in cards to be certain you are not short anything.

The next step is component configuration. Your computer will be made of parts from a variety of manufacturers, as occurs in most computers today. Each component will have configurable options. Many components have hardware jumpers to select those options. A jumper connects two circuits together and is like a switch. You can select options, such as clock speed on a motherboard or IRQ on an I/O card.

Read all documentation carefully and preset all jumpers to the default settings spelled out in the documentation supplied with each card. The cards are normally already set to default positions that provide the fewest conflicts. You are just performing a final check of someone else's work, but it is better to find any configuration problems early.

The documentation for the motherboard is the most critical guide because it will tell you how to set the configuration for your CPU type. *This is very important.*

Many CPUs run on different power-supply voltages and clock frequencies. If you have any doubt of the correct motherboard jumper settings, the vendor can help. The supplied documentation should help you find the correct settings. There is always a

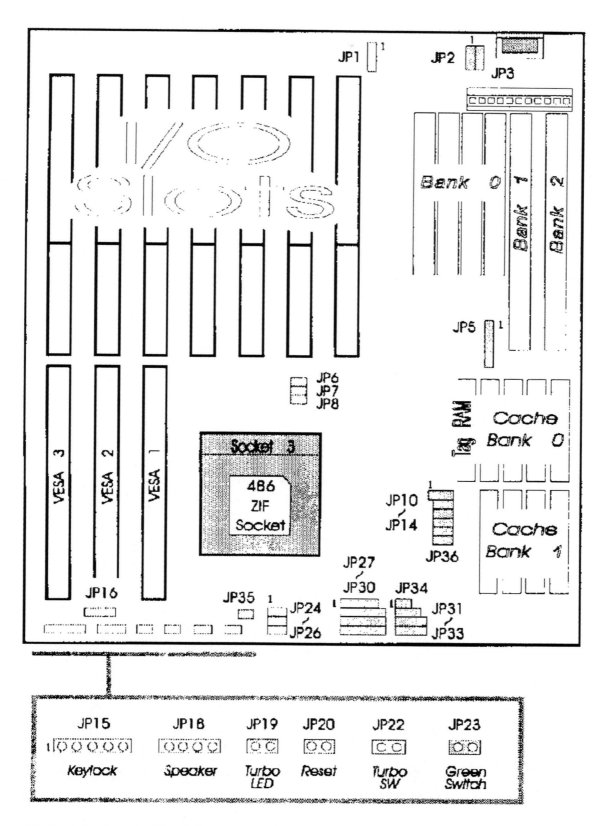

Figure 6-2. A motherboard with configuration jumpers.

diagram to follow if the written instructions are too confusing.

Other cards may have configuration jumpers but I have found that few use them today. The PnP motherboards and add-on cards set themselves up when you turn on the computer. Hopefully you have one or more of these components.

The Athalon 1800+ motherboard in my computer has no jumpers because it "auto-detects" the CPU, the cache, and the RAM. The first time I turned on my computer, the configuration was loaded into BIOS on the motherboard. This type of setup is the best and easiest because no manual configuration is required.

Nearly all motherboards built after March 1996 have BIOS that supports both Intel and clone microprocessors and auto-detects PnP add-in components. It is unlikely you will have to configure a motherboard but if you do, the following information will help.

Remember that even if you have configuration jumpers, the default positions are generally the best. Figure 6-2 shows a motherboard with configuration jumpers, each labeled **JP** followed by a number.

The jumpers on this motherboard set voltage to the CPU, clock frequency, IDE master or slave connector priority, and cache memory size. Some of these parameters change with each different type of CPU you can install.

If you have to set jumpers on the motherboard you selected, look at Figure 6-2. Your jumpers, if any, will be different. The documentation with your motherboard will help you perform any necessary configuration changes required by CPU type, RAM type, and cache size.

This is the most precise part of the entire computer-building experience, and the only task that requires anything more than a pair of screwdrivers. You might need a pair of tweezers or small needle-nose pliers to move the jumpers.

At this point the cards have either been configured by you or the factory. Jumpers have set default conditions and each component is ready to install. I normally perform one additional task. I find it easier to connect any ribbon cables to the add-on cards now. That way you do not have to fight the cable, case, and cards to install them while the card is inside the case, and you can see the connector pins better and ensure the connectors mate properly with the cables.

A quick word about alignment of connectors to cables: Normally, the connectors on the add-in cards and motherboards have a pin 1 designation. It is either an inverted triangle near the pin designated as pin 1, or a number 1. This pin aligns with the same type of designator on the cable connector. An added check is to look at the cable itself.

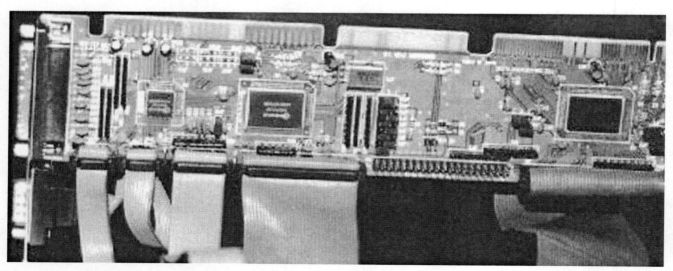

Figure 6-3. An IDE I/O card with cables.

Nearly all cables have a red wire on one end. This is pin 1 of the cable assembly. Power cables are the exception. They are keyed and can plug in only one way.

Cards with cables attached include a sound card, an IDE I/O card (if required), any tape controller card, and any CD-ROM add-on card, such as a SCSI interface card. Figure 6-3 shows an IDE I/O card with the cables attached.

Note: this card has jumpers for DMA and IRQ settings, which we discussed in detail earlier. Neither has to be moved from default, however, upon installation into the case. Use this card only if you need additional drives. The excellent documentation for the card depicts exactly how to connect each ribbon cable correctly.

Be certain to follow all connector polarities when installing the cables to the card. An inverted triangle mark on the connector or a red-colored wire on the cable normally identifies pin 1. The card should have a triangle-shaped mark showing pin 1, or a pin 1 designation. Consult the documentation for polarities if there is any uncertainty.

MOTHERBOARD MEMORY AND CPU INSTALLATION

You may have purchased a motherboard with memory, cache, and processors installed. If so, skip this step. If not, install the memory first. Memory will only install one way as the module is keyed. To install a SIMM or DIMM, place the module in a slanted position in the socket. To lock the SIMM in position, raise it to a vertical position and you will feel it snap into place.

Memory may have to be installed in certain banks on certain motherboards. If so, the documentation will assign certain pairs of sockets as bank 0, 1, 2, and 3, if so equipped. You must fill bank 0, then 1, and so on, until you run out of memory or all banks are filled. I recommend buying memory in a size that will fill only one bank so that memory upgrades mean just filling another bank. If you fill all your banks with lower capacity memory, you will have to replace the smaller capacity memory in order to upgrade.

Example: You buy memory in DIMM that are 128 MB in size. You have two banks of sockets on the motherboard. You fill the computer with two 128-MB DIMM, resulting in 256 MB of RAM. Now you must replace the DIMM with a larger capacity DIMM in order to upgrade RAM. If you had purchased one 256-MB DIMM, a RAM upgrade would require only adding more DIMM.

CPU INSTALLATION TIPS

Handle the processor as you would an add-on card. You will find a zero insertion force (ZIF) socket on your motherboard that allows you to easily remove and replace the CPU for upgrades. With the motherboard's documentation handy, install the processor and confirm any jumper changes necessary. To install the processor, lift up on the handle attached to the socket, drop the processor in, and return the handle to its original position. It's that easy.

All CPUs have a heat sink and usually a fan mounted on top of them for additional cooling. Installation of these processors is identical to the one mentioned above. If the CPU has a fan attached, the power cable mates with any of the power cables for hard drives that are in the case, or installs directly to a connector on the motherboard. The instruction manual gives details.

The only additional work you may have to perform on the motherboard is installing the cache memory heat sink or fan. Most motherboards for Pentium 4 and Athalon processors will already have this installed. Installation is simple.

Let's recap. The add-on cards are configured. They have the cables installed as required. The motherboard has memory, cache, and the CPU installed. The motherboard is configured for installation. So, what's keeping you?

MOTHERBOARD INSTALLATION

Open the case and remove the hardware inside. Most cases have one side that folds down where you install the motherboard. This

Figure 6-4. Installing the motherboard in the case.

is usually the right-hand side, with the front of the case facing you. The other side is open. There will be several screws holding the fold-down side in position. Remove them now, and remove or lay down the side.

Discharge static by touching the case anywhere on the bare metal surface. Remove the motherboard from its ESD protective container and lay it on the open side. Rotate the motherboard until the round keyboard connector faces the rear of the case. The two power connectors on the motherboard should also be to the rear of the case.

Align the motherboard with the mounting holes on the case side, and install the standoffs wherever possible. There should be enough metal standoffs in the hardware package.

Install them in all locations where a hole in the motherboard coincides with a location in the case. There may already be one there. This is the primary ground for the motherboard. Refer to figures 6-4, 6-6, and 6-9 for further visual assistance. Note: Figure 6-6 shows a plastic slide alternative to metal screws.

With the plastic standoffs, if supplied, attached to the bottom of the motherboard where they align with the slides on the case side, slide the motherboard into place. When the holes in the motherboard align with the ground standoffs, secure the motherboard with screws from the hardware kit. Refer to Figure 6-9 for screw types. The proper screws to use are the finely machined ones, not the rough sheet-metal screws. Figure 6-6 shows the plastic slides that sometimes are used to secure motherboards in lieu of metal screws.

The next steps apply to all types of cases.

Connect the cables from the turbo and reset switches and lights for turbo, power, and hard-disk operation. Connect the power cables from the case to the motherboard. In the non-ATX case, the two power cables have six wires each, of which two are black. When the power cables are properly installed, the four black wires should be alongside each other at the center of the two power connectors. In all other cases there is one connector supplied and it is keyed to eliminate errors in installation. (See Figure 6-5B.)

Figure 6-5A shows the angle of the power cables relative to the connector. They have to be hooked over the connector, stood up vertically, and pressed down. This type of connector reduces the possibility of the cables accidentally becoming disconnected.

If not already installed, install the power switch in the case. Pay particular attention to how it is installed, as an error might injure you or others.

Important: If there is any doubt in your mind as to the correctness of this step, return the case to the vendor and ask for help.

Refer to Figure 6-4 to see how you install a motherboard in a case with no fold-down side. On the cases without a fold-down side, installation is similar, but somewhat more cumbersome than the fold-down style. Install the plastic standoffs and slide the motherboard into position, aligning the ground screw with the metal standoff. Screw the motherboard to the metal standoff. Exercise care not to damage the motherboard while installing it in a case without a fold-down side. You have to carefully slide the motherboard in without hitting the hard drive and floppy disk installation bays.

With this type of case—and many of the purchased computers have this type—it is more difficult to upgrade a motherboard. Often you are better off removing the hard disk or disks first, then removing and reinstalling the motherboard. If you have a choice, always purchase a case that has a removable or fold-down side.

Cases may or may not come with a digital readout indicator for system speed. You will find it quite an experience programming the readout to properly indicate the processor speed of your system. From a bank of options you must select the digits corresponding to your system's speed. This programs the three-digit readout. Jumpers are removed or connected to select the row and column associated with each number in the readout. The documentation is accurate for every case I have used, but the process is time-consuming and occasionally frustrating.

This type of case is rapidly disappearing from the scene due to its difficulty in programming. I recommend purchasing a case that does not have this feature because of the annoyance associated with this task. Then, if you upgrade later and use the same case, you do not have to reacquaint yourself with this task. The range of processor speeds currently available makes this type of case obsolete.

Reinstall the fold-down case side and check the rear panel cutouts for alignment with the add-on card slots. You can loosen the ground screw and realign the motherboard for closer fit if required.

Test the alignment by plugging in a card. Ensure that the mounting screw that holds the add-on card aligns properly and tighten down the motherboard. Double-check the tightness of all screws. This test ensures the motherboard will not accidentally short out if you plug in a card with the power on.

Press lightly on each corner of the motherboard after it is installed. Ensure no portion of the motherboard contacts the case beneath it. If it does, you should install another standoff in the area. If there isn't a slide slot beneath the hole for a standoff on the motherboard, cut off the portion of the standoff that hooks under the slide slot and install the standoff in the board anyway. It will not hold the motherboard in position, but it will prevent the motherboard from contacting the case accidentally. Refer to Figure 6-6. When you install the motherboard, it will be elevated by this standoff and unable to short to the case in the

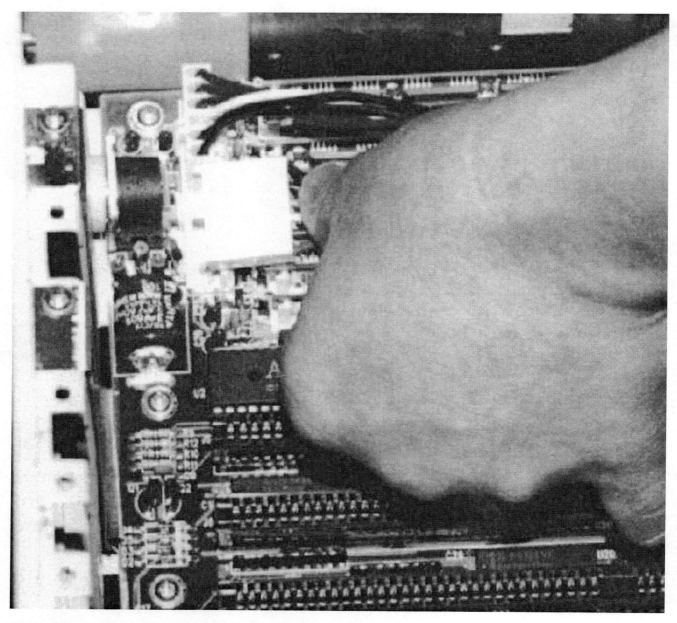

Figure 6-5A. Connecting power cables to the motherboard, non-ATX case.

event you must plug in an add-on card with the power applied. You are performing this operation because some add-on cards allow you to plug them in with power applied, though this is not the normal practice.

Once the motherboard is installed in the case, the hardest part of this project is completed. Now let's install add-on cards.

Installing the add-on cards is quite easy. Be certain you have observed polarity on all cables you connected to the add-on cards. If there is any doubt, consult the documentation or your supplier.

VIDEO CARD INSTALLATION

If you are using an AGP video card, place it in the AGP slot. If it's not an AGP card,

Figure 6-5B. Connecting power cables to the motherboard, ATX case.

place it in the PCI slot closest to the power supply. Figure 6-7 shows the installation.

Use care handling the video card. The RAM is sensitive to electrostatic shock. To prevent a damaging static discharge, ground yourself to the metal inside of the case once before unpacking the video card. Do this by touching any bright metal surface inside the case, preferably the power supply enclosure.

If your system has onboard IDE I/O, skip the next step (unless you are installing multiple hard disks and IDE CD-ROMS).

EIDE I/O CARD INSTALLATION

Refer to Figure 6-8 to see an Ethernet I/O card. This shows an EIDE I/O card being installed. The cables are already in place,

Figure 6-6: Plastic standoffs can be purchased separately.

Figure 6-7. An AGP video card installed.

which is the only way to easily connect all the cables. The only cable still remaining to install on this card is the hard drive LED indicator. The documentation for the case will identify this two-conductor cable for you.

To complete the EIDE I/O installation, install the rear panel add-in slot with the other two communication ports. Unless your motherboard fails you will probably never use these. This is permanently connected to one of the cables you attached to the EIDE I/O card earlier. Refer to Figure 6-10 for a quick look now.

If you ever experience problems with a serial communications port on your system and you have one unused port, you can easily reconfigure your system to use the second I/O port supplied with this add-in card. The hardware jumpers covered in your documentation will show you how to easily swap the two ports so you do not have to reconfigure your software. It is much easier to reconfigure your hardware settings than to peruse and change each software setting affected.

Some newer add-in IDE I/O cards, designed to replace defective onboard IDE I/O functions, have onboard BIOS that allows you to configure them automatically. The add-in card will query you during the first boot up after installation. You will answer questions about your hardware, and the add-in card will configure itself accordingly.

This add-in interface requires one unused

slot in your computer. You should pick a position near the center of the case so the cables will be easy to route away from normal case airflow. Keep airflow through the case in mind when routing all cables, ensuring that fans are not blocked.

Some motherboards have a slot position dedicated for this I/O slide. It is the one with the CMOS battery situated directly in the path of a potential add-in card, making the slot useless for any other purpose.

A basic computer requires only the add-on cards installed up to this point. Most people install a sound card, modem, and/or CD-ROM SCSI interface card as well.

At this point, you have completed the installation of all add-in cards, the motherboard, RAM, and CPU. You have connected all cables to the installed PC boards, including the motherboard. You still have several cables hanging from the computer, and a small pile of hardware remaining to install.

If you haven't done so already, connect the IDE and I/O cables to the motherboard with an onboard IDE I/O interface. Your motherboard documentation will show you where they go. Install the I/O interface as Figure 6-10 depicts, and check the attached cables one more time while some parts not yet installed are not in the way.

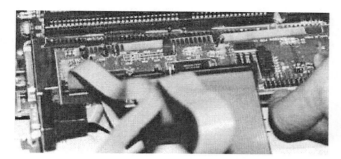

Figure 6-8. IDE I/O card installation.

Figure 6-9. Two mounting screws.

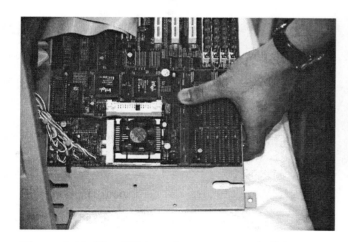

Figure 6-10. The I/O interface rear panel slide.

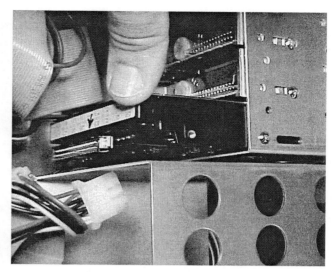

Figure 6-11. Hard disk installed.

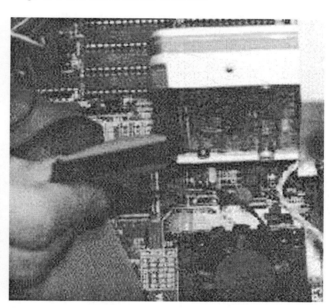

Figure 6-12. Hard disk cable.

Let's install the remaining hardware now. We will start with the hard drive. Refer to Figures 6-11 and 6-12 for installation and cable connections.

Configure the hard disk per instructions provided with it. Ensure the jumpers (shown in Figure 3-4 in Chapter 3) are properly set. The default is "single hard drive." If you have

multiple hard drives to install, you must set one up as master and one as slave using these jumpers. Make your boot drive the master. If you install a CD-ROM on this cable also, it's a slave drive.

Install the hard disk in the lowest 3.5-inch bay. Slide it into the bay until two holes align in the case and the hard drive. Install the short screws that came with the hard drive. Any other screws may be too long and could damage the hard disk's printed circuit board.

Install two screws on the other side of the case in a similar manner. Each hard drive should have four screws holding it in.

Install the hard disk control cable from the IDE add-on card or motherboard as shown on Figure 6-12. Ensure that the polarity is correct. For multiple disk installations, a two-connector cable is available with two identical connectors on the hard disk side so both drives can connect to the same cable. Be certain the master drive is the furthest from the end of the cable that connects to the IDE controller.

Installing the floppy drive is similar. I am showing installation of a 3.5-inch floppy drive in a 5.25-inch bay with a 5.25-inch adapter, sold separately. I used all of my 3.5-inch bays for hard disks because I installed multiple hard drives. For this reason I added an additional I/O card to support a total of six IDE drives.

Refer to Figures 6-13 and 6-14. They show installation of a 3.5-inch floppy drive and the cable that controls the drive. The cable end furthest from the floppy control card or motherboard must be connected to the floppy disk (in a single floppy installation). The cable is coded to assign drive letter A to the floppy drive installed on that end of the cable.

If you install a second floppy drive, use the remaining connector on the same cable. The second floppy drive will be assigned drive letter B.

With the floppy and hard drives installed and configured, the remaining task is to install the CD-ROM drive. Review Figures 6-15 and 6-16 for details on CD-ROM installation.

A typical IDE CD-ROM drive connects to the IDE interface through a cable identical to a hard-drive control cable. The cable connects to the secondary IDE interface in an EIDE system. If you do not have the EIDE interface, you must give up the slave hard disk drive position to install an IDE CD-ROM. The CD-ROM documentation gives an example.

Many users choose to install a CD-RW and a CD-ROM drive. If both are IDE, install them on the slave secondary IDE port and configure

Figure 6-13. The floppy drive.

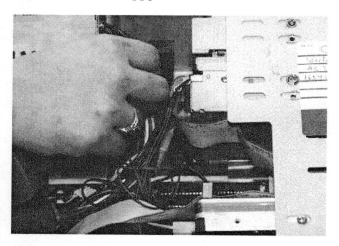

Figure 6-14. The floppy cable.

one as a slave. Refer to Figure 6-16 for slave jumper location on a CD-ROM.

A SCSI CD-ROM requires a SCSI controller card or a SCSI sound card as an interface card. The instructions for this type of installation are detailed and are included with the purchase. Review the documentation for the interface card and the CD-ROM drive.

The power cables to the drives were not discussed earlier, but they are specified in the documentation for the hard drive, floppy drive, and CD-ROM drive. Confirm all the power connections have been made to these components.

The power connectors come in two sizes, both plugging in only one way. With this task completed it is time to hook up the monitor,

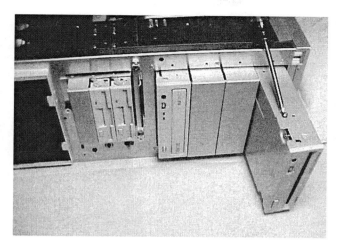

Figure 6-15. An IDE CD-ROM.

Figure 6-16. CD-ROM cables.

keyboard, and mouse. If you have speakers for your CD-ROM drive and sound card, install them now as well. The speakers connect either to the onboard sound card jacks on the rear of the case or to your purchased sound card.

Connect the keyboard at the round hole on the rear of the case. You can see the connector on the motherboard by looking into the left-hand side of the case.

Advances in technology have left you with several keyboard and mouse installation options. The mouse can be USB or remote infrared using the IR port option. The keyboard can have any of three connectors, so match the mouse and keyboard connectors with your intended application. Use the motherboard as the determining factor, as it

provides the interconnect options from which you must choose.

The mouse connects to the smallest of the I/O connectors you installed on the rear panel. If you installed an IDE I/O card, it is normally the top connector on this card and has nine pins.

For future reference, this configuration will default the mouse, as installed, on Com1 (the first serial I/O port). You have two of these. The second one has a 25-pin connector. Both serial I/O ports can perform this function but, since a mouse normally comes with the smaller nine-pin connector, it is usually installed on Com1.

The monitor connects to the video card through the rear panel. Connect and screw down the interface cable from the monitor. If the monitor has a special power cable to connect to the case, install it now.

Connect the speakers to the sound card. The sound card has an interface cable that you connected between the sound card and the CD-ROM. This interface cable, a small cable with three to four wires, transfers digital sound information from the CD-ROM to the sound card for processing into analog signals that will drive the speakers. You can see the connection point for the sound card in Figure 6-16, which is a rear view of the CD-ROM.

Connect your printer to the printer port, if you have a printer. When you finish with this portion of the installation, you should have a system similar in appearance to the one pictured in Figure 6-17.

STEP-BY-STEP INSTALLATION

Most people that evaluated the original proof of this book suggested the following step-by-step approach. Though information specific to the particular components you select for your system may differ from these directions, the pictorial nature of this presentation is very comfortable for many first time computer assemblers. These components are desirable to most of the individuals I queried, so the pictures presented here are representative of the most common system built today.

Figure 6-17. The completed system: Athalon 1800+, faster than anything sold.

Step 1

Prepare the motherboard as described next. Install the processor, heat sink, and fan. Install the cache RAM fan as shown in Figure 6-18 by pressing it down into the chip with your thumb and latching it. Install the DIMM RAM by placing it into the keyed socket and forcing it against the spring locks into an upright position, as shown in Figure 6-19. The motherboard is now ready to install into the case, on the fold-down side shown in Figure 6-20. Remove the three screws shown.

Step Two

Install the motherboard on the fold-down case. Review Figure 6-20 for a backside view, which shows the plastic standoffs and the case slides. Review the section on motherboard installation earlier in this chapter.

Locate and install the IDE I/O cables to the motherboard, as shown in Figure 6-21. These cables are keyed, with pin 1 of both the cable and connector identified clearly. Ensure the cables are routed away from all fans and heat sources, such as the power supply and anything with a heat sink.

Connect the remaining case cables for the power LED, reset switch, speaker, HDD activity LED, and any other applicable cables now. Since the options vary between cases and motherboards, you must use the installation documentation supplied with both. Refer to Figure 6-22 for one installation example.

If the documentation is not specific as to the proper polarity to observe with the power

Figure 6-18. Cache RAM fan installation.

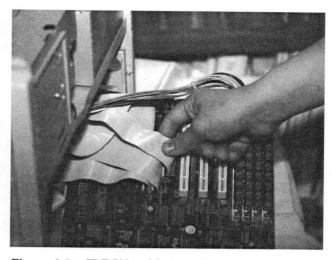

Figure 6-21. IDE I/O cable installation on motherboard.

Figure 6-19. DIMM RAM installation.

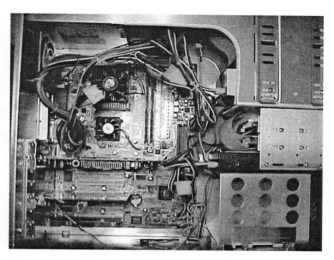

Figure 6-22. The remaining case cables are installed and routed.

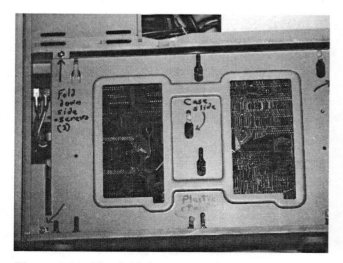

Figure 6-20. The fold-down case slide.

Figure 6-23. Case slide installation.

LED and HDD LED, do not worry. You can reverse them without damaging anything if they do not light when initially installed.

After completion, the case side can be pushed back into normal position and secured with the screws previously removed. Refer to Figure 6-23 for specifics. Note: *Before* tightening the mounting screws, ensure you are not pinching any wires as you reinstall the case side.

You have just finished the most difficult portion of the component installation phase. The remaining items simply plug into the motherboard or the case.

Step 3
Let's look at figures 6-24 through 6-28 to review the remaining hardware to be installed.

Step 4
The remainder of the installation is simple. Install the cards pictured previously in the motherboard slots corresponding to the bus type. The short connectors with the pins close together are the 64-bit PCI connectors. The AGP video connector is typically different in color and usually nearest to the power supply.

Install the video card in the AGP slot first.

Next, install the remaining cards—the Ethernet card, the additional I/O card, if required, the modem card, and the sound card. If possible, allow some space between the cards.

With all the cards installed, it is now time to install the remaining hardware, such as hard disks, floppy disks, and CD-ROM drives. Study the pictures in Steps 1 – 3 for the finer points.

Using the information in the beginning of this chapter and this step-by-step method, you have just built your own computer.

The sample systems pictured and described here are an Intel Celeron and an Athlon 1800+ computer with a full boat of accessories, including two printers and an external modem. When I started this book, the Athalon-based computer had a mere 1,400 GHz processor, but times change. Remember: the computer you choose may be anything the market has to offer, and the installation steps are basically the same.

This concludes the installation portion.

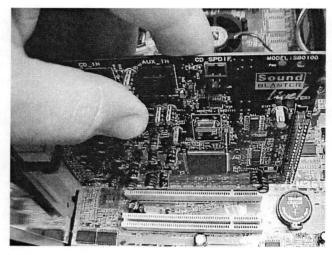
Figure 6-24. A premium sound card being installed.

Figure 6-25. An AGP video card being installed.

Figure 6-26. External backup systems: tape, hard drive, and removable disk.

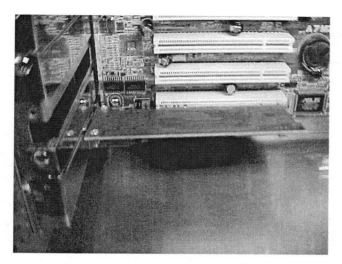

Figure 6-27. An Ethernet card has just been installed in the lower PCI slot.

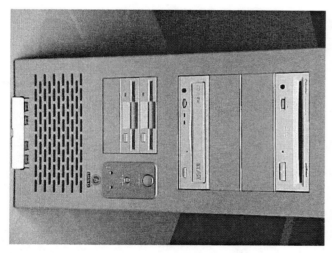

Figure 6-28. (from right to left) DVD recorder, CD-RW, two 3.5-inch floppies.

The next step is to power up and configure the computer as a complete system. You are about to turn on your new computer for the first time and enjoy the benefits of your substantial efforts. Congratulations!

STARTING YOUR SYSTEM FOR THE FIRST TIME

Plug in the main power cable for your system to both the wall socket and your computer. Have the following documentation handy: the motherboard manual turned to the section on CMOS setup, the hard drive manual

turned to the section on CMOS configuration data, and the phone book turned to the fire department's number. (Just kidding!)

You have to tell your computer something about the components you installed. The CMOS setup stores the information and uses it each time you turn on the computer. When you turn your computer on, check for any unacceptable signs, such as smoke, arcing noises, or flashes of light. If you see or hear anything that suggests a problem, shut the computer off and recheck all connections, including power cables and the power switch connections. If everything is normal, press the required keys on the keyboard to enter setup mode. Often the computer screen will tell you which keys to press. The motherboard manual will certainly give the information.

The CMOS setup screen should come up. If it doesn't, and you get an error message about some configuration issue, refer to Chapter 8 ("When Things Go Wrong"). Problems are discussed in detail so they can be quickly resolved.

If you have a blank screen or the computer locks up during initial power up, repeat the process once. If you get the same results, jump quickly to Chapter 8 and we will analyze and fix the problem together.

Once you are in CMOS setup, follow the motherboard documentation. Enter the date, time, hard drive information from the hard disk manual, and floppy disk size and type. Do not change anything in CMOS setup unless the documentation tells you to. We will optimize CMOS configuration later in this chapter.

The CMOS directions are fairly simple. Follow them carefully, particularly when setting the hard disk's parameters. If you only have one floppy disk drive, make certain that you designate it as floppy drive A. (Note: CMOS setup is volatile, which means temporary. If the CMOS battery on the motherboard dies, the setup is lost. Make sure you write the CMOS setup down and keep it inside your case. A floppy disk label is a good place to write it. Stick the label somewhere inside the case. Hopefully you will never need the information again, but if you do, it will be handy.)

When starting the computer with a hard disk that has no information on it, there are two ways to get going. The first is the most common for users that do not wish to make a multiboot system. If you are not familiar with a multiboot system, please follow the first example. It will prepare the computer to run on Windows 9X, NT, or 2K, the preferred way to set up a computer for home use.

Turn on your computer. As it begins to start up, you will see a message that allows you to press a keyboard key to get into the BIOS setup program. It is usually the "delete" key. Press it after you are requested to do so.

When the BIOS menu appears, follow the on-screen instructions to allow the computer to recognize your hard drive and floppy drives. Set the hard drive parameters to AUTO for both the master and slave IDE ports, and select the proper floppy drive as well. Set the date and time.

Move into the advanced setup and select your CD-ROM as the primary boot device. Exit and save the setup parameters, then turn off the computer.

Install your Windows 9X, 2K, or NT bootable CD-ROM disk into the CD-ROM drive and turn on the computer. It will boot on the CD-ROM. Follow the directions to FDISK and FORMAT your hard drive, then install the operating system per the on-screen instructions. Install the remaining software as well. After installing your Windows software, remember to return to the BIOS setup and set your primary boot device as your hard disk.

You are off and running!

The following method is the way I set up my hard disk for the first time:

With CMOS setup configured, reboot the system with a DOS boot disk. The Microsoft DOS boot disk has the necessary files to prepare your hard disk for use, but use DOS version 6.0 or later. The disk should have a label that says Disk 1 – setup.

When you exit CMOS setup your computer will boot, or initialize, from the floppy disk. You will receive a message allowing you to continue installing DOS or exit. The exit key is the F3 function key on the keyboard. Press

this now, because you cannot install DOS yet since DOS does not recognize your hard drive.

When setup returns you to the A> prompt, type *fdisk*. This drops you into the fixed disk setup program. It is necessary to prepare any hard disk that has not been previously formatted in order to allow you to install software on the drive. The fdisk and format programs prepare the hard drive to accept data from you or your programs.

The screen looks something like this:

MS-DOS Version 6.22
Fixed Disk Setup Program
Copyright Microsoft Corporation 1983, 1993

FDISK Options:
Choose one of the following:

1. Create DOS partition or logical DOS drive.
2. Set active partition.
3. Delete partition or logical DOS drive.
4. Display partition information.
5. Change current fixed disk drive. (Note: Number 5 shows up only if you have multiple hard drives.)

Enter choice: [1]
Press ESC to return to FDISK options.

You must do two things to use your hard disk. Choose option 1 to create a DOS partition, then return to the menu and choose option 2 to make the partition active. When asked if you want to use the entire disk for DOS, select "yes."

If you wish to partition your hard disk into several smaller logical drives, now is the time to do so. If you partition your hard drive *after* you format your hard disk and install software, you will destroy installed software. Refer to your hard disk manual to investigate the benefits of partitioning before you move on.

After you finish, press the ESC key to return to the A> prompt. You are ready to format your hard disk and create the boot block.

High level formatting organizes the disk area into sections in a manner that allows data to be easily stored and accessed. A FAT is created to index the stored data. Now, type format C: /S. This action high-level formats the hard drive C and transfers the system files to the hard drive. The next time you boot up, you will be able to do so from the hard drive.

Try this test. Remove the floppy boot disk and reboot your computer. To soft boot, hit the CTRL, ALT, and DEL keys simultaneously. Your hard disk should boot and you should have a message displayed asking for the date and time to be entered. This means your hard disk is successfully formatted and operational.

Now, reboot with the floppy disk installed. Install DOS according to the directions shown in the DOS setup program. You are on your way!

Install your software per the directions on the software package or documentation. It is best to install software in the following order:

---

1. Microsoft DOS.
2. Microsoft Windows 9X, NT, or 2K.
3. All DOS-only applications, particularly backup programs.
4. Combination DOS and Windows applications.
5. Windows applications.

Read your software documentation.

Software documentation is typically very good where installation issues are concerned. If you have any problems with software, the product support staff will help. I have even received good help from the software vendors.

THOROUGHLY TEST YOUR SYSTEM

The next few hours should be invested learning your system and checking for any glitches. Test everything, from the speakers to the modem, by running the software you have installed. Document anything that seems unusual. Keep an error log of your first 48 operational hours on the computer. Note the programs involved, the hardware being used and the operations you are performing. Hopefully the log will be an empty sheet of paper but if not, you have a good starting point to resolve the conflicts.

If you find any problems, check the documentation on the programs involved. See if you might be doing something the program doesn't agree with. Look in the hardware documentation and be certain you are within the proper operational guidelines for the hardware involved. Glitches and conflicts are discussed and corrected in Chapter 8.

Example 1: You are typing in a word processor and every time you hit the ENTER key, the text is reformatted.

Fix: Check the online help program or the software setup and look for auto-format options that are turned on.

Example 2: You are trying out the sound card software in Windows and something locks up the system, causing you have to reboot to restore operation.

Fix: Check to see if you installed the Windows sound card software before the DOS software. The DOS software may have modified your CONFIG.SYS and/or AUTOEXEC.BAT files, confusing the Windows setup. Reinstall the Windows software for the sound card.

Let the DOS programs have control over the AUTOEXEC.BAT and CONFIG.SYS routines by installing all DOS programs first. Windows will modify its WIN.INI and SYSTEM.INI files to run the DOS programs. Then, when Windows exits, it will restore the DOS settings. This is the primary reason to install DOS programs first.

BURN IN YOUR COMPUTER

If you can, leave your computer on for at least 24 consecutive hours. This burn-in period allows hardware issues to surface. Ninety percent of all hardware failures occur within the first 24 hours of operation. It is unlikely that you will experience any problems, but if you perform this operation you can be confident that you have reduced the chance of an unexpected failure considerably.

START A FOLDER ON YOUR COMPUTER

Save all documentation, receipts, and other paperwork associated with your system. If you

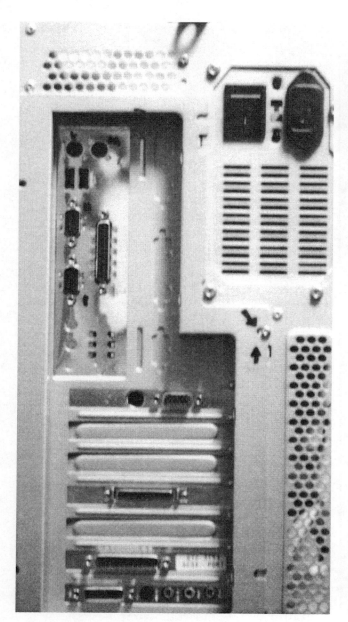

Figure 6-29. The ATX case.

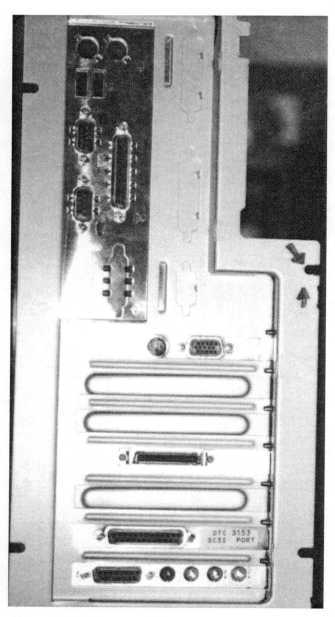

Figure 6-30. The case slide.

have a printer, enter the setup program and press the SHIFT and PRINT SCRN keys on the keyboard simultaneously. This will make a hard copy of your CMOS setup. Add this to your folder on your computer and keep it in a safe place along with other important paperwork.

The folder will help if you decide to upgrade because you will have all the information on your system in one place. Since you have documentation on everything you purchased, the folder is an excellent place

to keep the documentation and receipts.

Now, let's look at a significant performance upgrade. It's time to take a close look at the AMD Athalon XP 1800+. By any measurable standards, this is the best money can buy.

UPGRADING YOUR SYSTEM TO AN ATHALON XP 1800+

Many people involved with computers dream of having a new system with that

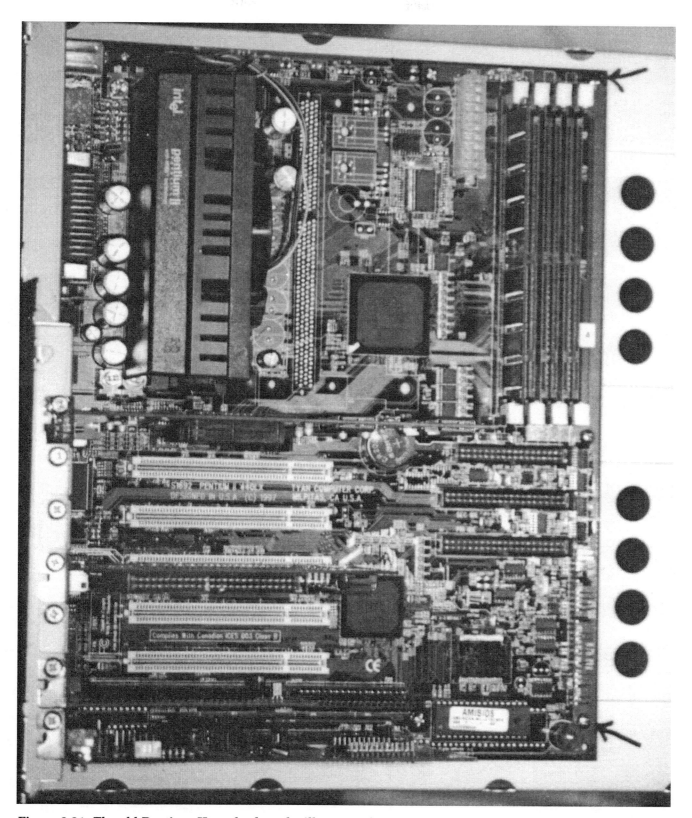

Figure 6-31. The old Pentium II motherboard still mounted on case slide.

leading-edge performance we read about in the computer magazines. Usually the super system we desire is priced just out of reach, so we pass on the dream for now. Maybe next year...

One way to have the dream system is to perform a competitive upgrade using most of the components in your existing system.

Let's look at one of the things that must change. Review Figure 6-29, the ATX case, rear-view, with a slide-out motherboard mount.

Figure 6-30 shows the case slide removed from the case. Removal consists of separating the case from its cover, then removing the one screw that retains the case slide. After doing so, lift up on the top of the case slide and pull rearward. It will come out easily. Now you have easy access for component installation.

Now, lay the case slide down on your work area with the inside facing upward. Place your motherboard over the case slide on the metal standoffs, aligning each standoff with a hole in the motherboard. Attach the motherboard to the case slide with the included screws. If any standoff does not align with a hole in the motherboard, remove it to prevent the possibility of shorting the motherboard to the case.

Assemble the cards onto the case slide and the motherboard as shown in Figure 6-31. If you have built a computer before, you remember how difficult this action was with the older cases, since installing the add-in cards had to occur inside the tight confines of the case.

Check to ensure that all add-in cards are properly seated in their slots and screwed down to the case slide. Confirm that both the RAM and Athalon CPU are seated tightly in their slots. Look once more to ensure that no possibility of a short exists between any component and the case.

Now, set this assembly in a safe place and prepare to install your drives in the case.

The next step is installing the case-mounted drives, including the CD-ROM(s), the hard disk(s), and the floppy disk(s). Install them in the new case in the same manner that they were installed in the old case. Review Figure 6-32 for a sample installation.

Now, connect all cables to these

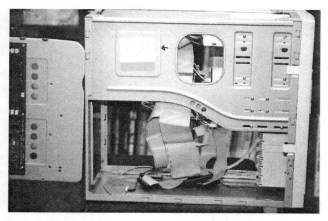

Figure 6-33. Cables and slides in position for cable connection.

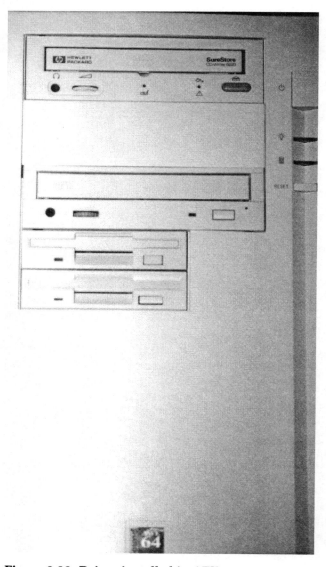

Figure 6-32. Drives installed in ATX case.

Figure 6-34. Case slide in position to complete wiring.

components, including the power cables, while the case is uncluttered by the circuit boards and their cables. By now you realize that most of the difficulty in installation has been eliminated by the ATX case designers.

After connecting the cables to the drives, place the case in the upright position, allowing the cables to hang freely. Figure 6-33 shows exactly what you should see during this step.

Place the case slide on the two tracks, and gently slide it forward, until the motherboard power connector reaches the power supply cable. Figure 6-34 is a good example.

There are a few things to be aware of as you continue. As you connect cables between the hard disks, floppy disks, and CD-ROMs, be absolutely certain that you observe the proper orientation of the cables to the connectors.

All cables have a red mark on the cable and a triangular indentation on the connector designating pin 1. There is a corresponding mark on both the drive and the motherboard connector designating pin 1. *Failure to follow cable orientation will result in damage to either the motherboard or the drive.*

Some peripherals and motherboards have keyed slots to prevent plugging in the cables incorrectly. Most CD-ROMs and a few newer motherboards share this safety feature.

Also, be certain you do not place any cables on or near the power supply fan or the CPU fan. Fan failure is the primary reason for microprocessor failure to date.

Check all cables to ensure that there is no possibility they will impede airflow. If possible, tape or wire all cables to a secure place in the chassis to eliminate the possibility of interaction with any fan or airflow interruption. You will be glad you did.

Now for the truth behind this adventure: My

wife, forever in my shadow because I had the Pentium 1.7 GHz blaster and she had my leftover Pentium 3, decided to ditch a day of work. Instead of running over to the local department store she visited the local computer parts vendors. Little did I realize she was planning a coup!

She had my draft of this book, about $600, and the desire to make me suffer, so she brought home a brand new ATX case and an AGP video card, compliments of the salesperson who knew it would improve her video graphics performance by 100 percent. She wrapped up the package by purchasing an Athalon 1.4 GHz processor, 512 MB of DDR RAM, and the latest American-made motherboard.

She had the system up and running in less than two hours. After she burned my tail in a total system benchmark contest, she showed me the system. She also duplicated the assembly at my request so I could document the process for your benefit.

Figure 6-35 shows her completing the assembly process by installing the case slide after connecting the cables to the motherboard that control the drives and connecting cables between the sound card and the CD-ROM. She wrapped up the process by installing the cover.

Of course, the system booted perfectly since the new motherboard was PnP compatible and had an auto-detect function for configuring the hard drives and CD-ROMs.

Figure 6-36 shows the completed system with the cover on, booting for the first time.

Not bad for a couple hour's work!

Please take note of the small label under her left hand in Figure 6-35. That's where she wrote the CMOS settings for her hard disk, in case the auto-detect feature in CMOS failed to accurately configure her hard disk. The information she wrote down is on the hard disk, but invisible when the hard disk is installed.

One other thing to remember when you do such a complete upgrade is, if you have an external modem, be certain that you take note of which com port the mouse is set to before you disassemble the old system. Swapping the com ports between the mouse and modem will cause some annoyance in reconfiguring them. The computer will auto-detect the modem and

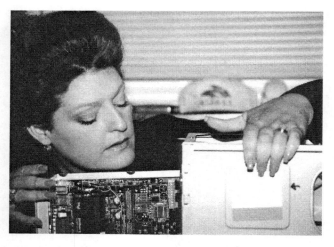

Figure 6-35. Seeing is believing: final assembly after cabling.

mouse, but any applications you have already installed that remember where the mouse or modem was before will be confused.

Now, let's look at some ways to speed up your computer. Note: CMOS setup parameters are normally preset very conservatively to allow the use of slower processors and RAM.

Performance Tricks

Several performance improvement methods are available in your CMOS setup, however, care must be taken in each case. Thoroughly test your system after each change and return the system to default values if any problems arise.

These tricks work only if you have a fast Pentium 4 or Athalon system. Implementing them on anything less will result in poor performance or lockup.

The advanced CMOS settings for each computer vary considerably. These settings assume a minimum of a Pentium 4, 2 GHz, Athalon 1400 or Athalon XP 1800+, and can be improved somewhat with faster processors.

- DRAM RAS Pulse Width: This is the number of cycles the row address strobe (RAS) is in width. Set this down from 6 to 5 to increase speed.
- DRAM RAS# Precharge time: Bump this down to 2.
- DRAM RAS to CAS Delay: Change to 2.
- DRAM R/W Burst Length: Change to 1T.
- Fast Command On: Enables quicker CPU access times.

These settings are normally set very conservatively by the manufacturers of the motherboards and can be set to faster positions, as we are doing, with the faster processors installed. The performance increase is significant.

Now let's speed up hard-drive access time.

Formatting the HDD with NTFS, the NT File System, increases hard disk access speeds and reduces file and directory location times. This only works for NT-based software such as Windows NT, 2K, Millennium and XP.

If these methods cause your computer to experience unexpected problems, such as locking up or rebooting by itself, reset your BIOS parameters more conservatively before looking at other reasons for the failures.

DDR SDRAM and a good, fast video-adapter card with 64 MB of memory also speed up a fast machine significantly. CD-ROM caching software will turn a 52X CD-ROM into the equivalent of a 100X or better without any hardware changes.

The most important upgrade capability involves the processor, as prices of the faster processors steadily fall. That is the best time to buy a processor-only upgrade. You can have today's $3,000 performance for few hundred dollars when the opportunity arises.

You have built the computer of your choice and saved a bundle doing it.

You have found and debugged the conflicts by reading documentation (or referring to Chapter 8). You have even taken a look at hot-rodding your system without spending another dime.

Now, let's look into the future and get an idea of how we can upgrade the system we have, when the time comes.

7

Keeping It New

UPGRADING OLDER COMPUTERS

When queried, most individuals would rather upgrade their existing computer than buy a new one. The reasons are varied as are their unique applications and needs. The two computers I presently have are hybrids of the numerous upgrades I have performed.

Upgrading saves money—this is a fact. It gives you the performance of a new machine at a fraction of the cost. It's also a way to buy a new computer one piece at a time, allowing you to have a new computer without the immense bill normally associated with a purchase of that magnitude.

The original title of this chapter was influenced by the actions of a friend. He is a published expert in the field of digital frequency synthesis and PLL digital communication techniques. He also proudly owns and uses a 386-40 ISA computer. This is the age of the Pentium 4, but he still clings tenaciously to the past. I have been leaving notes in his desk and e-mail with the message *upgrade or perish*. He pays me no mind and just pumps out another book or technical document. This leads me to the most important subject in this chapter: upgrading older computers.

Several options apply to upgrading older systems. The upgrade can be a simple memory increase, monitor upgrade, processor upgrade, motherboard and add-in card upgrade, or my favorite—empty the case and start over.

The most common upgrade is the motherboard swap. Let's look at this upgrade step by step. It can be the easiest and quickest way to get light-speed performance from an outdated and slow computer.

THE MOTHERBOARD

If you read Chapter 6, you know how very important it is to have your CMOS setup information preserved. Imagine trying to read the setup information from an installed hard drive's top cover. Make a copy of your CMOS setup before you attempt any upgrades.

To access your CMOS setup, most computers have a startup message telling you which key to press to enter setup. The most common key is the *Del* key, followed by the *Esc* key.

When the CMOS screen is displayed, press the *shift* and *print SCRN* keys to print the setup information. If you don't have a printer, write down the information for the hard drive. You will need the number of cylinders, heads, sectors, landing zone, and pre-comp data.

If you know the mode information of your hard drive, include it. Scan all areas of your CMOS setup for information on hard disks, CD-ROM devices and any other add-in devices, including pipeline cache and EDO RAM or SDRAM.

Shut off your computer and disconnect the power cables, monitor, keyboard, mouse and any other cables on the rear panel. Mark the cables and the connectors for future reconnection. Use a permanent marker to avoid confusion when you disconnect these cables sometime later.

Remove the rear panel screws that hold the cover on. They are located at each outside corner and in the top center on the rear panel of a desktop case. The typical tower cover has one screw in each outside corner on the rear panel. Many of the newer cases, designed for those that like to tamper, have hand-tightened lugs instead of screws.

The next step is documenting the cables and connections to the motherboard. If you have the manual for the motherboard, this is unnecessary. I recommend that first-time upgraders take a picture of the computer's interior in addition to documenting cable connection and placement. If you have the documentation on each add-in card and the motherboard, this level of care is unnecessary.

If you don't take a picture, make a sketch of each card and cable's placement in the system. Mark the interior cables and connectors to ensure correct replacement when the job is complete. Mark the cable and the connector on the same side to ensure you do not install the cable backwards. I recommend leaving the cables connected to the hard drive, CD-ROM, tape drive, and floppy disk drives, if possible, and only disconnecting the opposite end of the cable.

Remove the cables for front panel switches and LED indicators. These can normally be traced back to the switch or indicator, so marking them may not be necessary. Remove the two power connectors on the motherboard, at the rear near the power supply. To be removed, they must be pulled up and angled toward the center of the motherboard. For clarification, refer to Figure 6-5 in Chapter 6 and read the material about connecting to the motherboard. (ATX cases have a single power connector that is keyed for safety.)

You are now ready to remove the add-in cards. Remove the screws that hold in the cards. They are screwed in at the rear panel through the add-in card retainers. Ground yourself by touching the cover you removed. Place the add-in cards on this cover. Do not stack the cards on each other—it is possible to damage sensitive components that way.

Find the one or two screws that retain and ground the motherboard. Remove them and slide the motherboard from the case. The plastic standoffs will come free of the case slides, and the motherboard can be removed and placed on the cover with the other cards. Some motherboards do not have plastic slides, but are attached to metal standoffs by screws. In this case, all the screws need to be removed.

Make a mental note at this time to observe

the location of all the metal standoffs when installing the new motherboard; ensure that there is a hole in the motherboard for each metal standoff in the case. If not, remove each unused standoff by screwing it from the case so it will not damage the new motherboard when installed.

Refer to the documentation that came with the new motherboard and ensure the default jumper positions are correct for your processor and memory and types. Compare the two motherboards at this time and determine where each cable removed from the original motherboard will connect to its replacement. Refer to the section in Chapter 6 on motherboard installation for further useful information.

Check the mounting configuration on the new motherboard. Transfer the plastic standoffs to the new motherboard. Refer to Chapter 6 for the solution if one or more of the standoffs do not align with the case. Look at Figures 6-6 and 6-9 in Chapter 6.

Transfer any RAM you intend to use onto the new motherboard. If you have upgraded to a much faster processor, like the Athalon 1800+ or a Pentium 4, disregard this step. You should install RDRAM for the Pentium 4 and DDR RAM for the Athalon processor to receive the full benefit of this upgrade. The few dollars spent will be worth it.

The documentation will tell you if you must install the RAM in a specific slot or bank. You are now ready to install the new motherboard in the case.

Install the motherboard by reversing the procedure you used to remove the original. Connect the power cables first, making certain the black wires are alongside each other at the inside of the two connectors. If you incorrectly install these connectors, the black wires will be on the outside, and turning on the computer will send the motherboard to PC heaven.

Uses the motherboard documentation to place the remaining cables in their correct position and then install the video card and all other add-in cards.

If your new motherboard has onboard IDE I/O functions, do not install your existing IDE I/O card. This is the card that was connected to the hard disk, the floppy disk, and the extra I/O add-in rear panel slide. Figure 3-2 in Chapter 3 shows the card. Instead, refer to the motherboard documentation and install the cable from the hard and floppy drives, then the I/O rear panel slide to the motherboard.

All internal components are now hooked up. Reconnect everything disconnected from the back panel and replace the cover. *Never turn on anything plugged into the wall socket with the cover removed.*

A motherboard powered up for the first time must have the CMOS configuration information updated. Using the motherboard documentation, turn the computer on and start the setup routine. Type in the date, time, and all CMOS information concerning the hard and floppy drives, and CD-ROM if required. Use auto-detect functions for the hard drive and CD-ROM drives for simplicity, if available in standard CMOS.

Exit the setup routine and allow the computer to reboot. Pat yourself on the back, and then go to the bank with the hundreds of dollars you just saved.

Some people upgrade the video card to an AGP type when they upgrade their motherboard. I always install the motherboard first and then get the other goodies later. This allows me to thoroughly evaluate the motherboard alone and then check out the other parts later. It is no fun to do a complete upgrade and then have one bad part hang up the system. Always keep your older components for a while, in case you need to use them as troubleshooting aids later. Then sell them to a less fortunate friend.

Run your new motherboard overnight to burn it in. If anything is going to fail, it will probably do so in the first 24 to 48 hours of operation. Do a thorough test of your computer after 48 hours to ensure you have a functional system. After performing these operations, you will know the project was successful.

Now, let's discuss why anyone would want to upgrade a perfectly operational computer.

WHY UPGRADE?

Occasionally upgrades are forced upon us. For example, a friend of mine bought a version of Microsoft Office that slowed down his computer tremendously. Why? The program requires 64 MB of RAM to run effectively, and his computer only had 64 MB of RAM installed. A quick trek to the computer store and a modest purchase fixed his problem. He now has 128 MB of RAM and a much faster machine as well.

Another example: A client of mine likes multimedia packages. She bought a high-end computer game with embedded video clips, but hated the horrible performance. The video was jerky and unrealistic. She had invested a bundle on a six-CD game she couldn't play. The reason it was unacceptable was that she had a single-speed CD-ROM drive, which is good enough for data transfer but not fast enough for good, smooth video performance. Again, the solution was an easy upgrade she performed herself. The 52X CD-ROM drive she installed cost her very little money and just 20 minutes of her time.

I have built many hundreds of computers, ranging from DEC workstations and Tektronix information display systems in my years with Tektronix, to the faster Pentium 4 and Athalon machines my clients occasionally require. I have noted the primary reason a computer becomes obsolete to the user is a change in software requirements. This forces many good computers into a premature burial.

When is a computer obsolete? I've learned that a computer that fills its required purpose is *never* obsolete. If you never have the desire or need to upgrade your software, you may never want to upgrade your computer.

Why do software programmers write programs that have high hardware requirements? The primary reason is that programmers aim their software at the fastest computers available. They fear mortality.

The faster machines show off the programs better than slow ones, and the programmers have more flexibility writing programs for faster machines. More memory in a computer means the programmer has even more flexibility with his program code. All programmers write code for the best and fastest machines available so their hard work doesn't become obsolete in a few years.

It is hard to write programs with high levels of functionality for slow machines with small amounts of memory. The limitation of speed makes many visually oriented programs, such as Windows 9X and most multimedia programs, run slowly or not at all. Most programs today must grab the user's attention and keep it, so they must be visually oriented and interact with the user. And, of course, programs like these consume memory. These reasons make programmers constantly strive for speed and functionality in their programming.

If you plan on upgrading or replacing your current system, be certain you are doing it for the right reason. Upgrading or replacing a system that performs to your requirements may not be a good idea, particularly if increased speed is not a concern. Save your money until your system fails to meet your requirements and a real need arises. Do not succumb to advertising literature telling you that you must have the latest and greatest software update unless you actually need the improvements the upgrade offers.

TO UPGRADE OR REPLACE

When deciding between upgrading your system or replacing it entirely, consider the following items:

- How old is your monitor? If it is a 17-inch SVGA monitor, it is worth saving. A 17-inch SVGA non-interlaced monitor is worth between $100 and $150.
- How old is the motherboard? If it is a Pentium 2 or older, the expense of replacing the motherboard, all the add-in cards, and the memory will probably justify replacing the case and everything in it. You can sell your Pentium 2 to offset some of the cost. Also, if the monitor is not a non-interlaced SVGA monitor, you might want to replace it as well.

• Generally, replace a Pentium 2 or older system if the monitor is not a 17-inch SVGA non-interlaced monitor. The older monitors fall short in high-quality, visually oriented programs. The add-in cards will have to be upgraded to PCI or AGP to work in a new Pentium 4, Athalon 1400 or faster motherboard. This makes upgrading and replacing similar in price, assuming you plan to build the new system instead of buying a new one.

If you have an upgradeable Athalon or Pentium 4 motherboard, you probably also have a SVGA monitor. You can upgrade this system by replacing the processor alone and get performance improvements of twice the speed or better. The price of a fast Athalon processor is around $120, and $260 buys you the fastest Pentium 4 processor available today. I would suggest getting an Athalon processor and motherboard. Then you only have to add a $50 video card and you have a complete fast system. The IDE I/O function is built in. What this means is a complete upgrade (less RAM) will cost around $200, and your system will beat a comparable Pentium in performance and speed significantly.

In the decision to upgrade or replace, consider the age of the components in your system. If you can live with a slight improvement in performance, upgrade the motherboard and use the slower existing add-in cards from your original system. Obviously, for a few dollars more you can make the jump to light speed and be obsolescence worry free for a while.

If you want the full performance of an AGP/PCI system, it will be as cheap to buy a new case and build this system inside it. Remember the Athalon upgrade in Chapter 6? You can sell your old system for more than you will pay for the new case and the loaded motherboard. The price of the case is the only addition to the price of buying new versus upgrading. I am assuming you will use the same floppy and hard drives.

Now, let's look into upgrading systems that are less than two years old.

PROCESSOR OR MOTHERBOARD-RELATED UPGRADES

For some reason, most people shy away from upgrading the CPU. I find it the easiest and most beneficial upgrade you can perform. The CPU is a drop-in upgrade for most of the newer motherboards.

This upgrade starts with a quick perusal of your motherboard documentation. Verify which processors your motherboard supports and confirm the location of which jumpers, if any, you must move.

To upgrade a Pentium microprocessor-based motherboard, determine if its BIOS supports the Pentium 4 and Celeron processor line. If it does, you can upgrade to beyond Pentium 3 speed. If not, you may have to be satisfied with a little more than doubling your system performance.

Upgrading a Pentium 4 system is similar to upgrading a Celeron machine, though you have more options. The Athalon processor upgrades clobber a comparable Pentium processor's speed. Of course, the faster Pentium processors are drop-in upgrades to most Pentium motherboards. To upgrade to Athalon requires a new motherboard and RAM.

Another drop-in performance improvement is DDR RAM for the Athalon and RDRAM for the Pentium 4, which will buy you 30 to 35 percent improvement in overall speed. The speed difference is significant, as both of these types of RAM can transfer data on either edge of a clock pulse, making them twice as fast, minus latency and a few other things too hard to spell.

HARDWARE IMPROVEMENTS ON NEWER COMPUTERS

Generally, everything you can add to a computer gets faster with time and technical evolution. The improvement in video adapter cards is significant in departments other than speed. You can upgrade to hardware MPEG video movie support with the replacement of your existing video card. Watch the ads. The price of this upgrade is falling fast.

CD-ROM drives are constantly increasing in speed. No sooner did I find a good deal on a 32X drive than the 48X drives hit the market. I just test-drove a 52X recently. It is noteworthy to mention that I saw no difference in performance between my 48X and the 42X I evaluated, but software is currently being developed that will use the increase in speed.

SOUND CARDS

Since the new 64-voice sound cards are out in force, many gaming people have coded some extremely realistic games and multimedia programs that use the improvements. The sound card has come a long way and an upgrade of this nature will give some people an extreme rush. Live sound with surround-sound and full Dolby are commonplace. Most programs, however, do not make use of the improvements. Read all of the documentation regarding hardware and other requirements to make certain you will gain measurable performance.

SOFTWARE UPGRADES

When do you upgrade your software, and why? I have been asked this question many times. I upgrade when the newer version fixes a bug I wish to get rid of, or when new software offers something I can't live without.

The only other time I will upgrade is if the operating system I am using becomes obsolete. An example is DOS version 3 or earlier. Most DOS software requires DOS 4 or newer, and prefers DOS 5 or 6. You have to keep software for more than five years to run into a problem like this.

Upgrading software is an expensive process if you have 60 GB of software like me. Upgrade only if there is value to you in the result. Remember, if you keep upgrading

software, sooner or later you must upgrade your computer. It's a never-ending cycle.

Upgrading is the most inexpensive way to keep your computer current, if that is what you wish. I need to be on top of the current high end of computer technology since I work with many people who need the latest in performance. I have not purchased a new computer since 1994, yet two of my computers are state of the art.

I sell most of what is removed from my computer as I upgrade. Every year or so, I put everything I have removed into a new case and build a system. I install the software I no longer use on it and transfer the software licenses to the person who buys the system. I refer the buyer to a local vendor who buys and sells equipment, and the person buys an SVGA monitor for $110 and a keyboard and mouse pair for $15. They have a computer and I have the money.

This action accomplishes two things—it keeps me from becoming a pack rat and it reduces my upgrade costs. I found out that my Pentium 3 cost me about $600 after I subtracted revenue from selling the old stuff. The Pentium 3 had two 3.5-inch floppies, two 20-GB hard drives, a 5-GB tape backup system, a 32X CD-ROM drive, a flatbed color scanner, and printer. Not bad for a mere $600!

My wife just turned that computer into an Athalon XP 1800+ with a gig of RAM, a DVD recorder, A CD-RW, the same two floppies, and a 100 GB hard drive for less than $300 after selling the Pentium stuff and the CD-ROM.

As you can see, upgrading is the most inexpensive way to get a new machine if your existing computer is fairly new. If you have a very old machine, I recommend selling it and applying the money toward parts for the new system. (Be advised that computer software licenses must stay with the original software disks and you cannot sell copies of your software. You give up the right to use any software you sell.)

8

When Things Go Wrong

COMMON CONFLICT AREAS

Hopefully you have a successfully operating machine and you are reading this chapter for information only. Maybe you are intending to help an unfortunate friend ferret out a few bugs in his computer.

But if you and Murphy are good friends, we know why you are here.

Murphy's Law says if something can possibly go wrong, it will. *He is right.* Occasionally, I will come across his magic working in a friend's computer and sometimes it finds a way into mine.

I have seen a number of configuration issues in my time and have read numerous books and articles on these issues. These are the most common problems and ways to deal with them.

DMA CONFLICTS

Let's look at the DMA channels and see who uses what. Remember from the introductory chapter that many add-in cards require direct memory access channels and no two items in the computer can share the same address.

- DMA 0: This signal line is internal to the motherboard and is used to refresh memory. There is no conflict possibility with this line.

119

- DMA 1: This line is available and primarily used by sound cards. You may have a conflict here if you default install a sound card and then install a SCSI adapter for a scanner or other host device. This is a common mistake.
- DMA 2: This line is for the floppy disk drives to share. You may also piggyback a tape drive here. Occasional conflicts occur if you try to use a tape drive and floppy drive simultaneously.
- DMA 3: This line is available and is the primary choice for many Sound Blaster-compatible sound cards. I found out the hard way that some IEEE controller cards and network cards use this line as a default.
- DMA 4: This is the DMA controller line. It is unavailable in most machines for other applications.
- DMA 5: Available for sound cards and SCSI adapters. It is 16-bit stereo sound compatible. Watch for conflicts between sound cards and SCSI cards.
- DMA 6: Available for Sound Blaster-compatible sound cards.
- DMA 7: Like DMA 5, available for sound cards and SCSI adapters.

There is quite a bit of flexibility in setting up DMA channels. Remember that when you set up DMA channels, you need to set up the add-on cards with the least amount of flexibility first. The least flexibility normally can be found on any 8-bit card and many network cards.

Make a point to set up AGP and PCI cards last, and be certain to configure all manually configurable cards before installing and configuring PnP add-on cards. If you have any conflicts attributable to DMA settings, the information presented here should fix the problem.

IRQ CONFLICTS

You have control over which device uses certain IRQ lines. Let's take a look. Remember from the introduction that interrupt request

lines must also be unique between hardware add-on components.

- IRQ 0: The system timer uses this line. It is only available for the motherboard's use. If any conflicts are reported here, there is a problem with the motherboard.
- IRQ 1: This line is for the keyboard's use. The signal is available for the keyboard and motherboard only. The motherboard or the keyboard may cause problems with this line.
- IRQ 2: Once used for EGA video adapters, this line is available. Watch for conflicts if your video adapter is backward compatible to EGA or if you are using IRQ 9. IRQ 9 often uses this IRQ to talk to the processor. (Use this line for network cards. It is not an ideal choice for 16-bit stereo sound cards and may rob the card of stereo performance. Some systems assign this line to the programmable interrupt controller.)
- IRQ 3: This line is normally assigned to COM2 and COM4. Some older 8-bit network cards came with this setting as the default. This is a conflict in most systems and requires you to reconfigure the network card.
- IRQ 4: This line is normally assigned to COM1 and COM3. As with IRQ 3, this line can be configured on sound cards, network cards, and modems, so be aware of the numerous conflict possibilities.
- IRQ 5: This line was originally set up for a second parallel printer port. It is commonly used for sound cards, but most other devices can be set to this line. A tape drive may wind up being set to this line, particularly if it has a tape drive accelerator card.
- IRQ 6: The floppy-drive controllers grab this line. Often someone will use it for a tape drive or sound card if concurrent floppy drive use never occurs. This can be a conflict area in some systems, particularly if a sound card is set to this line.
- IRQ 7: The primary use for this line is the first parallel printer port. Watch out for conflicts when background printing if you

attempt to share this port with another add-on card.

- IRQ 8: Your motherboard uses this line for the real time clock. If something reports an error with this line, you must shoot the motherboard, i.e., return it to the vendor. (Note: the CMOS uses this line also. System information programs report this line as *"CMOS and real time clock."*)

- IRQ 9: Since this line shares with IRQ 2, it is a high-priority line. A high-speed network card will scream when set to this IRQ. Many 16-bit network cards are default set to this line.

- IRQ 10: Use this line for sound cards or network cards, particularly if all the lower numbers are utilized elsewhere.

- IRQ 11: SCSI cards often come set to this number. Multiple SCSI adapters may require the use of this line and others. Bump the network card down to IRQ 10 if you have network and SCSI cards installed.

- IRQ 12: This is the default line for the onboard PS/2 mouse. Most computers do not use this type of mouse, so this line is available for network, sound, or any other add-on card use.

- IRQ 13: The numeric processor operation ties up this line. Any error associated with this line means, of course, shoot the motherboard.

- IRQ 14: This is the secondary IDE hard-disk controller line. If you have no IDE hard disk or adapter present in your system, it is an ideal setting for a SCSI hard disk controller.

- IRQ 15: The primary IDE hard disk controller lives here. As with IRQ 14, you may do anything with this line if onboard or add-in IDE controller functions are not installed in your computer.

These bits of information cover most of the conflicts seen in the DMA and IRQ areas. Conflicts found here may be an indication of defective components, but 99 percent of all conflicts are in the setup of the add-in cards or motherboard jumpers.

Make a list of these DMA and IRQ settings and configure any items whose default settings conflict. Chances are this will solve any setup problems.

I/O ADDRESSES

Input/output devices require unique addresses to operate; two devices with the same address will not operate properly. The following list shows the addresses occupied by most add-in cards and resident operations.

These address schemes are the most common utilizations and give you an idea of how to clear addressing conflicts. The addresses are in hexadecimal notation.

- 130h: SCSI controller add-in cards often use this address.
- 140h: SCSI controller add-in cards often use this address.
- 220h: Sound Blaster emulation on compatible cards uses this address. This is the default setting for the real Sound Blaster sound card.
- 240h: This setting is the common alternative to Sound Blaster addressing.
- 278h: With IRQ 5, this address is commonly the default setting for the secondary printer port.
- 280h: This is a common choice for network, IEEE, and occasionally SCSI adapter cards.
- 2A0h: This is a common choice for network, IEEE, and occasionally SCSI adapter cards.
- 2E8h: Assigned as a default to COM4, as is IRQ 3.
- 2F8h: Assigned as a default to COM2, as is IRQ 3.
- 300h: Warning: Steer clear of this setting if you use Windows 95. Sometimes used for network cards, Windows 95 uses this address and causes conflicts with any devices set to this address.
- 320h: This is a common network card setting. Avoid it if you have a SCSI adapter at address 330h.
- 330h: This is a common choice for network, IEEE, and occasionally SCSI adapter cards.

- 340h: This is a common choice for network, IEEE, and occasionally SCSI adapter cards.
- 360h: Warning: Network cards set to this address will conflict with your primary printer port, unless you change the printer default from 378h.
- 378h: This is the default primary printer port address.
- 3BCh: This is a good alternate setting if you must move the primary printer port address default setting.
- 3E8h: This address is assigned to COM3, as is IRQ 4.
- 3F8h: This address is assigned to COM1, as is IRQ 4.

Occasionally, you will find intermittent or sporadic behavior. Be certain you check addresses for conflicts if any of these devices are inoperative or intermittent. The addresses normally are not a problem in systems with PnP cards installed.

Here's a problem I found in Windows 95 during the initial installation on a network machine. Remember the note about address 300h I mentioned earlier in this chapter? Yes, Murphy is alive and well. Things to avoid when installing Windows 95 on a network machine follow.

- If your network card is set to address 300h, reset it to either 340h or 280h.
- Avoid address 320h, since a SCSI device installed now or later at address 330h will screw up the system.
- Avoid address 360h, to eliminate a conflict possibility caused by a parallel port interface installed now or later at address 378h.

Network installation under Windows 95 is automatic, and you will not realize you have a conflict unless you try to network soon after installation. If you are missing the *Network Neighborhood* icon, or if you simply cannot access the network, you may have this type of conflict.

If you have to reconfigure a network card

for operation at another address, be sure you edit the *net.cfg* file in your system to reflect the changed address. You will find this file in your root directory on the drive your computer boots from, normally the C drive.

If you use Windows 9X, you must go to the control panel and change the resource configuration under either the *Windows 9X network* or *System* icons.

BACK TO HOME USE

Typically, if you set up your computer correctly and are starting a new system, very few conflicts will occur. In BIOS, set the PnP aware flag. It is worded differently in each motherboard BIOS, but will say something like: "Plug and Play Aware O/S" and the options will be "yes" or "no."

Always select "yes." Doing so will allow the BIOS to initialize PnP cards for boot purposes only. The affected cards will be any SCSI adapters, video adapters, and IDE/I/O cards and adapters necessary to display and control functions absolutely necessary for boot purposes.

When Windows 9X, NT, 2K, Millennium, or XP starts, the remaining cards and software will be allowed to grab the necessary resources required. This is the best way to eliminate conflicts before they can occur.

Most conflicts in a home computer come from sound card installation or configuration issues. To determine if your sound card is causing the headaches you are experiencing, remove it from your system. If the system works, the sound card was the culprit.

If your sound card is giving you fits, here's how to find out why. The sound card is a resource hog. It needs three of your resources: a DMA channel, an IRQ line, and a unique hardware address.

When you install the software for your sound card, it should create a record of these settings in your Windows *SYSTEM.INI* file. You will see a DOS record of the information in a line in your *CONFIG.SYS* file, too. Here are some examples.

Config.sys entry:

DEVICEHIGH = C:\PASTUDIO\MVSOUND.SY
S D:6 Q:7 S:1,220,1,5

This Pro Audio driver shows the DMA set to 6, the IRQ set to 7, and Sound Blaster emulation information.

Windows SYSTEM.INI entry:

```
[mvproaud]
dma = 7
irq = 7
```

What's wrong with this picture? First look shows that DMA settings for Windows and DOS differ. Is this a conflict? Absolutely not! This card, like many other sound cards, is completely software configurable.

The nice thing about software configurability is the capability of different settings on the card for different operating systems. This actually reduces conflicts, since different operating systems have different resources available.

What does this mean? If your DOS settings cause problems in Windows, set the sound card to another DMA or IRQ setting in the Windows configuration. The DOS settings are restored, if you specify, when exiting Windows.

If you have a sound card you must configure with jumpers, be certain your configuration files reflect the exact configuration specified by the jumpers.

UPGRADE HEADACHES

Some conflicts occur after upgrading one or more components. A new PCI motherboard and PCI video card may not like some of the older cards you transfer from your old motherboard. Generally, upgrades like this go flawlessly.

Try to isolate the questionable device or add-on card causing the conflict. If you are upgrading, you have a replacement for each new part. Try swapping in the original parts until the conflict is resolved.

When you find the offending component, try different configurations for DMA, IRQ, and I/O address, if possible. With the myriad of components available out there, occasionally one manufacturer's component may not work with other brands. If you cannot satisfy the conflict between one component and the others, try a different brand. This nearly always works. The best way to try a different setting when a conflict occurs is to remove the item by using the system resource tools shown in Figure 8-1. Figure 8-2 shows a clean screen with no conflict areas.

Figure 8-1 shows the hardware conflict screen. Note that the mouse shows up twice in this instance because a standard mouse was upgraded to a mouse that uses a USB port. The installer did not "turn off" the original mouse before installing the Logitech Marble USB mouse, and now he has two mice installed in the hardware configuration, causing a conflict and probably no mouse capabilities.

Now the fix: first, navigate through "my computer" to "control panel" and through "system" to show the system properties. Select the "hardware" button, then "device manager." Select the offending mouse button, the one with the red "X," and select "remove" from the options list. Reboot, and the correct mouse drivers will be correctly and automatically installed. If they are not, have the installation drivers handy and select the hardware conflict troubleshooter. Install the driver using the onscreen instructions.

These instructions are for Windows 9X, NT, 2K, Millennium, and XP. The screens will vary slightly, but the basic path is the same.

It is important to remember that a motherboard with onboard IDE I/O will *not* accept installation of an add-on IDE I/O card with the same DMA, IRQ, or I/O address settings. The default settings for both are the same. *Never* install an additional IDE I/O card without first setting the defaults differently. Remember, the only reason to install an additional IDE I/O card in your computer is if the function on the motherboard is either obsolete or defective.

Some video cards do not work well with certain brands of I/O card. You will have to get rid of one of the two. Of course, if your

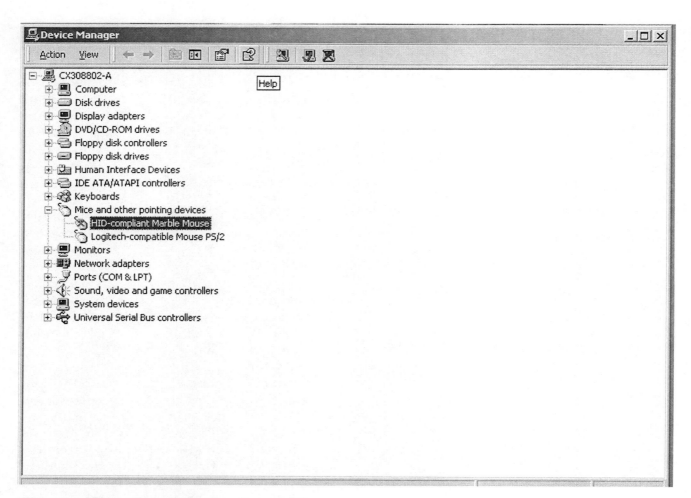

Figure 8-1. The resource screen showing a conflict.

motherboard has onboard IDE I/O functions, the problem is already solved.

Remember that a PCI motherboard with onboard IDE I/O needs only a video card to run. When upgrading, start with only the one card installed, then add the others one at a time. You will find the offending component quickly.

Now, let's examine problems with new systems.

New systems have their share of problems, but not as many as older computers. With the enhanced bus and additional 32-bit extended configuration additions, there are considerably fewer conflicts, and many more configuration options available.

Most conflicts in new systems occur due to more than one device sharing the same DMA, IRQ, or I/O setting. Confirming the default settings do not conflict and ensuring that components are configured properly with the default settings easily remedies these conflicts.

What if my computer doesn't initialize? If all portions of Chapter 6 are followed, this is the least frequently occurring problem. Common causes for a computer not starting are unseated RAM, unseated add-in cards, and configuration BIOS not set properly.

Confirm that all RAM is seated properly. Remove and reinstall each RAM SIMM or DIMM. Check the cards for proper seating. If you have onboard IDE I/O, confirm the plug-in cables are seated properly and installed correctly.

Try to boot up again. If this doesn't work, remove all add-in cards except the video card on motherboards with onboard IDE I/O. Leave the IDE I/O card installed on those motherboards without this option.

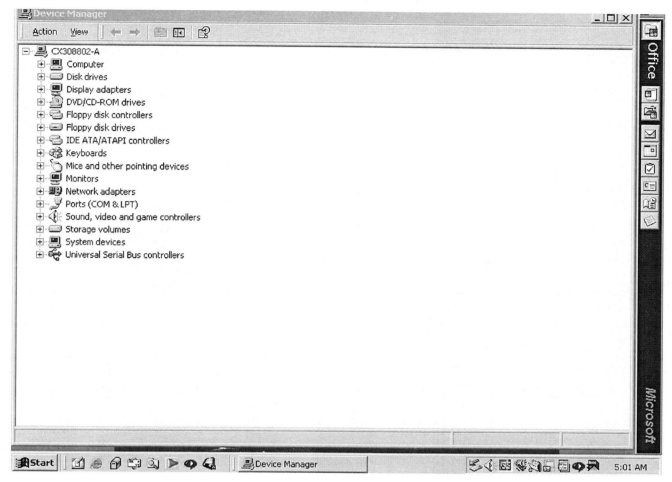

Figure 8-2. A clean, no-conflict hardware resource screen.

Try again. This time, the system should boot up. Refer to Chapter 6 and complete setting the system up. Now, install the add-in cards one at a time to find the culprit. Try everything mentioned above to reconfigure the card to work; if you still cannot get it to work, trade the card in for a new one or a different brand.

If the motherboard never enters the setup mode, it means the motherboard, processor, or RAM are defective. Return the parts to the vendor and he will test them. You will return home with the problem solved.

Reassemble the system and continue where you left off in Chapter 6.

SOFTWARE ISSUES

You now have an error-free system, but little or no software has been installed. We can really mess up a system by improperly installing software, believe me. Software normally installs flawlessly, but you *must read and understand* the instructions to install software properly.

Beware of software that modifies configuration files without prompting you. Understand exactly what is being changed. Chances are, if your system is hardware filled, something else may be affected. The software you install today may reconfigure the add-in component you installed yesterday, particularly sound cards.

Software that modifies the CONFIG.SYS, AUTOEXEC.BAT, WIN.INI and SYSTEM.INI files can cause unpredictable results. Always make a copy of each of these files and name them uniquely *before* installing a new software package, and make notes on which programs change the files.

This instruction set assumes you have a single hard drive with no partitions. Change the paths to reflect your directories and disks as required. Be sure you can remember what you name the file copies, or write them down and save them in your computer's folder.

From the C: prompt type:

```
copy config.sys config.sav
copy autoexec.bat autoexec.sav
copy c:\windows\win.ini
c:\windows\win.sav
copy c:\windows\system.ini
c:\windows\system.sav
```

This creates uniquely named backup files of the configuration files new software installation might screw up. I assume you have a boot disk, so even if the CONFIG.SYS and AUTOEXEC.BAT files are modified to the extent that they do not allow you to start your computer, you can still boot up and copy over them with the saved files.

Most modern software has extensive error detection and corrective measures embedded within the programs. You will be able to fix most software problems after a few minutes of reading the manuals but, since everything in life is nonlinear, some problems may escape the programmer's scrutiny. This is why the industry invented software hot lines and put them in the documentation.

New versions, new operating systems, and initial releases of games typically have the largest number of errors.

Most problems will be small compatibility glitches with certain hardware packages, particularly involving sound-card support. Video support is a close second when it comes to software incompatibility. Most software compatibility problems are divided between these two hardware components.

We have looked at the primary sources of problems occurring in new and upgraded computers. A basic understanding of addressing and the conflicts associated with address, IRQ and DMA sharing has been acquired. We have the knowledge to find and identify problem devices and know what to do when the computer isn't feeling well.

9

Diagnostic Software

Programs that fall into the category of diagnostic software generally do not top most software buyers' priority lists. This is very unfortunate. Without a good diagnostic program of some kind, you may become very unhappy someday soon.

Bad things can happen with computers. Some you may never notice, and some make themselves the central focus of your life if you are in the middle of something important on your computer. Hard disks occasionally lose small bits of data, a common occurrence in systems that are shut off accidentally or turned off without properly closing programs.

Small bits of data may be the missing link in your important graphics application, or they may be part of a program you installed improperly. When you use the program again, or look for the missing data and can't find it, you will wish you had a good diagnostic program.

Occasionally you do something like this.

You put a floppy disk in a:
    dir a:
You see nothing on the a-drive that you want to save. Then you do it. You are at the c prompt, but think you are erasing the floppy in the a-drive.
    Erase *.*

When you hit the enter key, everything at the root directory on the c-drive is erased.

You just lost your C O N F I G . S Y S , AUTOEXEC.BAT and many other important files. Guess whose computer can't boot anymore?

If you had installed Norton Utilities and created a rescue disk, guess who would be back online in minutes?

This is only one horror story. You will be able to create your own in time. You might do this a few times before you get a tool to recover data you accidentally lose.

There are many programs available to identify and correct the many little things that can go wrong while using and abusing your computer. I will discuss several I am familiar with in the remainder of this chapter and will mention some cool tune-up programs and their uses. After reading this chapter, you will know which program suits your unique needs.

THE PROGRAMS

I am going to list these in alphabetical order, since my preferences should not influence your decision on which best suits your needs. Remember, these are but a few of the many programs available. Check out your local dealer and evaluate as many programs as possible before making your purchases.

Checkit Pro: Analyst
This extensive program details performance and diagnoses all aspects of your

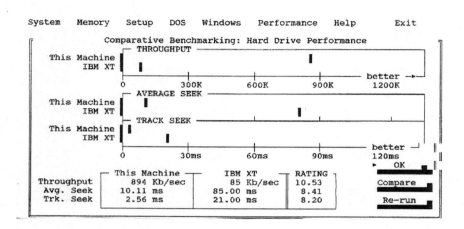

Figure 9-1. Checkit Pro benchmarks and system information.

computer. A burn-in feature allows you to run unattended tests on your computer, a procedure I highly recommend you perform during the first 24 hours of continuous use. If your hardware is going to mess up, it will probably do so in the first day of constant use.

Figure 9-1 shows some of the features available. (Newer benchmarks are at the end of this chapter. They cover the latest benchmark data from the experts.)

This program caters to new and experienced users alike. The Windows version is the latest release, and is feature loaded. It can provide performance data, configuration data, benchmark your system and test all aspects of your hardware.

Checkit Pro is available from **TouchStone Software** < www.touchstonesoftware >.

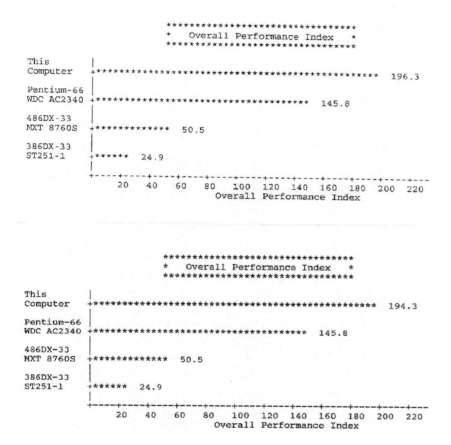

```
          **********************************
          *    Overall Performance Index    *
          **********************************
This      |
Computer  +**************************************************  196.3
          |
Pentium-66|
WDC AC2340+**************************************  145.8
          |
486DX-33  |
MXT 8760S +*************  50.5
          |
386DX-33  |
ST251-1   +******  24.9
          |
          +----+----+----+----+----+----+----+----+----+----+----+----
              20   40   60   80  100  120  140  160  180  200  220
                         Overall Performance Index


          *********************************
          *    Overall Performance Index    *
          *********************************
This      |
Computer  +*************************************************  194.3
          |
Pentium-66|
WDC AC2340+*******************************  145.8
          |
486DX-33  |
MXT 8760S +*************  50.5
          |
386DX-33  |
ST251-1   +******  24.9
          |
          +----+----+----+----+----+----+----+----+----+----+----+---
              20   40   60   80  100  120  140  160  180  200  220
                         Overall Performance Index
```

Figure 9-2. Norton benchmark running in DOS.

Dunford's Disk Error Monitor

A superior method of detecting errors on and recovering data from your hard disk is Dunford's disk error monitor, found at <www.filelibrary.com>. It will repair files by relocating data to a safe area on your hard disk. It can be configured to check your disk for errors on boot up, if you desire.

IniExpert

Windows configuration has always been an issue, particularly for new computer users. Programs use and abuse both the WIN.INI and SYSTEM.INI files. This program steps you through each line, allowing you to change anything and giving you information on the significance of each line item.

The program also tracks any changes that programs make to these files. This is particularly important if a newly installed program adversely affects something you previously installed.

IniExpert is a product of Chattahoochee Software. Look them up on the Internet at <www.cdw.com>.

Ashampoo WinOptimizer Suite

Speaking of Internet, this program rolls all aspects of surfing and peeking into one clean, user-friendly package. The user interface is the best I have used. This set of matched programs satisfies my appetite and increases my Internet mobility considerably. Formerly known as Internet Suite, it can be found at <www.ashampoo.com/products/>.

Micro-Scope

Volumes of praise have been written about this this full-featured program from Micro 2000 <www.micro2000.com>. It can analyze all aspects of your hardware and report on DMA, IRQ, and I/O addresses, finding conflicts quickly.

It does a complete memory allocation test, shows CMOS contents, and allows you to modify CMOS setup.

MSD

Microsoft Diagnostics is a program resident in DOS. It gives a snapshot of all aspects of computer activity at the moment it is invoked. To initialize it, just type MSD anywhere in your computer and it will work if a path to your DOS directory is spelled out in your AUTOEXEC.BAT file.

You can perform searches for subjects and files from MSD and print out about 15 pages of detailed system information, including your AUTOEXEC.BAT, CONFIG.SYS, WIN.INI, and

SYSTEM.INI files. MSD is available in MS-DOS versions 6.0 and later.

The Norton Utilities

Peter Norton put together a suite of diagnostic routines that dominates the market for superior and easy-to-use diagnostics. Both Windows 9X and Windows 2K are supported. Figure 9-2 shows benchmarks using Norton Utilities. Figures 9-3 and 9-4 complete the look at Norton Utilities benchmarking.

Now, let's look at the Windows 9X version of the same test. The Windows 9X version is a 32-bit program and tests your computer's ability to use 32-bit code. The performance will be different than that presented by a 16-bit test program, even the 16-bit version of Norton Utilities shown above.

This program is representative of the type of programming becoming available as computer software experts become proficient at 32-bit program skills. Programmers who use 32-bit programming have more flexibility, since the programs run very fast on current machines if the computer's operating system supports them. Examples of 32-bit operating systems are Windows 9X (a hybrid incorporating both 16- and 32-bit code), OS-2 WARP, Windows NT, Windows 2K, Millennium, and Windows XP all of which are straight 32-bit code.

Virtually all programs available today are Windows 9X compatible and written in 32-bit code. It is refreshing to note the previous benchmarks and test data that once was the

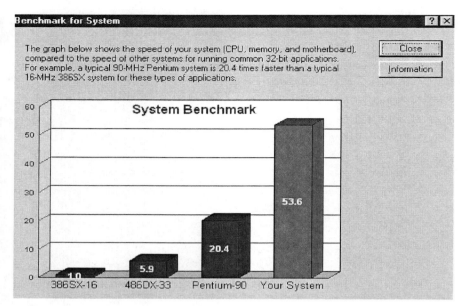

Figure 9-3. Pentium 200 MMX benchmark, SDRAM, on Norton.

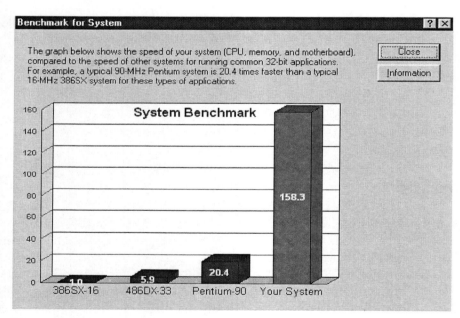

Figure 9-4. Pentium II-333 MHz benchmark, SDRAM, on Norton.

standard for measurement and analysis of the PC. As you read further, note the migration of both the diagnostic software and the performance improvements of the hardware being tested.

Now, let's take a look at the current state of the art when it comes to benchmarking programs. Norton and the other programs mentioned have the handle on protecting,

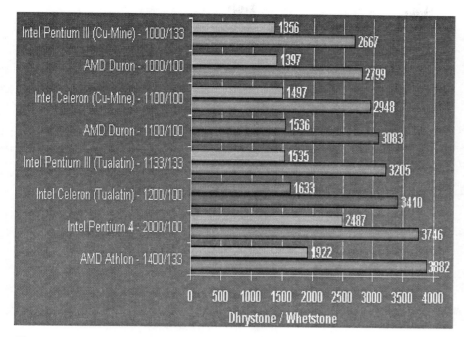

Figure 9-5. Benchmarks for AMD and Pentium Processors, moderate price and speed.

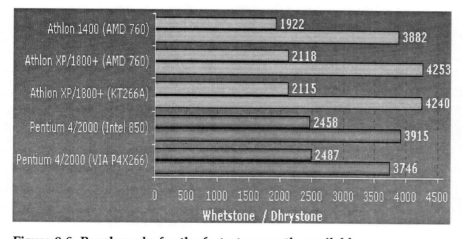

Figure 9-6. Benchmarks for the fastest currently available processors.

In addition to system information and benchmark testing, the Norton utility package provides comprehensive data protection. In Windows 9X, you can protect the trashcan from being accidentally emptied, which has saved many important files from destruction. The image program creates an exact duplicate of your file archive table in case the hard disk area beneath it becomes damaged.

The speed disk program arranges files and directories in contiguous order, so fewer disk revolutions are required to store and retrieve data. There are many other features but I will let you discover them for yourself.

Norton Disk Doctor is a program that I cannot do without. I'm constantly screwing up my system, though not intentionally. Trying some new and exciting global commands, I hang up even the most stable environments. Can you say fatal disk error?

Both Diskfix and Unerase have bailed me out of trouble when I tried something new and different to save time. I invariably find a way to hang my system with open folders, which creates nasty things called widows and orphans. Norton Utilities has restored my disk integrity, and sanity, on each occasion.

The most informative program, Ndiags, provides information on your CPU, memory, DMA, IRQ, and CMOS information. This information is necessary if you plan to upgrade your system.

Let's not forget the Norton Rescue Disk. When you install Norton Utilities, you have the capability of creating a rescue disk on a bootable

diagnosing, and correcting problems, but the following examples of benchmarks have exclusive dominion over actual performance variances between computer types.

Now let's look at the faster processors currently offered by AMD and Intel. The benchmarks are a composite of the combined performance of the processor combined with the fastest possible components available to support that processor and motherboard combination.

floppy. This will allow you to boot your system and fix it, even if you damage the data on it.

The Norton Utilities package is available from **Symantec Corporation** <www.symantec.com>.

PC TOOLS

If you need extensive and comprehensive utilities, this is the program you want. You can find and fix hard disk boot records and partitions, lost clusters and damaged file archive tables. Like Norton Utilities, this lets you create an emergency disk.

PC Tools has an extensive virus scan and cleanup program that supports identification of more than 1,000 viruses. It can be updated online by subscription, like Norton Antivirus, so it is extremely useful in the very sensitive business environment.

PC Tools and Central Point Software have merged with Symantec, the creator of the Norton Utility package.

Central Point Software can be reached through <www.symantec.com>.

PC911

Normally considered a companion to First Aid for Windows Users, this program tracks all changes to PC configuration files. Found at <www.pcnineoneone.com>, it offers a low-cost alternative to some of the expensive utility programs previously mentioned.

QAInfo

Another writer once told me QAInfo is the most comprehensive source of PC configuration information. Along with QAPlus, it has been known as a technician's tool rather than a home computer jockey's workhorse. The times are changing.

Hardware manufacturers often seek DiagSoft's expertise in software rather than investing their resources. This makes DiagSoft's programmers among the best at diagnostic programs. DiagSoft's programs cover more hardware than any program I have used.

QAPlus

This program runs diagnostics and burns in your computer for you. The burn-in portion

of this program alone is worth the price. It also comprehensively and repeatedly tests your computer while you sleep.

What if you find something wrong and don't know what to do next? QAPlus Windows version allows you to connect via modem to their electronic technical support center. You can electronically compose and send a test report. You will be notified by DiagSoft about how to alleviate the pain associated with a sick computer.

The QA series of products is available at <www.pchelplocator.com> by selecting DiagSoft, the manufacturer.

QEMM

This memory manager from Quarterdeck Office Systems first interested me in the early '90s when I needed a more sophisticated method of controlling memory use. Embedded in it is a nice system information program called Manifest.

Quarterdeck Office Systems has several good utility programs on the market, including Sidebar and Internet Suite. The entire package is a cost-effective and realistic support group for anyone interested in keeping their computer in top shape. Quarterdeck programs are available from local retailers or the Computer Discount Warehouse <www.cdw.com>.

ScanDisk

This Microsoft DOS 6.2 utility is a basic diagnostic tool for hard disks and floppies. It performs basic analysis of file structure and analyzes the disk surface. If it finds disk surface errors, it can move the data to a safe part of the disk.

SpinRite

Gibson Research <www.grc.com> developed a program that can actually read and recover data that DOS thinks is gone forever. This inexpensive program is a must. Its use in a DOS environment is unquestionably the best for finding, moving, and restoring lost data.

SYSCHK

This shareware program, available from <www.syschk.com> is an easy-to-use diagnostic program for the beginner and experienced user alike. The system information utility is simple and fun to use and provides comprehensive information.

The Troubleshooter

AllMicro <www.quickerwit.com> has an inexpensive diagnostic program that allows you to bypass your computer's normal boot routine. It thoroughly tests all hardware and allows you to print the results. If you have software conflicts you can eliminate the hardware as the cause with this program.

What's-In-That-Box

Jeff Napier has created the ultimate PC tutor. He describes entertainingly the intricate goings on inside the case of your computer. More of an educational tool than a utility, this program gives the user an enjoyable trip through the inner workings of a PC. The program is available on CompuServe, just GO PCFF.

WinSleuth

This program, available at <www.quickerwit.com> is a low-cost alternative. It performs all the tests the big guys do at a fraction of the cost.

WinProbe

The Landmark Company <www.cyberstreet.com> makes the burn-in program I like best. You can select as many tests as you like and run them as many times as you like. This program is tops in the documentation department, and many companies like the technician form printout with the diagnostic information and a signature block.

These programs are but a small sample of what is available, mentioned because I have experienced them or had positive input from other users. You must select the programs that suit you best. When you find one that suits you, expend the money to keep it current by upgrading and you will have a friend for life.

TUNING AND OPTIMIZATION

If you have purchased any one of the good diagnostic programs mentioned, you have the necessary tools to keep your computer in top operating shape. Here are a few tips on how to do what is necessary.

First, create backup copies of your CONFIG.SYS and AUTOEXEC.BAT files. Use the technique mentioned in Chapter 8. Do the same with your WIN.INI and SYSTEM.INI files. Again, Chapter 8 gives real-life examples for you to follow.

Write down the names of the backup files and keep them in a safe place. This will allow you to get moving again if a new program adds a conflicting line to any of your configuration files. To recover from a problem affecting any configuration file, just copy the saved backup file onto the existing configuration file. Make certain you rename the saved file the same as the original file you are replacing.

Second, review the performance tricks at the end of Chapter 6. Utilize any that apply to your system and expect some increased speed and flexibility from your system.

Third, run memmaker, a DOS-based program, to increase the available DOS (or low) memory available to DOS and certain Windows programs.

Finally, utilize your diagnostic program (the program of your choosing) to perform a disk optimization on your hard disk. Select the option that allows you to optimize directories first and files second. This way, when your computer tells the hard drive to find programs, they are in one contiguous track or series of tracks.

Optimization takes the pieces of files scattered over the disk surface and places them in sequential order on your hard drive. This means the hard drive travels a smaller distance to load programs into memory for utilization by the computer. Obviously, this saves time and wear and tear on your hard-disk assembly. It also cleans up fragmented files and returns your computer to optimal operating performance. Optimize your hard drive several times a year.

10

Other Things You Will Need

When I prepared quotes on computer systems for this book several weeks ago, the going price for 128 MB of RAM was $18. I could get it for around $15, but I did not believe it would be fair to quote prices not *easily* available.

Today I found an advertisement in one of the magazines listed in this chapter with a price for 128 MB of 168-pin PC-100 DIMM for less than $10. Not believing the reduction in price, I checked out some of my local component vendors. Sure enough, their advertising literature indicated similar reductions in price.

There is one certainty in computer and component prices: *They always go down.*

This chapter is devoted to where the home computing industry is going and how you and I will be affected, both as consumers and proficient upgrade specialists. If you are reading this chapter, I'll bet you know more about building and upgrading computers than 99.9 percent of the other consumers.

My wild guesses are based on trends I have observed and hardware I have gotten my hands on. Some of these factors are good indications of the future in home computing. We are in for an E-ticket ride if I am even close on my predictions.

Most of the advances affecting computers will occur in the peripheral devices. You can expect increased functionality from printers, fax machines, and modems. Other improvements will occur in motherboard technology as even faster bus speeds and microprocessors become available.

Speaking of microprocessors, expect sneakier processing schemes. For example, the Pentium Pro (Intel's boy wonder) uses a trick to change x86 (or complex instructions) into reduced instruction sets. RISC sets can be run in parallel. This makes the Pentium Pro a RISC microprocessor after all, even though externally it looks like a CISC CPU. The Pentium 3 and 4 have the best of both!

Complex instruction set microprocessors are the type you already are familiar with. They include everything from the Pentium 4 on down to the 286. The section of Chapter 1 on motherboards gives a detailed description of the differences between CISC and RISC processors and systems.

Even the fastest microprocessor is limited by external bus speed, commonly called the motherboard clock speed. Look for vast improvements here to get the most out of the faster processors. Example: A Pentium 4, 2 GHz processor sitting on a 100 MHz bus performs no better than a Pentium 4, 1.5 GHz processor using a 133 MHz bus or CPU clock.

For the short term, rather than change motherboard architecture most CPUs will probably increase internal cache size. The Pentium 4 has the L2, or secondary cache, built into the chip already, which is one reason it is so fast. The new Pentium microprocessors from Intel have already doubled the Pentium's internal cache size from that of a year or so ago. The trace cache has already increased to six times the size of the Pentium 3.

Let's examine some of these future additions in more detail.

I've mentioned the addition of MMX technology to the Pentium line, but what is it exactly?

MMX is a set of additional instructions added to the existing Pentium's instruction set, which is designed to accelerate operations that commonly occur during multimedia tasks. What this means from the computer user standpoint is a considerable increase in speed and data throughput in these areas.

The benefits from these instructions go beyond the games and presentation graphics normally thought of as unused by the casual user, since so many programs use calculations commonly thought of as multimedia-related.

Some of the tasks that will see the 50 to 100 percent improvement are MPEG video, speech recognition, modem conferencing, all audio processing, and both 2-D and 3-D image processing.

The casual user with an office suite will see significant improvement, as will the heavy game player. Some of the MMX updated programs, such as Microsoft Office and Macromedia Director, will provide eight times the execution speed with this processor update.

The coming year will see Intel and other microprocessor developers refine MMX technology to their entire product line. Intel is already incorporating MMX technology in the Pentium II processor line. The software developers are already taking advantage of the additional instruction sets in new revisions of existing programs and all new releases.

Last year I got my first look at an experimental CD-ROM drive that can read two-sided CD-ROM disks. It was about twice the size of the existing CD-ROM drive, requiring two 5.25-inch bays in a tower-style case. The first thing I wondered is why? CD-ROM drives exist that can handle six or more CD-ROM disks. The access time is at least 52X on the ones I have used. This system makes a double-sided CD-ROM disk unnecessary, or so I thought.

The real reason for research into double-sided CD-ROM drives is not just for reading the disks, but also for writing to them. With the drives rapidly approaching the access times of some hard disks, it is only a matter of time before a double-sided CD-ROM writer replaces your floppy or hard disk. With CD-ROM writer media at or below the cost of a tape cartridge, the CD-R will become the standard for backup systems. Do you really need a floppy disk in this case? I think not.

The drive I looked at had a different method of data storage than conventional CD-ROM drives. A typical drive reads data in one continuous track, starting at the inside of the CD and spiraling outward; this one-track recording method was not utilized in the new drive. The new drive stored data exactly like a hard disk, in concentric tracks. Obviously, this type of CD-ROM drive is not intended to replace the existing type, just as VHS never intended to replace BETA.

The real future in CD-ROM technology is limited by laser color. The higher frequency of light that can be used, the closer together the data can be packed. This is because a higher frequency of light has a smaller wavelength. Samsung has a green laser that can store more than 100 minutes of MPEG video on one side of a laser disk. If you are counting, that is about five times the current amount.

The blue laser currently being worked on will more than double that storage to about 3 GB for the green laser and more than 6 GB for the blue.

Some laser disk drives have onboard cache to speed up access times. Look for larger caches, probably in the 100- to 200-MB range in the next few years. A CD-ROM with a large cache will be faster than a hard disk performing the same operations.

By now you know color laser printers are available. They are extremely expensive currently, but so were color ink-jet printers when I got one. Soon, color laser printers will be in the $500 range or less. (I have a special gift. I will go out and buy something when I think the price has bottomed out, only to have it drop 50 percent in price as I walk to the car with my new purchase. People hire me to buy things so they can get a good price after I make my purchase. And I have been threatening to buy a color laser printer.)

The modem in your computer is another area slated for vast improvement in the next year or so. Since the advent and increasing popularity of cable and DSL, modems running at 10 Mbps, the 56K bps modems are rapidly approaching obsolescence. Internet cable will obsolete them unless something even faster does.

For those unfamiliar with ISDN, the integrated services digital network is the digital alternative to your analog phone line. It replaces your analog phone line and modem with a digital system. Though the two copper wires coming out the back of your computer look not unlike standard phone cables, they are capable of up to 1 megabit transmission rates with 8:1 compression.

Many phone lines are already ISDN compatible since Ma Bell has been so influential in bringing out and supporting ISDN-ready cables. If your area is compatible, the only costs are a one-time setup fee (refunded after two years) and the modem.

Now for the really fast alternative. Your computer has an interface in it that can probably communicate at 300K to 644K bits per second. It is your parallel printer port.

The next generation of communications packages will make use of this port and your cable network. Parallel communication over video channels is being experimented with today, and serial communication over satellite is available already with 10 megabit speed.

Expect communications speeds in the 100 MB per second rate soon. Note the emphasis on *byte*. Parallel communication, as you remember, uses multiple lines to transfer data, so you can multiply existing speeds by at least a factor of eight.

Other communications breakthroughs to expect are digital cellular phones with modems embedded in notebook computers. Expect to be able to rent a system like this at airports when you pick up your rental car. No reason to buy if you only use the thing when traveling or on vacation.

Look for portable computers like this to continue to shrink in size considerably and to run on smaller batteries. CPU speeds will not be the fastest on such a system, but power consumption will be minimized.

As speech recognition becomes more commonplace, the need for a keyboard will be lessened. My wife talks to her computer all the time and it does *exactly* what she tells it to do, just like me.

The Chinese proverb "If you tell me, I will listen./If you show me, I will see./If you let me experience, I will learn." describes the importance of VRML (virtual reality modeling language) in the standardization of 3-D simulations for use on the Internet. As modem speeds increase, the Internet will become a home tutorial system, which will aid tremendously in instruction of bedridden and homebound students. Interactive training already exists on CD-ROM.

In the "what will they come up with next" department, I want to talk a bit about the DVD player. This system, primarily designed for video playback, has found its way into the computer market.

DVDs (digital versatile disks) will be able to hold about 17 GB of MPEG 2 video. The players will be double-sided and double-layered, similar to a floppy disk drive's architecture. They will be able to copy a disk on the fly, as you are viewing it.

The transfer rates have to be at least 3.3 meg per second to provide the 24X performance specified. This drive, unlike the one I mentioned previously, will be compatible with existing CD-ROM technology.

The players have been available since 1997 at about $300 and recorders are now available.

Motherboard innovations are coming up to speed. I read an advertisement recently about a dual Pentium 4 motherboard with 1 MB of cache. It had onboard RAID hard-disk control included. The motherboard price, without either CPU was $175.

Motherboard bus speed will increase significantly in the next few years. The newer processors will force the issue, but how do you get more speed from the bus? With fiber optic bus interconnections. They are proven in high-speed analog computers, and some special purpose single-board computers used in industrial applications. This will require expensive retooling and innovative bus design, but will be necessary to break the 3 GHz barrier for CPU speed.

Back to the price of RAM. This single element of your computer will become a turning point if the price descends significantly.

Look for larger RAM installations in computers. Typical RAM installations today are 128 and 256 MB. I expect a typical RAM installation to be 3 GB by the end of 2002. This, of course, assumes RAM prices will continue to decline.

These are a few predictions based on what I have seen. I know based on past performance that it will always be much cheaper to build your own computer and perform your own upgrades. Some things never change.

Following this page are lists of periodicals available with advertisements on computer parts and accessories. You will also find a list of free magazines. Be sure you enhance your qualifications on the questionnaire in order to ensure a free subscription. A list of catalogs that provide computer parts and accessories wraps up this chapter. Please review the notes on the next page regarding Internet connection speeds and performance.

Let's talk a bit about Internet connection speeds. Please review the following chart for an indication of connection speeds compared to the 56K modem speed of 54K bits per second (bps).

Pricing is another story.

It is safe to say that networking pricing is one of the most variable things going on in the world today. The two most common methods of interconnection with full authorization, are priced as follows:

Modem connection is usually $19.95/month and cable access with full permission is typically $39.95 if you have your own cable modem and Ethernet card, and $49.95 otherwise.

DSL is broken down a bit differently. Unlimited dial-up usually costs $14.95/month. Home DSL runs $49.95/month, while business DSL is $99.95/month. A usage-based T1 line goes for $100/month. Wireless megabit DSL is going for $250/month, and a dedicated T1 line can cost up to $850/month.

Needless to say, the cost of the entire computer could pale considerably when measured against the high cost for light speed on the Internet.

INTERNET CONNECTION SPEED COMPARISON CHART

Carrier Technology	Description	Speed	Physical Medium	Comments
Dial-up Access	On-demand access using a modem and regular telephone line.	2,400 bps to 56K bps	Twisted pair (regular phone lines)	Available throughout most of the U.S. Cheap but slow compared with other technologies. Speed may degrade due to the amount of line noise.
ISDN	Dedicated telephone line and router required.	64K bps to 128K bps	Twisted pair	Not available throughout the U.S. but becoming more widespread. An ISDN line costs slightly more than a regular telephone line.
Cable	Special cable modem and cable line required.	512K bps to 52K bps	Coaxial cable; in some cases telephone lines used for upstream requests.	Must have existing cable access in area. Cost of bringing service into an area and trenching cable can be prohibitive. Networkable.
ADSL Asymmetric Digital Subscriber Line	This new technology uses the unused digital portion of a regular copper telephone line to transmit and receive information. ADSL is asymmetric since it receives at 6 to 8 Mbps per second but can only *send* data at 64K bps. A special modem and adapter card are required.	512K bps to 8 Mbps	Twisted pair (used as adigital, broadband medium)	Doesn't interfere with normal telephone use. Bandwidth is dedicated, not shared as with cable. Bandwidth is affected by the distance from the network hubs. Must be within 5 km (3.1 miles) of telephone company switch. Limited availability across the U.S. Only available at a few urban regions at present. Not networkable.
Wireless (LMCS)	Access is gained by connection to a high speed cellular like local multi-point communications system (LMCS) network via wireless transmitter/receiver.	2 Mbps or more	Airwaves. Requires outside antenna.	Still in the early test stages. In theory it's capable of super speeds of 10 Mbps or more. Can be used for high speed data, broadcast TV and wireless telephone service.
Satellite	The computer sends request for information to an ISP via normal phone dial-up communications and data is returned via high speed satellite to rooftop dish, which relays it to the computer via a decoder box.	400K bps	Airwaves. Requires outside antenna.	Bandwidth is not shared. Satellite companies are set to join the fray soon, which could lead to integrated TV and Internet service using the same equipment and WebTV-like integrated Services. Service is one-way with a slow uplink speed. Requires an Internet service account. Phone line is busy while online.
Frame Relay	Provides a type of "party line" connection to the Internet. Requires a FRAD (Frame Relay Access Device) similar to a modem, or a DSU/CSU.	56K bps to 1.544 Mbps	Various	May cost less than ISDN in some locations. Limited availability across the U.S.
Fractional T1 (Flexible DS1)	Only a portion of the 23 channels available in a T1 line is actually used.	64K bps to 1.544 Mbps	Twisted-pair or coaxial cable	Cheaper than a full T1 line with growth options of 56K bps or 64K bps increments as required.
T1	Special lines and equipment (DSU/CSU and router) required.	1.544 Mbps	Twisted-pair, coaxial cable, or optical fiber	Typically used for high bandwidth demands such as videoconferencing and heavy graphic file transfers. Many large businesses and ISP use T1. Expensive.
T3	Typically used for ISP to Internet infrastructure.	44.736 Mbps	Optical fiber	Very large bandwidth. Extremely expensive and complex.
OC-1	Typically used for ISP to Internet infrastructure within Internet infrastructure.	51.84 Mbps	Optical fiber	
OC-3	Typically used for large company backbone or Internet backbone.	155.52 Mbps	Optical fiber	

A Appendix

COMPUTER MAGAZINES

Here is a list of magazines that cater to the computer-oriented individual. There are many others, and you will become aware of them if you read several of these.

Audio Forum
96 Broad Street
Guilford, CT 06437

Black Box Corp.
P.O. Box 12800
Pittsburgh, PA 15241

Byte Magazine
P.O. Box 558
Hightstown, NJ 08520

CD-I World
P.O. Box 1358
Camden, ME 04843-1358

CD-ROM Multimedia
720 Sycamore Street
Columbus, IN 47201

CD-ROM Today
P.O. Box 51478
Boulder, CO 80321-1478

CD-ROM
Professional
462 Danbury Rd.
Wilton, CT 06897-2126

Compute!
P.O. Box 3245
Harlan, IA 51593-2424

ComputerCraft
76 N. Broadway
Hicksville, NJ 11801-9962

Computer Currents
5720 Hollis Street
Emeryville, CA 94608

Computer Graphics World
P.O. Box 122
Tulsa, OK 74101-9966

Computer Pictures
Montage Publishing, Inc.
701 Winchester Ave.
White Plains, NY 10604

Computer Shopper
P.O. Box 51020
Boulder, CO 80321-1020

Computer World
P.O. Box 2044
Marion, OH 43306-2144

Desktop Video World
P.O. Box 594
Mt. Morris, IL 61054-7902

Digital Imaging
Micro Publishing
21150 Hawthorne Boulevard #104
Torrance, CA 90503

Digital Video Magazine
P.O. Box 594
Mt. Morris, IL 61054-7902

Electronic Musician
P.O. Box 41525
Nashville, TN 37204-9829

High Color
P.O. Box 1347
Camden, ME 04843-9956

Home and Studio Recording
Music Maker Pub.
7318 Topanga Cyn Boulevard, Suite 200
Canoga Park, CA 91303

Home Office Computing
P.O. Box 51344
Boulder, CO 80321-1344

Imaging Magazine
1265 Industrial Highway
Southampton, PA 18966

Insight Direct, Inc.
1912 W. 4th Street
Tempe, AZ 85281

International Spectrum
10675 Treena Street, Suite 103
San Diego, CA 92131

Internet
P.O. Box 713
Mt. Morris, IL 61054-9965

Kidsoft Magazine
718 University Avenue, Suite 112
Los Gatos, CA 95030-9958

LAN Magazine
P.O. Box 50047
Boulder, CO 80321-0047

MicroComputer Journal
Classified Department
76 N. Broadway
Hicksville, NY 11801

Micro Times Magazine
5951 Canning Street
Oakland, CA 94609

Musician's Friend
P.O. Box 4520
Medford, OR 97501

Nuts and Volts
430 Princeland Court
Corona, CA 91719-1343

Open Computing
P.O. Box 570
Hightstown, NJ 08520-9328

PC Computing
P.O. Box 50253
Boulder, CO 80321-0253

PC Magazine
P.O. Box 51524
Boulder, CO 80321-1524

PC Novice
P.O. Box 85380
Lincoln, NE 68501-9807

PC Today
P.O. Box 85380
Lincoln, NE 68501-5380

PC World Magazine
P.O. Box 51833
Boulder, CO 80321-1833

PRE-
8340 Mission Road, Number 106
Prairie Village, KS 66206

Publish!
P.O. Box 51966
Boulder, CO 80321-1966

Video Magazine
P.O. Box 56293
Boulder, CO 80322-6293

Videomaker Magazine
P.O. Box 469026
Escondido, CA 92046

Voice Processing Magazine
P.O. Box 6016
Duluth, MN 55806-9797

Windows Magazine
P.O. Box 58649
Boulder, CO 80322-8649

MAGAZINES THAT ARE FREE TO QUALIFIED SUBSCRIBERS

Advanced Imaging
445 Broad Hollow Road
Melville, NY 11747-4722

Automatic ID News
P.O. Box 6158
Duluth, MN 55806-9870

AV Video Production
and Presentation Technology
701 Winchester Avenue
White Plains, NY 10604

Beyond Computing
1133 Westchester Avenue
White Plains, NY 10604

California Business
P.O. Box 70735
Pasadena, CA 91117-9947

CD-ROM News Extra
462 Danbury Road
Wilton, CT 06897-2126

Client/Server Computing
Sentry Publishing Co.
1900 W. Park Drive
Westborough, MA 01581-3907

Communications News
2504 Tamiami Trail N.
Nokomis, FL 34275

Communications Week
P.O. Box 2070
Manhasset, NY 11030

Computer Design
P.O. Box 3466
Tulsa, OK 74101-3466

Computer Products
P.O. Box 14000
Dover, NJ 07801-9990

Computer Reseller News
P.O. Box 2040
Manhasset, NY 11030

Computer System News
600 Community Drive
Manhasset, NY 11030

Computer Tech. Review
924 Westwood Blvd. #65
Los Angeles, CA 90024

Computer Telephony
P.O. Box 40706
Nashville, TN 37204-9919

Data Communications
P.O. Box 477
Hightstown, NJ 08520-9362

Designfax
P.O. Box 1151
Skokie, IL 60076-9917

Document Management & Windows Imaging
8711 E. Pinnacle Peak Road, # 249
Scottsdale AZ 85255

EE Product News
P.O. Box 12982
Overland Park, KS 66212

Electronic Design
P.O. Box 985007
Cleveland, OH 44198-5007

Electronic Mfg.
P.O. Box 159
Libertyville, IL 60048

Electronic Publish & Print
650 S. Clark Street
Chicago, IL 60605-9960

Electronics
P.O. Box 985061
Cleveland, OH 44198

Federal Computer Week
P.O. Box 602
Winchester, MA 01890

Identification Journal
2640 N. Halsted Street
Chicago, IL 60614-9962

ID Systems
P.O. Box 874
Peterborough, NH 03458

Imaging Business
Phillips Business Info
P.O. Box 61130
Potomac, MD 20897-5915

InfoWorld
P.O. Box 1172
Skokie, IL 60076

LAN Times
122 E. 1700 S.
Provo, UT 84606

Lasers and Optronics
301 Gibraltar Drive
Morris Plains, NJ 07950

Machine Design
P.O. Box 985015
Cleveland, OH 44198-5015

Managing Office Technology
1100 Superior Avenue
Cleveland, OH 44197-8092

Manufacturing Systems
P.O. Box 3008
Wheaton, IL 60189-9972

Medical Equipment Designer
29100 Aurora Road, Number 200
Cleveland, OH 44139

Micro Publishing News
21150 Hawthorne Boulevard, # 104
Torrance, CA 90503

Mini-Micro Systems
P.O. Box 5051
Denver, CO 80217-9872

Mobile Office
Subscriptions Department
P.O. Box 57268
Boulder, CO 80323-7268

Modern Office Technology
1100 Superior Avenue
Cleveland, OH 44197-8032

Mr. CD-ROM
MAXMEDIA Dist. Inc.
P.O. Box 1087
Winter Garden, FL 34787

Network World
161 Worcester Road
Framingham, MA 01701

Network Computing
P.O. Box 1095
Skokie, IL 60076-9662

Network Journal
600 Harrison Street
San Francisco, CA 94107

New Media Magazine
P.O. Box 1771
Riverton, NJ 08077-7331

Office Systems
P.O. Box 3116
Woburn, MA 01888-9878

Office Systems Dealer
P.O. Box 2281
Woburn, MA 01888-9873

PC Week
P.O. Box 1770
Riverton, NJ 08077-7370

Photo Business
1515 Broadway
New York, NY 10036

The Programmer's Shop
5 Pond Park Road
Hingham, MA 02043-9845

Quality
P.O. Box 3002
Wheaton, IL 60189-9929

Reseller Management
Box 601
Morris Plains, NJ, 07950

Robotics World
6255 Barfield Road
Atlanta, GA 30328-9988

Scientific Computing
301 Gibraltar Drive
Morris Plains, NJ 07950

Software Magazine
Westborough Office Park
1900 W. Park Drive
Westborough, MA 01581-3907

Sun Expert
P.O. Box 5274
Pittsfield, MA 01203-9479

Surface Mount Technology
P.O. Box 159
Libertyville, IL 60048

STACKS
P.O. Box 5031
Brentwood, TN 37024-5031
Skokie, IL 60076-9662

B | Appendix

RESOURCES ON THE WORLD WIDE WEB

BIOS
AMI	www.amibios.com
Award	www.award.com
Micro Firmware	www.firmware.com
Mr. Bios (Microid Research)	www.mrbios.com
Phoenix	www.ptltd.com

Chipsets
Intel	www.intel.com
OPTi	www.opti.com
SiS	www.sis.com.tw
UMC	www.umc.com.tw
VIA Tech	www.via.com.tw
VLSI	www.vlsi.com
Winbond	www.winbond.com

Computers
Acer	www.acer.com
Acorn	www.acorn.com.uk
ALR	www.alr.com
Amiga	www.amiga.de
AMS	www.amsnote.com
Apache	www.apache.com
Apple	www.apple.com
Appro	www.appro.com
Apricot	www.apricot.com.uk
Aris	www.aris.com.sg
Aspen	www.aspsys.com
AST	www.ast.com
Astro Research	www.astronote.com
Axil	www.axil.com
Be	www.be.com
Bull	www.bull.com
Chicony	www.chicony.com
Compaq	www.compaq.com
Convex	www.convex.com
Daystar Digital	www.daystar.com
Data General	www.dg.com
Datalux	www.datalux.com
Dell	www.dell.com
Digital	www.dec.com
Dolch	www.dolch.com
Encore	www.encore.com
Epson	www.epson.com
Everex	www.everex.com
Gateway	www.gw2k.com
HAL	www.hal.com
HP	www.hp.com
IBM	www.pc.ibm.com
Integrix	www.integrix.com
Intergraph	www.intergraph.com
Jepssen	www.vol.it/jepssen/
Magitronic	www.magitronic.com
Micron	www.mei.micron.com
Mitsuba	www.mitsuba.com
NEC	www.nec.com
Next	www.next.com

Newchip	www.newchip.i
Nimantics	www.nimantics.com
Olidata	www.olidata.it
Olivetti	www.olivetti.it
Packard Bell	www.packardbell.com
Panasonic	www.panasonic.com
Polywell	www.polywell.com
Power Computing	www.powercc.com
Pyramid	www.pyramid.com
RDI	www.rdi.com
Ross	www.ross.com
Samsung	www.samsung.com
Sequent	www.sequent.com
Silicon Graphics	www.sgi.com
Siliconrax	www.siliconrax.com
Sony	www.sel.sony.com
Stratus	www.stratus.com
Swan Technologies	www.swantech.com
Tadpole	www.tadpole.com
Tandy	www.tandy.com
Tera	www.tera.com
Toshiba	www.toshiba.com
XI	www.win.net/xi_comp
Zenith	www.zds.com

Controllers and I/O

Adaptec	www.adaptec.com
Advance Storage	www.eden.com
Advansys	www.advansys.com
Advantech	www.advantech.com
AMI	www.megaraid.com
Atronics	www.atronicsintl.com
Berkshire	www.berkprod.com
Buslogic	www.buslogic.com
Byterunner	www.byterunner.com
Centennial	www.cent-tech.com
CMD	www.cmd.com
Comtrol	www.comtrol.com
Crestor	www.crestor.com
Cyclades	www.cyclades.com
Digi Intl.	www.digibd.com
DPT	www.dpt.com
DTC	www.datatechnology.com
Dynatek	www.zstarr.com/dynatek/
Future Domain	www.adaptec.com
Gtek	www.gtek.com
Infotrend	www.infotrend.com.tw
Initio	www.initio.com
Iwill	www.itwill.com

Mylex	www.mylex.com
NCR	www.ncr.com
New Media	www.newmediacorp.com
Pathlight	www.pathlight.com
Promise	www.promise.com
Qlogic	www.qlc.com
Specialix	www.specialix.co.uk
Symbios	www.symbios.com
Tandy	support.tandy.com
Tekram	www.tekram.com
TURBOstor	www.genroco.com
Tyan	www.tyan.com
Winbond	www.winbond.com.tw
Z-World	www.zworld.com

Input Devices

Acecad	
www.acecad.com	
ACT Lab	www.actlab.com
Advanced Input	www.advanced-input.com
Advanced Gravis	www.gravis.com
Alps Electric	www.alpsusa.com
BTC	www.btc.com.tw
Calcomp	www.calcomp.com
Casco	www.casco.com
CFX	www.cfx.com.au
CH	www.chproducts.com
Chicony	www.chicony.com
Contour	www.contourdes.com
Cybernet	www.cybernet.com
DataHand Systems	www.datahand.com
Datalux	www.datalux.com
Eurgonics	www.eurgonics.com
Evergreen	www.trackballs.com
Exos	www.exos.com
Focustaipei	www.focustaipei.com.tw
Gefen	www.gefen.com
Genius	www.genius-kye.com
Genovation	www.genovation.com
Glidepoint	www.glidepoint.com
The Glove	www.theglove.com
Gyration	www.gyration.com
Infogrip	www.infogrip.com
Interlink Electronics	www.interlinkelec.com
Jag Tech	www.clearlight.com
Kernel	www.kernel.com
Keytronic	www.keytronic.com
Kurta	www.mutoh.com
Left-Handed	www.lefthanded.com

Logitech	www.logitech.com
Memtron	www.memtron.com
Microsoft	www.microsoft.com
Microspeed	www.microspeed.com
Mitsumi	www.mitsumi.com
Mouse Burger	www.unipac-usa.com
Mouse Systems	www.mousesystems.com
Mouse Trak	www.mousetrak.com
Mutoh	www.mutoh.com
NMB	www.nmbtech.com
No Hands Mouse	www.footmouse.com
Paneltec	www.paleltec.com
Polytel	www.polytel.com
Primax	www.primax.nl
Sejin	www.sejin.com
Sicos	www.sicos.com
Spacetec	www.spacetec.com
Spec Research	www.spec-research.com
Star Trak	www.am-group.com
Summagraphics	www.summagraphics.com
Supermouse	www.supermouse.com
Sym Media	www.symmedia.com
Synaptics	www.synaptics.com
Sysgration	www.sysgration.com
Tandy	www.support.tandy.com
Texas Ind. Periph	www.ikey.com
Thrustmaster	www.thrustmaster.com
Trust	www.trust.box.nl
U&C	www.superpen.com
USAR	www.usar.com
Vector	www.mbws.com
Wacom	www.wacom.com
Wireless Computing	www.cpgs.com

Memory

Centron	www.centron.com
Century	www.century.micro.com
Cypress	www.cypress.com
Dallas	www.dalsemi.com
Hsin Lin	www.hsinlin.com.tw
Hyundai	www.hea.com
IDT	www.idt.com
Jaton	www.jaton.com
Kingston	www.kingston.com
Memtron	www.memtron.com
Micro Memory	www.micromemory.com
Micron Memory	www.micron.com
Newer Technology	www.newertech.com
Nutek	www.nutekmen.com

PNY	www.pny.com
Rambus	www.rambus.com
Simm Expander	www.minden.com
Simple Technology	www.simpletech.com
Sony	www.sony.com
Visiontech	www.visiontech.com

Microprocessors

AMD	www.amd.com
Analog	www.analog.com
ARM	www.arm.com
Cyrix	www.cyrix.com
Evergreen Tech	www.evertech.com
Kingston	www.kingston.com
IDT	www.idt.com
Intel	www.intel.com
IBM	www.ibm.com
Motorola	www.mot.com
Nexgen	www.nexgen.com
Quantum Effect Design	www.qedinc.com
SGS-Thomson	www.st.com
Texas Instruments	www.ti.com
Zilog	www.zilog.com

Modems and FAX

Aceex	www.aceex.com
Aetherworks	www.aetherworks.com
Amquest	www.amquest.com
Anchor	www.anchor.nl
Apex Data	www.warrior.com
Angia	www.angia.com
Archtek	www.arctek.com.tw
Askey	www.askey.com
Asuscom	www.asuscom.tw
AT&T	
www.paradyne.att.com	
Banksia	www.banksia.com
Best Data	www.bestdata.com
Boca Research	www.bocaresearch.com
Cardinal	www.cardtech.com
Com 21	www.com21.com
Comcorp	www.comcorp.com.au
Communicate	www.commuicate.co.uk
Creatix	www.creatix.com
Digicom Systems	www.digicomsys.com
Dr. Neuhaus	www.neuhaus.com
Echo	www.echousa.com
Eiger Labs	www.eigerlabs.com
Elebra	www.elebra.com.br

E-Tech	www.e-tech.com	Barco	www.mindspring.com
EXP	www.expnet.com	CTX	www.ctxintl.com
Gammalink	www.gammalink.com	Daewo	www.daewo-display.com
Gavi	www.hwgavi.com	Datalux	www.datalux.com
Genoa	www.genoasys.com	Daytek	www.daytek.com
Hayes	www.hayes.com	DIGIview	www.digivew.com
Intertex	www.intertex.se	Dotronix	www.dotronix.com
J-Mark	www.j-mark.com	EDL	www.edldisplays.com
KM Engineering	www.kme.com	EIZO	www.eizo.co.jp
Konexx	www.konexx.com	Hitachi	www.hitachi.com
Logicode	www.logicode.com	Hyundai	www.hea.com
Maestro	www.maestro.com.au	IBM	www.pc.ibm.com
Max Link	www.askey.com	Iiyama	www.iiyama.com
Maxtech	www.maxcorp.com	KDS	www.kdsusa.com
Megahertz	www.megahertz.com	MAG	www.maginnovision.com
Min	www.kct.com	Magnavox	www.magnavox.com
Motorola	www.mot.com	Maxtech	www.maxcorp.com
Multitech	www.multitech.com	Miro	www.miro.com
Netcom	www.netcom.com.au	Mitac	www.mitac.com
Newcom	www.newcominc.com	Mitsubishi	www.mela-itg.com
Novalink	www.novalinktech.com	Nanao	www.traveller.com
Olitech	www.olitech.com	NEC	webserver.nectech.com
Practical Peripherals	www.practinet.com	Nokia	www.nokia.com
Psion Dacom	www.psiondacom.com	No Rad	www.noradcorp.com
Quantum Data Systems	www.quantum.co.uk	Pacom	www.pacomdata.com
Rockwell	www.rockwell.com	Panasonic	www.panasonic.com
RSA	www.rsacode.com	Philips	www.philips.com
Sidin	www.inrete.it.com	Portrait	www.portrtrait.com
Smart Line	www.queen.shiny.it	Princeton Graphics	www.prgr.com
Spectrum	www.sprectumsignal.com	Radius	www.radius.com
Tandy	www.support.tandy.com	JVC	www.jvc.com
TDK	www.tdksystems.com	Samsung	www.sec.samsung.co.kr
Telindus	www.telindus.be	Sceptre	www.gus.com
Trust	www.trust.box.nl	Smile	www.smile.com.tw
US Robotics	www.usr.com	Sony	www.sony.com
Western Data	www.western-data.com	Tandy	www.support.tandy.com
Wisecom	www.wisecominc.com	Tatung	www.tatung.com.tw
Zentech	www.zentech.com	Taxan	www.taxan.com.uk
Zoltrix	www.xoltrix.com	Viewsonic	www.viessonic.com
Zoom	www.zoomtel.com	Visionmaster	www.kom.com
Zyxel	www.zyxel.com	Wen Technology	www.iiactive.com
		Wyse	www.wyse.com

Monitors

Acer	www.aci.acer.com
Acula	www.acula.com
ADI	www.adi.com.tw
AOC Spectrum	www.aocltd.com
Artmedia	www.artmedia.com
AST	www.ast.com

Motherboards

Abit	www.abit.com.tw
Achme	www.achme.com
AIR	www.airwebs.com
AMI	www.megatrends.com
Amptron	www.deltanet.com

A-Open	www.aopen.com.tw	Boffin	www.boffin.com
Arvida	www.arvida.ca	BTC	www.btc.com.tw
Asustek	www.asustek.asus.com.tw	Casio	www.casio-usa.com
Biostar	www.biostar.net	Chromatic Research	www.impact.com
California Graphics	www.calgraph.com	Connectix	www.connectix.com
Chaintech	www.bdcc-nl.com	Coreco	www.coreco.com
DataExpert	www.dataexpert.com	Creative Labs	www.creaf.com
DFI	www.dfiusa.com	Crystal Lake	www.teleport.com
ECS	www.ecs.com.tw	DFI	www.difusa.com
Edom	www.netindex.com	Digital Audio Labs	www.digitalaudio.com
Epox	www.epox.com	Dycam	www.dycam.com
FIC	www.fic.com.tw	Ensoniq	www.ensoniq.com
Free Tech (Pride)	www.freetech.com	ESS	www.esstech.com
Fugutech	www.fugu.com.tw	Frontier Design	www.frontierdesign.com
Gemlight	www.gemlight.co.tw	Futurecho	www.futurecho.com
Genoa	www.genoasys.com	Genius	www.genius-kye.com
Gigabyte	www.giga-byte.com	Giltronix	www.giltronix.com
Intel	www.intel.com	Goldstar	www.goldstar.co.kr
Iwill (Side)	www.iwill.com.tw	Gravis	www.gravis.com
J Bond	www.jbond.com	H45 Technologies	www.h45.com
J Mark	www.j-mark.com	Hitachi	www.hitachi.com
Megastar (TMC)	megastar.kamtronic.com	Hisi Lin	www.hsinlin.com.tw
Micronics	www.micronics.com	In Focus	www.infs.com
Microstar	www.msi.com.tw	Interactive EFX	www.interactive-efx.com
Microway	www.microway.com	IPC	www.ipctechinc.com
Mitac	www.mitac.com.tw	Jazz Multimedia	www.jazzmm.com
Mitsubishi	www.apricot.com.uk	Konton	www.kontron.com
M Technology	www.mtiusa.com	Koss	www.koss.com
Ocean	www.Ocean-usa.com	Labtec	www.labec.com
Octek	www.oceanhk.com	Logicode	www.logicode.com
Pc Chips	www.pcchips.com	MediaVision	www.mediavis.com
QDI	www.qdigrp.com	Mediatrix	www.mediatrix.com
See Thru	www.seethru.com	Minolta	www.minolta.com
Shuttle	www.spacewalker.com	Mitsumi	www.mitsumi.com
Soyo	www.soyo.de	Multimedia Labs	204.174.94.120
SuperMicro	www.supermicro.com	Multiwave	www.multiwave.com
Tyan	www.tyan.com	Nakamichi	www.nakamichicdrom.com
Vextrec	www.vextrec.com	NEC	webserver.nectech.com
Zida	www.zida.com	Newcom	www.newcominc.com
		Nikon	www.klt.co.jp

Multimedia/CD-ROM

3DO	www.3d0.com	NSM Jukebox	www.nsmjukebox.com
8x8	www.8x8.com	NuReality	www.nureality.com
Acer	www.acer.com	Ocean	www.oceanusa.com
Advanced Digital Systems	www.ads-mm.com	Octek	www.oceanhk.com
Altec Lansing	www.altecmm.com	Olympus	www.olympus.co.jp
Animation Technologies	www.lifeview.com.tw	OPTi	www.opti.com
Aria	ftp.wi.leidenuniv.nl	Panasonic	www.panasonic.com
Aztech	www.aztechca.com	Philips	www.philips.com
		Pioneer	www.pioneer.co.uk

Plasmon	www.plasmon.com	Cayman	www.cayman.com
Play Inc	www.play.com	Cellware	www.cellware.de
Plexor	www.plexor.com	Chipcom	www.chipcom.com
Poloroid	www.poloroid.com	Cisco	www.cisco.com
Primax	www.primax.nl	Cnet	www.cnet.com.tw
Reveal	www.reveal.com	Cogent Data	www.cogentdata.com
Roland	www.rolandus.com	Compatible	www.compatible.com
Samsung	www.sec.samsung.co.kr	Compex	www.cpx.com
SC&T2	www.platinumsound.com	Connectware	www.conectware.com
SIC	www.sicresource.com	Cray	www.cray.com
Sony	www.sel.sony.com	Crosscom	www.crosscom.com
SRS Labs	www.srslabs.com	Cybex	www.cybex.com
Star Multimedia	www.starusa.com	Danpex	www.danpex.com
Taiwan Multimedia	www.tmi.at-taiwan.com	Dayna	www.dayna.com
Tandy	support.tandy.com	Develcon	www.develcon.com
Teac	www.teac.co.jp	Diamond Chips	www.dchip.com
Teac (us)	www.teac.com	Digital	www.dlink.com
Terratec	www.terratec.com	D-Link Systems	www.dlink.com
Toshiba	www.toshiba.com	DPI	www.dgiprod.com
Trust	www.trust.box.nl	DTC	www.datatechnology.com
Turtle Beach	www.tbeach.com	Dynatech	www.dynatech.com
Vertos	www.ecusa.com	Edimax	www.edimax.com
Vine Micros	www.vinemicros.com	Efficient Networks	www.efficient.com
Wearnes	www.asiabiz.com.sg	Eicon	www.eicon.com
Willow	www.willow.com	Ethercom	www.ethercom.com
		Equinox	www.equnox.com
Networking		Eversys	www.eversys.com
3Com	www.3com.com	Extended Systems	www.extendsys.com
ACC	www.sys.acc.com	Farallon	www.farallon.com
Accton	www.accton.com.tw	Fastcom	www.fastcom.com
Adax	www.adax.com	Fibronics	www.fibronics.co.il
ADC	www.adc.com	FORE Systems	www.fore.com
Agile Networks	www.agile.com	Gandalf	www.gandalf.ca
Alcatel	www.and.alcatel.com	Global Village	www.globalvillage.com
Allied Telesyn	www.allied-telesyn.cm	Grand Junction	www.grandjunction.com
Amber Wave	www.amberwave.com	Hewlett Packard	www.hp.com
AMP	www.amp.com	IBM	www.ibm.com
Apple	www.apple.com	ICL	www.icl.com
Asante	www.asante.com	IMC	www.imcnetworks.com
Ascend	www.ascend.com	Interlan	www.interlan.com
AT&T	www.att.com	Interphase	www.iphase.com
Axis	www.axis.se	Intel	www.intel.com
Banyan Systems	www.banyan.com	Jolt	www.jolt.co.il
Bay Networks	www.baynetworks.com	Katron (KTI)	www.ktinet.com
Black Box	www.blackbox.com	Kentrox	www.kentrox.com
Boca Research	www.bocaresearch.com	Klever	www.klever.com
Cabletron	www.ctron.com	LANart	www.lanart.com
Cameo	www.cameo.com	Lantronix	www.lantronix.com
Canary	www.canarynet.com	Linksys	www.linksys.cm

Longshine	www.longshin.com.tw	Xedia	www.xedia.com
Luxcom	www.luxcom.com	Xircom	www.xircom.com
Madge	www.madge.com	XLNT	www.xlnt.com
Microcom	www.microcom.com	Xylan	www.xylan.com
Microdyne	www.mcdy.com	Xyplex	www.xyplex.com
Microplex	www.microplex.com	Zeitnet	www.zeitnet.com
Mitron	www.gus.com		
Morning Star	www.morningstar.com	**Printers**	
Multitech	www.multitech.com	Brother	www.brother.co.jp
Nbase	www.nbase.com	Calcomp	www.calcomp.com
NetCorp	www.netcorp.com	Canon	www.usa.canon.com
Net Edge	www.netedge.com	Citizen	www.citizen-america.com
Network Peripherals	www.npix.com	Colorocs	www.nav.com
Networth	www.networth.com	CoStar	www.costar.com
Newbridge	www.newbridge.com	Dataproducts	www.dpc.com
NHC	www.nhc.com	Encad	www.encad.com
Novell	www.novell.com	Epsom	www.epsom.com
Optical Data Systems	www.ods.com	Excellink	www.excellink.com
Olicom	www.olicom.com	Fargo	www.fargo.com
OST SA	www.ost-us.com	GCC	www.gcctech.com
Penril	www.penril.com	Genicom	www.genicom.com
Performance Tech	www.pt.com	Hewlett Packard	www.hp.com
Plaintree	www.plaintree.on.ca	IBM	www.can.ibm.com
Plexcom	www.plexcom.com	JRL	www.jrl.com
Proteon	www.proteon.com	Kodak	www.kodak.com
PureData	www.puredata.com	Kyocera	www.kyocera.co.uk
Racal	www.racal.com	Lasermaster	www.lasermaster.com
Racore	www.racore.com	Lexmark	www.lexmark.com
Raritan	www.raritan.com	Mannesmann Tally	www.tally.com
Retix	www.retix.com	Microcom	www.micromcomp.com
Rockwell	www.rns.rockwell.com	Mutoh	www.mutoh.com
Shiva	www.shiva.com	NEC	webserver.nectech.com
Sonic Systems	www.sonicsys.com	OKI	www.oki.com
SMC	www.smc.com	Okidata	www.okidata.com
Spider	www.spider.com	Olivetti Lexicon	www.olivettilolexicon.com
Stallion	www.stallion.com	Panasonic	www.panasonic.com
Standard Microsystems	www.smc.com	Printer Works	www.printerworks.com
Startech	www.startech.com	QMS	www.qms.com
Symplex	www.symplex.com	Ricoh	www.ricohcorp.com
Syskonnect	www.syskonnect.de	Samsung	www.samsung.com.kr
Telebit	www.telebit.com	Seiko	www.cgg.seiko.com
Telindus	www.telindus.com	Sharp	www.sharp-usa.com
Thomas Conrad	www.tci.com	Star Micronics	www.starmicronics.com
Transition	www.transition.com	Talaris	www.talaris.com
Tribe	www.tribe.com	Tandem	www.tandem.com
UB	www.ub.com	Tandy	www.support.tandy.com
Webster	www.webstercc.com	Tektronix	www.tek.com
Whitetree	www.whitetree.com	Texas Instruments	www.ti.com
Whittaker	www.whittaker.com	Zerox	www.xerox.com

Scanners

3Dscanners	www.3dscanners.com
Adara	www.adara.com
AGFA	www.agfa.com
Artec	www.artecusa.com
Astro Research	www.astronote.com
Avision Labs	www.avision-labs.com
Bantec	www.bti-ok.com
Bell&Howell	www.bellhowell.com
Blackwidow	www.blackwidow.co.uk
Envisions	www.envisions.com
Epson	www.epson.com
Genius	www.genius-kye.com
Hewlett Packard	www.hp.com
Howtek	www.howtek.com
Ideal	www.ideal.com
Imacon	www.imacon.com
Interactive EFX	www.interactive-efx.com
Logitech	www.logitech.com
Lumina	www.lumina2000.com
Microtek	www.mteklab.com
Mustek	www.mustek.com
Nikon	www.klt.co.jp
Paktek	www.paktek.com
Panasonic	www.Panasonic.com
Plustek	www.plustek.com
Polaroid	www.polaroid.com
Primax	www.primax.nl
Relisys	www.relisys.com
Ricoh	www.ricohcorp.com
SunRise Imaging	www.sunriseimg.com
Suvil	www.suvil.com
Trust	www.trust.box.com
Umax	www.umax.com
Visioneer	www.visioneer.com
WordWand	www.wordwand.com

Software

3Com	www.3com.com
Adobe	www.adobe.com
Apple	www.apple.com
Autodesk FTP	ftp.autodesk.com
Banyan	www.banyan.com
Banyan FTP	ftp.banyan.com
Borland	www.borland.com
Cnet Sorftare Library	vsl.cnet.com
Compuserve	www.compuserve.com
Digital	www.dec.com
Digital FTP	ftp dec.com

FTP, Inc	www.ftp.com
Hewlett Packard	www.hp.com
Hewlett Packard FTP	ftp-boi.external.HP.com
IBM	www.ibm.com
McAfee FTP	ftp.mcafee.com
Microsoft	www.microsoft.com
Novel FTP	ftp.novell.com
Lotus	www.lotus.com
Next	www.next.com
Symantec	www.symantec.com
Winsite	www.winsite.com
Ziff-Davis	www.ziff.com

Storage

3M	www.3m.com
Advanced Digital Info	www.adic.com
Aiwa	www.aiwa.com
Amdahl	www.amdahl.com
Andataco	www.andataco.com
APS Technologies	www.apstech.com
Artecon	www.artecon.com
Atronics	www.atronicsintl.com
Boxhill	www.boxhill.com
Centennial	www.cent-tech.com
Ciprico	www.ciprrico.com
Conner	www.conner.com
Cutting Edge	www.cuttedge.com
CRU	www.cruinc.com
Digi-Data	www.digidata.com
Disctec	www.disctec.com
ECCS	www.eccs.com
EMC	www.emc.com
Eurologic	www.eurologic.com
Exabyte	www.exabyte.com
Filetek	www.filetek.com
Fujitsu	www.fujitsu.co.jp
FWB	www.fwb.com
H45 Technologies	www.h45.com
Hitachi	www.hitchi.com
HP Colorado	www.hp.com
IBM Storage	www.almaden.ibm.com
Intek	www.Intek.net
Iomega	www.iomega.com
JVC	www.jvcservice.com
Maxtor	www.maxtor.com
Megadrive	www.megadrive.com
Micro Hut	www.microhut.com
Micronet	www.micronet.com
Micropolis	www.microp.com

Mindflight	www.mindflight.com	Storage Tech	www.stortek.com
MTI	www.mti.com	Syquest	www.syquest.com
Optical Access	www.oai.com	Tapedisk	www.tapedisk.com
Optima Technology	www.optimatech.com	Tandberg	www.tandberg.com
Panasonic	www.panasonic.com	Tandy	www.support.tandy.com
Pinnacle	www.pinnaclemicro.com	Tecmar	www.tecmar.com
Procom	www.procom.com	Texas Isa	www.texasisa.com
Reveal	www.reveal.com	Toray	www.toray.com
Ricoh	www.ricohcorp.com	Tri-Plex	www.triplex.com
Quantum	www.quantum.com	Valitek	www.contagious.com
Samsung	tongky.sec.samsung.co.kr	Western Digital	www.wdc.com
Seagate	www.seagate.com	Winchester	www.winsys.com
SonyStorage	www.mmmg.com	Xyratek	www.xyratek.com

Appendix

CATALOGS OF COMPUTERS, COMPONENTS, AND SOFTWARE

CompuClassics
P.O. Box 10598
Canoga Park, CA 91309

Compute Ability
P.O. Box 17882
Milwaukee, WI 53217

Computers and Music
647 Mission Street
San Francisco, CA 94105

DAMARK
7101 Winnetka Avenue N.
P.O. Box 29900
Minneapolis, MN 55429-0900

Data Cal Corp.
531 E. Elliot Road
Chandler, AZ 85222-1152

Dell Direct Sales
11209 Metric Boulevard
Austin, TX 78758-4093

Digi-key Corporation
701 Brooks Avenue S.
Thief River Falls, MN 56701-0677

DTP Direct
5198 W. 76th Street
Edina, MN 55439

Edmund Scientific Co.
101 E. Gloucester Pike
Barrington, NJ 08007-1380

Global Computer Supplies
11 Harbor Park Drive
Dept. 48
Port Washington, NY 11050

Global Office Products
11 Harbor Park Drive
Dept. 30
Port Washington, NY 11050

Hello Direct
5884 Eden Park Place
San Jose, CA 95138-1859

IBM PC Direct
P.O. Box 12195
Bldg. 203/Dept. WN4
Research Triangle Park, NC 27709-9767

JDR Microdevices
2233 Samaritan Drive
San Jose, CA 95124

KidSoft Software Catalog
10275 N. De Anza Blvd.
Cupertino, CA 95014

MAILER'S Software
970 Calle Negocio
San Clemente, CA 92673

MicroWarehouse
1720 Oak Street
P.O. Box 3014
Lakewood, NJ 08701-3014

Momentum Graphics
16290 Shoemaker
Cerritos, CA 90701-2243

Mr. CD-ROM
P.O. Box 1087
Winter Garden, FL 34787

Multimedia World
P.O. Box 58690
Boulder, CO 80323-8690

One Network Place
4711 Golf Road
Skokie, IL 60076

Paper Catalog
205 Chubb Avenue
Lyndhurst, NJ 07071

Pasternak Enterprises
P.O. Box 16759
Irvine, CA 92713

PC Connection
6 Mill Street
Marlow, NH 03456

Personal Computing
90 Industrial Park Road
Hingham, MA 02043

Power Up!
P.O. Box 7600
San Mateo, CA 94403-7600

PrePress
11 Mt. Pleasant Avenue
East Hanover, NJ 07936-9925

Presentations
Lakewood Building
50 S. 9th Street
Minneapolis, MN 55402-9973

Processor
P.O. Box 85518
Lincoln, NE 68501

Projections
Business Park Drive
Branford, CT 06405

Queblo
1000 Florida Avenue
Hagerstown, MD 21741

Software Labs
100 Corporate Pointe, #195
Culver City, CA 90230-7616

Soundware
200 Menlo Oaks Drive
Menlo Park, CA 94025

South Hills Datacomm
760 Beechnut Drive
Pittsburg, PA 15205

TENEX Computers
56800 Magnetic Drive
Mishawaka, IN 46545

Tiger Software
800 Douglas Tower, 7th Floor
Coral Gables, FL 33134

Tools For Exploration
4460 Redwood Highway, Suite 2
San Rafael, CA 94903

United Video and Computer
724 7th Ave.
New York, NY 10019

UnixReview
P.O. Box 420035
Palm Coast, FL 32142-0035